"Democracy is under assault, not least from white evangelical Christians nostalgic for a full-blown theocracy. In *Democracy after Christendom*, James Paul Lusk provides an unapologetic and timely justification for a religiously pluralist democracy. His argument draws heavily on the much-neglected political theology of Roger Williams, the founder of Rhode Island. Lusk's retrieval of Williams in defense of democracy is worth the price of admission."

—DOUGLAS HYND, Australian Centre for Christianity and Culture

"In *Democracy After Christendom*, Paul Lusk tackles a subject central to the debates of our age. Taking as a definition of democracy that draws on Roger Williams of Rhode Island fame, a system of rule 'held by consent,' and insisting on the religious freedoms that the First Amendment calls 'non-establishment' and 'free exercise,' Paul traces the history of democracy after Christendom, principally in the UK and US. His analyses of the various definitions and forms of democracy are informative and stimulating, as is his discussion of the current malaise of democracy in the West. To commend a book is not necessarily to agree with all of it, and I do not agree with some of Paul's interpretations and assertions, but I have benefited from this book and will turn to it again. Be assured that you will gain from it too."

—MOSTYN ROBERTS, author of *The Subversive Puritan: Roger Williams and Freedom of Conscience*

"In this intriguing book, Paul Lusk explores the connections between the development of modern western democracy and the unravelling of Christendom. In a time when democracy is under attack in its modern backyard, Christians who recognize they are in the minority need a coherent political stance that guarantees religious freedom. This is a major contribution!"

—JEREMY THOMSON, author of *Interpreting the Old Testament After Christendom*

"Who knew that the blueprint for modern democracy came from Rhode Island, the smallest colony of North America? And who has ever heard of Roger Williams? It's good to be reminded of how democracy arose and to refocus our attention on the functions of church and state in a modern nation. I found this book to bring real clarity to these issues and helpful in understanding how to navigate today's society."

—RICHARD BARRETT, Partner, Emmanuel Church Canterbury, United Kingdom

"A very carefully argued work that weaves history, political theory, and theology and integrates UK and US examples seamlessly toward the goal of reviewing and re-laying the post-Christendom foundations of democracy. Lusk rejects Christian nationalism as the primary diagnostic category and identifies problems on both the culture war left and right. A brisk, straight-talking, and significant contribution to current Christian thinking about democracy in these troubled times."

—DAVID P. GUSHEE, Distinguished University Professor of Christian Ethics, Mercer University

"Democracy and two world wars, it turns out, did not achieve the 'end of history.' In our day, democracy is threatened in ways that two decades ago would have been inconceivable. In this book the masterful Paul Lusk sets out a vision for a democratic nation that does not require a 'sacred canopy' to unite it—a vision that is theologically-informed but non-coercive. It is an urgent and important book for our time."

—HELEN PAYNTER, Director, Centre for the Study of Bible and Violence

Democracy After Christendom

AFTER CHRISTENDOM Series

Christendom was a historical era, a geographical region, a political arrangement, a sacral culture, and an ideology. For many centuries Europeans have lived in a society that was nominally Christian. Church and state have been the pillars of a remarkable civilisation that can be traced back to the decision of the emperor Constantine I early in the fourth century to replace paganism with Christianity as the imperial religion.

Christendom, a brilliant but brutal culture, flourished in the Middle Ages, fragmented in the Reformation of the sixteenth century, but persisted despite the onslaught of modernity. While exporting its values and practices to other parts of the world, however, it has been slowly declining during the past three centuries. In the twenty-first century Christendom is unravelling.

What will emerge from the demise of Christendom is not yet clear, but we can now describe much of western culture as "post-Christendom."

Post-Christendom is the culture that emerges as the Christian faith loses coherence within a society that has been definitively shaped by the Christian story and as the institutions that have been developed to express Christian convictions decline in influence.

This definition, proposed and unpacked in *Post-Christendom*, the first book in the After Christendom series,[1] has gained widespread acceptance. *Post-Christendom* investigated the Christendom legacy and raised numerous issues that are explored in the rest of the series. The authors of this series, who write from within the Anabaptist tradition or in sympathy with it, see the current challenges facing the church not as the loss of a golden age but as opportunities to recover a more biblical and more Christian way of being God's people in God's world.

This extensive series addresses a wide range of issues, including theology, social and political engagement, how we read Scripture, youth work, mission, worship, relationships, and the shape and ethos of the church after Christendom.

---

1. Stuart Murray: *Post-Christendom: Church and Mission in a Strange New World* (Carlisle: Paternoster, 2004), 19.

Volumes include:

Stuart Murray, *Post-Christendom*
Stuart Murray, *Church After Christendom*
Jonathan Bartley, *Faith and Politics After Christendom*
Jo and Nigel Pimlott, *Youth Work After Christendom*
Alan and Eleanor Kreider, *Worship and Mission After Christendom*
Lloyd Pietersen, *Reading the Bible After Christendom*
Andrew Francis, *Hospitality and Community After Christendom*
Fran Porter, *Women and Men After Christendom*
Simon Perry, *Atheism After Christendom*
Brian Haymes and Kyle Gingerich Hiebert, *God After Christendom?*
Jeremy Thomson, *Relationships and Emotions After Christendom*
Dan Yarnell and Andy Hardy, *Missional Discipleship After Christendom*
Joshua Searle, *Theology After Christendom*
Andrew Francis and Janet Sutton, *Sacraments After Christendom*
Lina Toth, *Singleness and Marriage After Christendom*
Jeremy Thomson, *Interpreting the Old Testament After Christendom*
Douglas Hynd, *Community Engagement After Christendom*

These books are not intended to be the last word on the subjects they address, but an invitation to discussion and further exploration. Additional material, including extracts from published books and articles on related topics, can be found at https://amnetwork.uk/resource_tag/after-christendom-series/.

Stuart Murray
Series Editor

Democracy After Christendom

James Paul Lusk

CASCADE *Books* • Eugene, Oregon

DEMOCRACY AFTER CHRISTENDOM

After Christendom

Copyright © 2025 James Paul Lusk. All rights reserved. Except for brief quotations in critical publications or reviews, no part of this book may be reproduced in any manner without prior written permission from the publisher. Write: Permissions, Wipf and Stock Publishers, 199 W. 8th Ave., Suite 3, Eugene, OR 97401.

Cascade Books
An Imprint of Wipf and Stock Publishers
199 W. 8th Ave., Suite 3
Eugene, OR 97401

www.wipfandstock.com

PAPERBACK ISBN: 978-1-6667-5713-2
HARDCOVER ISBN: 978-1-6667-5714-9
EBOOK ISBN: 978-1-6667-5715-6

Cataloguing-in-Publication data:

Names: Lusk, James Paul [author].

Title: Democracy after Christendom / James Paul Lusk.

Description: Eugene, OR: Cascade Books, 2025 | Series: After Christendom | Includes bibliographical references and index.

Identifiers: ISBN 978-1-6667-5713-2 (paperback) | ISBN 978-1-6667-5714-9 (hardcover) | ISBN 978-1-6667-5715-6 (ebook)

Subjects: LCSH: Christianity and politics. | Political theology. | Democracy—Religious aspects—Christianity. | Democracy. | Church and state. | Church and the world.

Classification: BR115.P7 L87 2025 (paperback) | BR115.P7 (ebook)

11/11/25

Scriptures taken from the Holy Bible, New International Version®, NIV®. Copyright © 2011 by Biblica, Inc.™ Used by permission of Zondervan. All rights reserved worldwide. www.zondervan.com The "NIV" and "New International Version" are trademarks registered in the United States Patent and Trademark Office by Biblica, Inc.™

Contents

Acknowledgments ix

Prologue xi

Introduction 1

1: Christendom 11

2: The Invention of Democracy 20

3: Freedom and Slavery 34

4: Culture War 42

5: Education and the Rise of Theonomy 53

6: Politics and the State 70

7: Democracy in Public 90

8: Democracy's Crisis of Trust 110

9: Religious Freedom 124

Final Reflections 144

Bibliography 147

Subject Index 161

Scripture Index 167

Acknowledgments

This book would not have been written without the inspiration of the UK Anabaptist Theology Forum and its members. Special and profound thanks are due to Stuart and Sian Murray Williams. Fuel for the book also came through Tortoise Media[1] and its "think-ins" on democracy. Special thanks go to James Harding. Some material was first published in *Anabaptism Today*. Many thanks to its then editor, Lloyd Pietersen, for his support and openness.

Deepest thanks are due to my wife, Kay Lusk, for her unwavering patience and comments on the final draft.

Many have taken time and effort to read drafts, comment, and suggest reading and lines of enquiry. Thanks go to Richard Barrett, John Barry, Andrew Bartlett, Teresa Bejan, Andrew Bolton, Chris Catherwood, Polly Curtis, Roger Dean, Rupert Greville, John Heathershaw, Douglas Hynd, Francis Koppschall, James and Katie Linforth, Andy Lusk, Sean Lusk, Monica Minott, Mostyn Roberts, Richard Rogers, Jeremy Thomson, Joe Twyman, and John Wakeham.

None can be held responsible for the final contents. Some profoundly disagree. Many other conversations have helped. Sorry to anyone whose name is missing. I am deeply grateful to all who have shared thoughts and interest.

While writing this, I belonged to a loving and prayerful community in Emmanuel Church, Canterbury. Many thanks go to the leaders and congregation of this diverse, exciting fellowship. The ideas in the book were planted and grew in Belvidere Road Church in Liverpool, Woodgreen Church in Worcester, and City Church in Birmingham.

This is far from a full list of all who have encouraged and helpfully criticized. None of you is to blame for the result, but each of you has helped.

---

1. In April 2025, Tortoise Media acquired the *Observer* newspaper and is now known as "The Observer."

Prologue

Before we start, may I tell you a story?

It begins with a small boy, and a photograph. The picture shows a couple in mid-life, sitting beside each other. The man, slim-faced with a trimmed moustache, wears a white shirt and neatly knotted tie. His face is turned a little to his left. From this guarded angle, he looks into the lens.

The woman smiles into the camera. Even in black and white, her dress suggests a will to be cheerful. Her eyes sit behind thick, round lenses.

Behind these two, above them with a hand on each shoulder, is a young woman. I recognize her: it's my mother, Inge. She looks away, well to her left, as if to her future, and her eyes do not engage with the camera.

This image, mounted in the living room of my home, is a familiar part of my domestic landscape.

But the time has come to ask my mother: who are these people? Why, she says, they are my father and mother. I say: so, these are my grandparents? Yes, she says, they are Paul and Paula. She pronounces these names in the German way: Powl and Powla. You are named for them, Paul.

My name is pronounced the English way: Porl. For I am English, already determined so to remain.

Now I ask: where are they? When can I meet them?

I saw them last when I left Hamburg in 1939, says Inge. After that they were made to go to the East. They did not come back. They probably died there. Probably in a *concentration camp*. A picture of this place enters my seven-year-old mind: flat, desolate, wired in, guarded, a place of hunger, cold, fear.

I ask: why? What had they done wrong? For that must be a punishment, and punishment is for those who deserve it.

Nothing wrong, she says. They were Jews. I am a Jew. You, according to the laws of our people, are a Jew, though your blue-eyed father is not. All Jews in Germany were banished in this way. It was the government's doing.

Prologue

I press. What sort of *government* does that? A Nazi government, she says. I wrestle with this information. Nazi? What does that mean? Inge speaks the full name, in German, and then translates it: National Socialist German Workers' Party. My horizons suddenly expand. Socialist? Like Mr. Attlee's party?

For "Socialist" here in this English suburb means "*Labour*," with government-run railways, coal mines, medicine, and schools. No, she explains, the Labour Party is a *democratic* Socialist party; the Nazis were *National* Socialists. Though both are *workers'* parties, I notice, dawningly aware of a lifetime's mission to understand. But I've reached the edge of her patience with politics. Now I say: but this is so wrong! So unjust! How many people know about this? Don't you want *justice*?

Only much later do I learn of the early efforts to seek compensation from the courts in British-occupied Western Germany. Judges spoke of Paul and Paula as among those who "went East" and "never returned."

For now though, Inge says: no memory of this will remain. The Germans have "moved on." They are rebuilding. They will not want to be reminded of this past.

But she turns out to be wrong about that. Children and grandchildren of the Nazi generation interrogate their elders: you did *what?* They locate the efficiently compiled lists of those with one-way "tickets," purchased—using property confiscated from the unwilling passengers—from the state railway. They publish these. They publish *everything*. They commission museums and monuments.

Seventy years on from the death of my grandparents, my wife and I visit the Polish city of Łódź, where Paul and Paula spent their last months in the designated "ghetto." First, they were compressed into a commandeered school building ("the Hamburg Collective"). Then they were moved to a house near the high wire of the boundary fence; then "onward deported"—the euphemism for "sent to a place made for efficient mass murder."

Germans who never knew Inge find records of my grandparents' life, and publish their research. Together we—family, researchers, a neighbor of the apartment where Paul and Paula and Inge had lived—lay two memorial plates, called *Stolpersteine* ("stumbling stones") in the sidewalk fronting their home on Beim Schlump in Hamburg. These brass plaques—headed "*Hier Wohnte*" ("here lived")—record my grandparents' names, dates of birth, date and destination of deportation, and date and place of death.

There are now some eighty thousand of these *Stolpersteine* across Europe: once aware of them, you notice them all over Germany and elsewhere. Mostly they record Jews, but also other Nazi targets: Romanies, gays, Communists.

Prologue

The handcrafting and laying of these plaques started in 1992 as an art project by Gunther Demnig. It continues as an initiative of local community groups and foundations, funded by giving. They are the work of what we call "civil society"—the "space of uncoerced human association" belonging neither to state nor to market.[2]

Germans today, when they hear my story, often say: I am so *sorry*. I say: no German now lives who voted in 1930, 1932, and 1933, in the three national elections that carried the Nazis to power. You are not to blame, and you have no need to apologize. Neither do those who look away and prefer to think about something else.

But, if you do turn your mind to these truths, examining them not just as "history" but as part of your own people's story, then you are doing a service to humankind. You know the truth that "those who cannot remember the past are condemned to repeat it."[3]

Through a Saturday in May 1955, flash cards pop up on the new television in our family living room. Each card shows the result of voting in a general election held two days previously. Six hundred and thirty areas—"constituencies," they call them—have chosen someone to represent them in the House of Commons. There, a party's leader will become prime minister. In this election, nineteen votes out of every twenty are cast either for a candidate of the Conservative Anthony Eden, or of his Labour opponent, former Prime Minister Clement Attlee.

Eden is winning. I am eager to share the news with my mother. But she refuses to watch. She is distressed. A general election recalls memories of the Hamburg gutters running with the blood of those parading against Adolf Hitler's party. More than four out of every ten voters endorsed his Nazi vision of the state.

In 1923, Hitler led an armed uprising, and was locked up for treason. He emerged with a smarter idea: to use democracy itself as the means of its own destruction.

Democracy relies on the renewed bond of consent by which the people accept this system of government. When consent falters, democracy fails.

---

2. Walzer, "Civil Society," 89.
3. Santayana, *Life of Reason*, 264.

Introduction

In 1863, President Abraham Lincoln gave a short address at the opening of the Gettysburg Cemetery. These warriors died, he said, so that "government of the people, by the people, for the people should not perish from the earth."[1]

Thus, he made "democracy" the cause for which the USA was at civil war: not just so that democracy may continue in its North American homeland, but that it should survive on the planet at all.

Now over a third of the world's population lives in recognized democracies. But democracy's advance is faltering. The Washington observatory Freedom House reports that, worldwide, democratic freedoms have been on the decline for eighteen years.[2] Three-quarters of Americans think their democracy is under threat.[3]

On November 7, 2024, the world awoke to news of Donald Trump's return to the US presidency, for a second term. In the vote on November 5, he won both in the Constitution's electoral college and in the total of votes counted (the "popular vote"). His party gained a majority in both the Senate and the House of Representatives. The Supreme Court has a majority shaped by three Trump nominations in his first term. The count went more quickly and smoothly than in 2020, when delay helped feed the suspicion of those ready to agree the whole thing was "rigged." These all help confer power, legitimacy, and the ability to govern.

But many were ready to proclaim that America had elected a "tyrant" who would end democracy. Some of President Trump's announcements during the campaign—about governing as a dictator on "day one,"[4] deploying the military against "the enemy from within,"[5] and saving his supporters the

1. Lincoln, "Gettysburg Address."
2. Freedom House, *Freedom in the World 2024*.
3. Corasaniti et al., "Voters."
4. Michael and Agencies, "Trump."
5. "We have some very bad people. We have some sick people, radical left lunatics.

trouble of ever having to vote again[6]—fed this concern. Then he chose to place the USA's armed forces under the control of a "Christian" political activist recorded saying that "our founders did not want . . . democracy."[7]

No one now shares Lincoln's fear that the fall of democracy in the USA will mean its end in the world. But America's hesitation brings comfort to those, in such places as Russia, China, and Iran, who expect their alternative systems to outlast democracy[8].

This book proposes that, in advancing the case for a democratic revival, we face three problems. We do not know where democracy started. Related to that, we do not know what it is. Consequently, we do not know where it is going.

Leading scholars agree that democracy is "widely advocated and sought, but its meaning is widely contested."[9] Robert Dahl found "democracy" to be a word "used in a staggering variety of ways."[10] It is a "hotly contested term"[11] that "defies definition."[12] The topic is "confusing due to the many definitions applied." With "hundreds of definitions" in use, it is "almost impossible" to work out where academic study of the subject is heading.[13]

"Hundreds" turns out to be an understatement. Jean-Paul Gagnon, a "philosopher of democracy" at the University of Canberra, documents this "staggering variety."

> Much as an archaeologist would spread out . . . the many pieces of a shattered artefact on a table, a scholar of democracy needs to identify and interrogate, and compare and contrast each description of democracy in turn.[14]

And I think they're . . . very easily handled by, if necessary, by National Guard, or . . . the military," he said to Fox News on Oct. 13, 2024. Groves, "Trump Suggests," para. 7.

6. "Christians, get out and vote! This just time—you won't have to do it any more," he said in a speech on July 26, 2024. Vargas, "Trump."

7. Herman, "Hegseth."

As Robert Dahl explained, the founder Madison published an influential paper on the difference between Greek "democracy" and the Roman "Republic." Madison was trying to promote the new Constitution to those who shared eighteenth-century skepticism about "democracy." However, the Greek word for "democracy" and the Latin for "republic" mean the same thing: "popular government." (Dahl, *Democracy*, 16–17).

8. To understand the Chinese alternative, see Bell, *Beyond*.

9. Inoguchi et al., introduction to *Changing Nature*, 1.

10. Dahl, *Democracy*, 35.

11. Manville and Ober, *Bargain*, 16.

12. Lijphart, *Democracy*, 4.

13. Storm, "Elemental Definition," 215.

14. Gagnon, "Update," 93.

Introduction

By 2020, Dr. Gagnon had found 3,539 different meanings in use of the word "democracy."[15]

Does this matter? There are contrasting answers to this question. One is that democracy is an "evolved gift."[16] Self-determination is a "human ability" disclosed through the Enlightenment and then enhanced in a natural process. The task of political thought is to observe, identify, and classify the "many pieces" which result.

The other view is that democracy is the *product* of thought. Giovanni Sartori warned that "wrong ideas about democracy make democracy go wrong."[17]

> If we wish to keep "democracy," then we must understand what it is. The artifact "democracy" has to be conceived and constructed before being observed. Democracies exist because we have invented them, because they are in our minds, and insofar as we grasp how to keep them well and alive.[18]

Democracy is invented and must be reinvented in successive generations. Some of those inventions may turn out to be correct and sustainable. Others will not; they will produce effects opposite to what their inventors expect. Professor David Held agreed that it "is a remarkably difficult form of government to create and sustain . . . democracy has evolved through intensive social struggles and is frequently sacrificed in such struggles."[19]

The usual story of democracy maps a route from ancient Athens and through the city-states of Renaissance Italy. Then the Enlightenment and the Industrial Revolution fed demand for popular sovereignty and representative government. This account is not useless. But almost every book on the subject overlooks the moment of its modern invention.

In May of 1647 the colony of Providence Plantations gave its political arrangements the name "democracy." Up to that point, "democracy" was known to mean a system where "the greater part of the people have authority to command not only each particular citizen as such, but the minority of the people as a body."[20] Providence—the province now called Rhode Island—defined theirs differently. Democracy meant rule "held by consent." It aimed to give "as good and hopeful assurance as we are able" of "each man's peaceable and

---

15. Gagnon, "Database, at 3,539."
16. Welzel et al., "(Still)," 160.
17. Sartori, *Revisited*, 3.
18. Sartori, *Revisited*, 17.
19. Held, *Models of Democracy*, 1.
20. Bodin, *Six Books*, 72.

quiet enjoyment of his lawful right and Libertie" notwithstanding different "consciences."[21] Individuals were to govern their own lives, as far as possible, according to "conscience." Here, in rudimentary form, was the first *liberal* democracy.

The system was "held by consent." This meant that *consent* legitimized the state.[22] This was a concept of state legitimacy that replaced Christendom.

Christendom required all (or most) citizens to be "Christians." This meant the state had to define the mandated form of "Christianity." This, necessarily, resulted in the persecution of those who disagreed—including dissenting Christians. Refugees fled the Massachusetts version of Christendom. They established Providence Plantations. When the English Parliament gave them the right to their own government, they decided that "democracy" would be the form it would take.

Here was "democracy after Christendom." It was a solution to the problem of religious diversity. The state should not concern itself with questions of religious truth. It should stick to "civil matters." The mind behind this solution belonged to Roger Williams.

In America, these ideas, practiced only in Rhode Island, were considered wildly disordered. Williams was ignored until the 1840s. Then he was discovered as a father of American democracy, with its flourishing evangelical Christianity. Frontiersman, trader, intellectual, preacher, soldier, and statesman, he became a hero both of American nationalism and of Reformed Protestant Christianity.[23] At the turn of the twentieth century, his statue joined those of Calvin and Knox on the "Reformation Wall" in Geneva. Then Christianity fell from intellectual fashion. Williams was returned to obscurity. Hardly anyone now sees his importance to democratic history. The Oxford professor Teresa Bejan is a rare exception. Her title for her study is *Mere Civility*—Williams's own term for his central idea.

Democracy developed within Christian societies as they moved *out* of political Christendom.[24] The United States of America flourished as a Christian people *without* a Christian state. Though not Christendom *politically*, it remained Christendom *culturally*. The abolition of political Christendom appeared, for a time, to strengthen Christian culture. This would not have

---

21. Lutz, *Colonial Origins*, 172.

22. See p. 108 for the difference between this notion of "consent" and the theory of state origins famously put forward by Hobbes.

23. Coyle, *Roger Williams*.

24. This does not mean that every democracy occurs "after Christendom." For example, Japan, Singapore, and India would not fit that model. It means that democracy as we know it was first devised as a successor to Christendom.

Introduction

surprised the authors of the Rhode Island democracy. They understood that when the state mandates a form of religion to be observed by all citizens, then politics, not faith, will define the "god" to be worshiped.

However, this Christian cultural moment is now passing. In the United Kingdom, a majority of citizens say they are not Christians. The United States is on its way to that position. A rising generation says it has no religion.[25] The democracy we have enjoyed in the West was an interlude between the end of political Christendom and the later end of cultural Christendom.

So, after Christendom, democracy has a problem. As David Gushee explains:

> It is highly doubtful whether human communities can function without any kind of shared values or a vision of what a good life and good community look like. . . . But no such substantive vision is on offer, because the individualist-libertarian vision prevails, quite intentionally. There is no collective common good; there is only the aggregation of individual goods as we each pursue our own version of happiness.[26]

All human communities need "shared values." But, within the modern pluralistic state, there is not one community: there are many. Christians take their definition of "good" from the Bible and a relationship they believe they have with God, since "no one is good but God."[27] Other communities generate different visions of "goodness," which may oppose Christian values.

With the end of the Christian majority, the "aggregation of individual goods" results in a moral consensus that challenges Christianity. How are Christians to deal with this? The response that has come to dominate American politics is "culture war." Moral community is essential, but moral community between Christians and others is impossible. Therefore, political life must be a struggle between Christians and the rest over which community is to rule.

President Trump is one beneficiary of this. But its origins long precede his arrival on the scene. Many books highlight the racism, nationalism, and misogyny said to animate his political base. To focus on these sins of the

---

25. This trend appears to have reversed in recent years. The proportion of active Christians among the UK population is now rising, driven especially by growth among young men. Churchgoers have risen from 8 percent of the population in 2018 to 12 percent in 2025. At the same time, "those who don't engage in practices such as churchgoing or Bible reading are less likely than ever to identify themselves as Christian." Christianity is a small but growing minority commitment. A growing majority identifies as non-Christian. See McAleer and Barward-Symmons, *Quiet Revival*, 6–7.

26. Gushee, *Defending Democracy*, 10.

27. Mark 10:18.

"religious right" is to take up arms in the culture war, rather than understand it. If we are to understand the problems now facing democracy, then we need to *understand* "culture war."

The origins of culture war are found deep in the roots of American democracy. Providence defined democracy as meaning:

> Government held by ye free and voluntarie consent of all, or the greater parte of the free Inhabitants.[28]

The "free inhabitants" did not mean *everyone*. It meant heads of households owning some land. Generally, these were males. The early laws of the colony forbade slaveholding, though this ban was poorly enforced. "Indentured," time-limited servitude was normal. Indentured servants belonged to their master's household. They had the prospect of completing their bonded servitude and then buying land. But until then, they were not "free."

Two centuries later, Lincoln redefined democracy as "government of the people, by the people, for the people." The key words are three prepositions: *of* the people, *by* the people, *for* the people. The first, "of," defines "the people" as *those who are governed*. The second, "by," says "the people" are the rulers. The third, "for," says that government exists for their benefit.

Lincoln tells us that the "people" in a democracy are *all* those subject to the authority of the state. So slaves and their descendants are "people." This was six years after the US Supreme Court ruled that descendants of slaves brought from Africa were not "people" in terms of the US federal Constitution.[29] Gettysburg signalled the reversal of this judgment.

Democracy evolves through struggles. People use the resources of democracy to make their claims on the system. Since modern democracy's inception, slaves and their descendants, working men, and women have claimed their equal right to belong to "the people."

Equality leaves losers and winners. The losers in the Civil War were protected by Lincoln's "Democrat" opponents in restoring their racially coded superiority. This survived for two generations before the Democrats themselves decided to become the party of civil rights and Black liberation. This left a body of white southerners seeking a voice. This body did not share the Republican right's free-market, small-state "conservatism." But Republican strategists learned that it was devoutly evangelical. A Supreme Court decision to ban prayer in public schools had already fed suspicion that the federal government and its Democrat-appointed judges were on a mission to suppress Christianity. Was there an opportunity to capture a bloc for the "right"?

---

28. Lutz, *Colonial Origins*, 172.
29. Dred Scott v. Sandford (1857).

Introduction

In a famous lecture, Professor Isaiah Berlin said that a group in society with a shared interest is like a naked "body." It needs "clothing" to enter the political arena. A body of people without ideas is blind and directionless. The "clothing" of ideas gives that body direction and purpose.[30]

What then is the idea that "clothed" this disaffected body of white Christians? Is there an idea that gives it a purpose beyond a grievance about racial privilege and religious education? An idea that makes it the "religious right," with enough substance and purpose to challenge democracy as the legitimizing theory of the state?

There is. It is belief in the Bible as a legal text to be applied in civil law. The word for this doctrine is "theonomy." The "hard" version of this was developed in the 1970s by Rousas Rushdoony.[31] It holds that Old Testament law should be applied in full, with civil penalties for nonbelief. A more acceptable "soft" theonomy came a little later, especially through the widely disseminated work of Francis Schaeffer.[32] This holds that God's law allows religious freedom. Both hard and soft theonomy agree on the strategy of "evangelism through law."[33] This says that arguing for civil law to conform more closely to God's law is a way to show people their wrongdoing before God. Theonomy promises a restored Christendom: not now on the basis that most citizens are "Christian," but on the basis that Christians can use political power to compel submission to God's law.

Liberal democracy has freed people to follow their own conscience. J. S. Mill said this means that personal freedom may be limited only to prevent harm to others.[34] That raises the question of what is considered "harmful." Article 4 of the 1789 French Declaration of the Rights of Man and of the Citizen explains it thus:

> Liberty consists in being able to do anything that does not harm others: thus, the exercise of the natural rights of every man has no bounds other than those that ensure to the other members of society the enjoyment of these same rights.[35]

---

30. Berlin, "Two Concepts," 193. Marxists say that a "class in itself" must become a "class for itself" before it can enter the political arena: it needs a set of ideas that identifies and expresses the nature and purpose of its interest. Berlin was not a Marxist. He did not believe that all social relations could be reduced to "relations of production" or that a correct "analysis" would lead to human liberation and the decline of the state.

31. Rushdoony, *Institutes*.

32. F. Schaeffer, *Christian Manifesto*.

33. North, "Kingdom," 37.

34. Mill, "On Liberty," 78.

35. Élysée, "Declaration," art. 4.

So "harm" refers to an action that diminishes the freedom of others. Otherwise, the "rights of every man"[36] are "boundless." A liberal democratic state aims to maximize the *equal* level of individual self-government.

Is this an end in itself? Can we make this version of "freedom" the center of a revived moral community? The Christian answer is that we cannot. The highest freedom, Roger Williams said, is the "soul liberty" found in following Christ.[37] Liberal democracy does not itself achieve "soul liberty." Furthermore, this liberty may be found outside democracy. Why therefore should Christians want to sustain democracy?

Here are two answers to this question.

The first is a biblical answer. God calls people to follow him and submit to him freely: not compelled, like horses, by "bit and bridle."[38] Conditions of civil freedom are ones in which we may *freely* delight God by proclaiming his love and submitting to him without compulsion. Theonomy cannot achieve this liberation. Only loving and willing submission can.

The second is a political answer. Modern conditions create a technically accomplished state which can project its power into every corner of our lives. This is not a "zero-sum game" where the rights of individuals are traded off against the rights of the state. Rather, technical advances also empower individuals. This in turn demands a greater role for the state in protecting people against the harms capable of being inflicted by the power of others.

Perhaps the smartest thing I've read on politics was by a journalist called Claud Cockburn. In the 1930s, Cockburn exposed how sections of the British elite were preparing to submit to the waves of fascism rolling in from Italy and Germany. He wrote that government does "as much harm as it can, and as much good as it must."[39] The state will do bad things, unless citizens apply themselves to creating the conditions in which it *must* do something better. The thought is along the same lines as Sir Winston Churchill's famous remark that "democracy is the worst form of Government except all those other forms that have been tried from time to time."[40] Democracy does not necessarily produce a better outcome than its nondemocratic alternative. However, it should give those receiving this outcome—the people subject to a state's control—the means to change it.

---

36. Now understood to mean "every adult human."
37. Roberts, *Subversive Puritan*, 18.
38. Ps 32:9.
39. Cockburn, *Discord*, 204.
40. In a speech in the House of Commons on Nov. 11, 1947. Hansard, "Commons Chamber Volume 444."

Introduction

This book appears in an After Christendom series. Our writing is by Christians who see the end of state-sponsored Christianity as a matter of both fact and celebration. We know that with that change—welcome as it is—come challenges and pressures. We need to prepare for these.

Democracy is a system "held by consent." It legitimizes the state through the consent of all or most of those subject to its authority. This conceives self-governing power as properly lying with individuals. The transfer of power requires consent based on good reasons. "Consent" means, as Roger Williams said, *renewed* consent. It cannot mean, as his more famous contemporary Thomas Hobbes suggested, that the state is legitimized by consent given once, and never renewed.

"Consent" does not mean the same thing as "consensus." "Consensus" means shared agreement to decisions. The "consent" that legitimizes the state still leaves room for decisions to be disputed. It confirms, however, that there is a process in place that confers the *right* to take those decisions.

This needs each of us to consider not just *our* terms for consent, but also those on which *others* are ready to consent. This needs some people ready to act not just in their own interests but also in the interests of others.

Paul told Roman Christians to be "content to do what is right in the eyes of everyone" in relating to a hostile world.[41] They are to "overcome evil with good." "After Christendom" there are new opportunities to respond to this challenge. Christianity could—and arguably should—be part of reinventing "democracy" for a new generation.

Worldwide surveys find that people think democracy consists in the "rights that give people choices in governing their personal lives, and a voice and vote to shape public life."[42] This makes a good starting point. Democracy confers "rights." These apply at two levels. One is "personal." Individuals have the right to govern their own lives, subject to protecting the equal right of others. The other is "public life": things that, through the mechanism of the state, are made binding on all citizens. These two levels of democratic freedom are linked by two key rights. The first is the right to communicate—the right of "free speech"—through which we may persuade others to support a cause. The second is the right to associate with others to pursue a shared goal. These rights form the basis for the existence of "civil society": the uncoerced space where we pursue common aims beyond the forces of state and market.[43]

---

41. Rom 12:17, 21.
42. Alexander and Welzel, "Measuring Effective Democracy," 272.
43. Walzer, "Civil Society," 89.

With the passing of cultural Christendom, we are now entering a new period after Christendom. In this democracy after Christendom, can we pursue freedom to love Christ in the framework of everyone's equal freedom to seek what is good? And how can "voice and vote" enable all citizens to "shape public life"?

The first two chapters examine the political crisis following the end of classical Christendom. New England was a laboratory for experiments in state legitimacy. Old England's Civil War became a battle for religious freedom. The invention of the first liberal democracy was an outcome of transatlantic exchange. Chapters 3 to 5 consider America's struggles for religious liberty, equality, and democracy, through the Revolution, the spread of Evangelical Christianity, and civil war. Culture war is the outcome of these struggles. "Nationalism" and "racism" do not explain the potency of the movement at work here. "Theonomy," meaning the application of God's law as civil law, is the driving idea offering to replace consent as the basis of state legitimacy. Democracy is "political," but that word is used too loosely. Chapter 6 clarifies the meaning of "politics" and what theory of the state may be found in the Bible. Chapter 7 examines the different ways in which democracy may install state government. This leads to chapter 8 and the roots of, and solutions to, the crisis of trust in mature democracies, especially in the United States and the United Kingdom. Chapter 9 looks at challenges to religious freedom in modern democracies. Brief "final reflections" draw out some conclusions.

1

Christendom

The word "Christendom" refers to a system of order in society. Christendom expected all in its territory, with some possible exceptions,[1] to be Christians by birth and to come under the authority of the church.

As the Roman Empire declined, the Catholic and Orthodox Churches filled its space as the source of authority. Christendom lasted for a thousand years, before giving way to Islam in the East. In the West, monarchies freed themselves from the papal system, while Anabaptist movements sought a church free of state control. The English Civil War became a battle for religious freedom, outside state control.

Its Rise

Christendom became the ruling order in a period starting in the fifth century CE. Its power extended over those parts of the world—in Europe, North Africa, and West Asia—previously under the Roman Empire. It had two capitals, in the East at Constantinople—later known as Istanbul—and in the West at Rome. Eastern Christendom nurtured a Greek-speaking culture in its Byzantine Empire. It eventually gave way to Islam, and the Ottoman Empire replaced Byzantium after conquering Istanbul in May 1453 CE, or 857 in the Muslim calendar.

In the West, the pope ruled over and through the Roman Catholic Church. Latin was the language of law, government, and the educated elite. The church had the organizational structure, community services, and loyal

---

1. Such as Jews.

support to take the place of the Roman Empire as the preeminent source of public authority. According to the historian R. W. Southern:

> The medieval church was a state. It had all the apparatus of the state administrative: laws and law-courts, taxes and tax-collectors, a great machine, power of life and death over the citizens of Christendom and their enemies within and without. It was the state at its highest power.[2]

The ruling church, however, lacked one attribute of a "state": domination through its armed forces. For physical enforcement, the church looked to the local rulers in the shape of monarchs and leading aristocrats. As Pope Gelasius explained to a Byzantine emperor in 494 CE:

> Two swords there are . . . by which this world is chiefly ruled, the sacred power of the priesthood and the royal power. Of these the responsibility of the priests is more weighty insofar as they will answer for the kings of men themselves at the divine judgment.[3]

To discipline local rulers and elites, the church carried the threat of excommunication—exclusion from many aspects of church life, including Christian burial. The spiritual authority of the church rested on belief that its word was that of God, and the excommunicated individual would go to hell. As long as the rulers, or influential subjects, acted on this belief, the church could truly be "the state at its highest power."

And Its Fall

Eastern Christendom succumbed to Islam. The decline of the Western church followed, in the face of two forces.

Divine Right of Monarchs

One was the rise of monarchs claiming "divine right" to rule directly on behalf of God. Newly powerful states standardized national languages to replace Latin as the medium of cultural and political communication, channeled through the technology of the printing press. A major driver of the rise of the national monarchs was their ability to map the world accurately and to navigate the oceans. Portugal and Spain led the way in sending fleets to "discover" regions

---

2. Southern, *Western Society*, 17–18.
3. Robinson, *Readings*, 72–73.

where they found immense wealth. Native powers were subdued. Slaves provided captive manpower for mines and plantations.

Biblical Christianity and the Anabaptists

The other force was the rediscovery of biblical Christianity and the dissemination—through the printing presses—of an understanding of Christianity that contradicted some Roman Catholic doctrine. At first, this did not dismantle Christendom itself. The emergent sovereign states continued to enforce a common Christian religion, either the "old" Catholicism or the "new" teachings of leaders like Zwingli in Zurich, Luther in Germany, and Calvin in Geneva.

With the Bible supreme as the source of Christian authority, it was hard to confine popular Christianity within any Protestant orthodoxy. So-called "Anabaptists"—having read the New Testament—maintained that a true church must consist only of believers, baptized out of their own choice: the church should govern itself without interference from the state. In Zurich, in German-speaking Switzerland, a plaque on the riverfront commemorates the capital punishment of the first known Anabaptist martyrs. On the orders of the newly formed Protestant city-state, they were tied up and drowned in 1527. They were followed by many others, burned, hanged, beheaded, or, more benevolently, expelled, all over Catholic and Protestant Europe.

The continent wracked itself in war over which version of Christianity the state should enforce on its population. The most devastating effects of this struggle fell on Germany, where numerous micro-states were gathered into the Holy Roman Empire, and the French and Austrian powers competed for the spoils of religious war. Two international settlements made peace. The first, in Augsburg in 1555, resolved that each German state be either Catholic or Lutheran on the principle of *cuius regio, eius religio*: whoever rules the state decides on the religion all must follow. Subjects not ready to comply were allowed time to move to another territory. The Thirty Years' War followed the breakdown of Augsburg. The 1648 settlement of Westphalia—two parallel treaties between different combatants—followed the Augsburg principle, but allowed for the new Calvinist option. It further provided that dissidents who chose not to move home could follow their own inclinations in private.

Protestants understood that the circumstances of birth and citizenship could not, by themselves, make someone a Christian. The New Testament clearly says that belief in Christ is the sole and sufficient condition of becoming a Christian. But did that mean that the Anabaptists were right, and the church must consist only of those who are "born again"?[4] And that the state should have no say in running the church? Few were yet ready for such a radical "separation of church and state." Some early Anabaptists—for example, Balthasar Hubmaier (1480–1528)—began to grasp this possibility, but they were rapidly killed off. Anabaptists survived in physically separated communities, protected by sympathetic aristocratic landowners. The doctrine of these survivors was that true Christianity did not need the existence of a state. The state was needed only to provide order for the unbelieving community who followed a false version of Christianity. These Anabaptists held that true Christians should not take office in the state.[5]

The Priesthood of All Believers

From Luther's study of the New Testament came the doctrine of the "priesthood of all believers."[6] There is no special "spiritual order" of priests, as prescribed in the Old Testament. All Christians are equally "spiritual."[7] The pope has no authority over the head of state (the "emperor") except the right to crown and anoint that person.[8]

> [The] pope and his followers have no right to boast that they have done the German nation a great favor by giving us the Roman Empire.[9]

Luther appealed to German rulers to defend his new church against violent attack. Conventional warfare was waged by Catholic states. Peasants rose in revolt. One faction of "Anabaptists" seized the city of Muenster in 1534. Their deranged regime was suppressed by a Lutheran-Catholic alliance. Though repudiated by most Anabaptists, it was nonetheless an episode that left a lasting stain on the reputation of Anabaptism.

England: Searching for the True Church

Lutheran theory gave cover for King Henry VIII as he took control of the English church. This freed him to divorce his Spanish Catholic queen and

4. John 3:3.
5. Lusk, "Reappraising."
6. 1 Pet 2:9; Rev 5:10.
7. Luther, "To the German," 15.
8. Luther, "To the German," 53.
9. Luther, "To the German," 103.

marry his Protestant second wife. He then plundered the massive assets of the church to buy support among aristocrats and gentry to build the English state. Henry was followed by the reigns of his three children. The boy-king Edward, ruling from 1547 to 1553, pushed the established church in a more Reformed Protestant direction. After his early death, Mary reigned from 1553 to 1558. She restored Roman Catholicism, with broad popular support for the "old religion." Elizabeth, from 1558 to 1603, brought back Protestant establishment, though with concessions to Catholic sensibility in worship.

Particularly during Mary's reign, leading English Protestants took refuge in Geneva. They learned the doctrines and practices of the Swiss divines, notably Jean Calvin. Calvin's teaching became the basis for the Scottish Reformation, led by John Knox, in 1560. But it had less traction in England. Elizabeth resisted attempts to reform the church that she regarded, ultimately, as belonging to the Crown first and to Jesus Christ only via herself.

Calvinists seeking to "purify" the national church along Swiss and Scottish lines were at the heart of the movement known as the "Puritans." Frustrated at the imposition of what they regarded as Catholic forms of service and church government, some chose to meet for worship outside the local Church of England parish system. These illegal "separatist" gatherings were eventually made punishable by death under the Conventicles Act of 1592. Persecution propelled some to seek shelter in tolerant Holland and, a little later, in the "New World" opening up in America.

In Calvin's system, the church was self-governing through "presbyteries" and a national "synod." All citizens were considered church members, whether or not they attended church or made a specific Christian profession. The church could claim them as members unless their conduct showed otherwise. All infants should therefore be baptized, on the basis of their ancestral membership of the Christian community. The state had no authority to appoint clergy or control the life of the church. The state did, however, have a duty to enforce "true religion" as defined by the church.

Luther and Calvin differed over the organization of the church and its relationship with the state. All in society are (supposedly) Christians. Both church and state have authority over all Christians under their care. Who is ultimately in charge? Which of the "two kingdoms" has the final say? The English solution, derived from Luther, was: the state. The monarch must protect the true church: but the monarch ultimately says what that true church is. The Calvinist solution was: the church. The church tells the state the true religion to be enforced. If the state resists, then the community—through what Calvin called the "lesser magistrates"—has the right to rise up and replace their ruler.

What is the true church, and how is this church to be secured in society? How is the state to be established? These questions remained unresolved in Europe by the end of the sixteenth century. To solve these questions in a practical way meant accommodation with the existing state system. Catholics looked to Rome and loyal rulers to restore pre-Reformation Christendom. Protestants looked to protection from Protestant monarchs able to resist the Catholic states. Anabaptists were able to survive in semi-independent communities through deals with tolerant authorities, notably in Moravia, Holland, and Bavaria.

Christendom Renewed? The "City on a Hill"

English settlers on the Atlantic coast of North America found no deposits of gold and silver to make them wealthy. In time they prospered through farming and trade. Their "plantations" followed the pattern of late Christendom in adopting a version of Christianity to which to conform. The first English colony, Virginia, was established in 1607 as a mainly commercial venture, with the Protestant Church of England as the established religious institution and very limited tolerance for deviation. Maryland was formed in 1632 to be a haven for Catholics, albeit settled by a Protestant majority.

In the American Northeast, "New England" became a test bed for Puritan conceptions of church and state. In 1620, the vessel *Mayflower* brought "separatist" English refugees who were able to give their famous "Thanksgiving" for survival, made possible by the aid of indigenous Wampanoags. Their "Mayflower Compact" records their journey as "undertaken for the Glory of God, and Advancement of the Christian Faith, and the Honour of our King and Country."[10]

Another venture to "New England" followed. The Royal Charter of the Massachusetts Bay Company was signed in 1628. It allowed the government of the new company to be conducted wholly within New England itself. The effect was to diminish the English state's power over the new colony.

Massachusetts became the laboratory for a model of Puritan rule over church and state. Its church followed the "Congregational Way."[11] Local church membership was restricted to the "visible saints"—those with a convincing testimony of "saving grace." This did not mean just assenting to Christianity. It meant a heartfelt commitment which showed, as far as humanly discernible, the work of the Holy Spirit in an individual. Church ministers were appointed by the local congregation. They must live within the locality, and were not

---

10. Mayflower Society, "Mayflower Compact."
11. Hall, *Puritans*, 229–30.

allowed to preach outside it. Only members of state-approved churches, conforming to this model, could be "freemen." They had the right to manage town business and vote in elections for the government of the colony.

Under the "Congregational Way," the church could not alter "forms of civil government," and church ministers were barred from holding state office. This was seen as maintaining appropriate separation between the functions of church and state. But in reality, church and state were tightly integrated, under the control of the "visible saints." This system absorbed the Anabaptist understanding of the church: it is an association of believers controlling their own assembly and clergy.[12] But, in contrast with Anabaptism, it endorsed the Calvinist claim to the control of church over state. Its authors refused formal "separation" from the Church of England on the grounds that this would mean schism within the church. Those who established it

> came to Massachusetts confident that their congregational polity answered all the basic questions and preserved the essential characteristics of truly reformed churches: congregational autonomy, limited membership, and religious uniformity ... they discarded the hierarchal structure of Anglicanism and erected in its place independent churches free from the compulsion of bishops.[13]

This was the "city on a hill" proclaimed by its first governor, John Winthrop.

However, far from proving the model for a Reformed Christendom, the Massachusetts system rapidly collapsed under the weight of its own contradictions. On the Calvinist model, church members brought their infants for baptism. The children grew up as church members. But mostly they turned out not to show the evidence of the "quickening of the spirit" enjoyed by their parents. This second generation wanted their own children to be baptized. Agonized debate took place, climaxing in a synod in 1662.

> [This] created a class of half-way members, persons capable of transmitting baptism, recognized as members, but barred from the Lord's Supper[14] and from voting in church affairs. To qualify for this partial membership an individual was not required to give evidence that he had attained saving grace; he had only to renew or "own" the baptismal covenant made for him by his parents. Owning the covenant enabled parents as yet unqualified for

---

12. Hall, *Puritans*, 228.
13. Pope, *Half-Way*, 3–4.
14. The "Lord's Supper" is the sacrament also called "communion" in Protestant churches, and roughly corresponds to the Catholic "Mass," though with significant differences in interpretation.

communion to present for baptism children who would formerly have been excluded.¹⁵

The spiritual community of freemen was always a minority of the adult population in seventeenth-century Massachusetts. Others declined to join the approved Congregational churches, or would have been refused had they tried. Then, as just described, there arose new generations, descended from the first "saints," who were not seen to enjoy the same blessed qualification. The system was resented among the many it excluded and fell into disrepute. It was abolished on the orders of the English monarchy in the 1690s, replaced by a property qualification for freeman status.

The Battle for Religious Freedom

Meanwhile, in London, King Charles I, sure of his "divine right" to rule over his domains, tried to enforce conformity to his royal rule over the Scottish church, in the face of Calvinist resistance. When he convened the English Parliament to approve the taxes needed to pay for the results of defeat, his own legislature turned out to have a significant presence both of Calvinists wanting to reform the state church, and (in fewer numbers) of sympathizers with Anabaptism and religious liberty. Civil war broke out in 1642. It is sometimes called the "war of the three kingdoms." Charles occupied the three separate thrones of England and Wales,¹⁶ Scotland, and Ireland. The English Civil War was fought in England over the sovereignty claims of Parliament and Throne—which has final authority? It involved, simultaneously and inseparably, wars over national claims made in Scotland and Ireland.

The English Civil War became a struggle for religious freedom. Oliver Cromwell's "new model" parliamentary army emerged triumphant from the bloody chaos of the 1640s. The war cry of its troops was "liberty of conscience":

> That is, that the civil magistrate had nothing to do to determine of anything in matters of religion by constraint or restraint, but every man might not only hold, but preach and do, in matters of religion what he pleased; that the civil magistrate hath nothing to do but with civil things, to keep the peace, and protect the churches' liberties.¹⁷

15. Pope, *Half-Way*, 7–8.
16. Wales was conquered and colonized by the English King Edward in the thirteenth century.
17. According to an eyewitness report by the Calvinist minister Richard Baxter. See Woodhouse, *Puritanism*, 388.

The Breakthrough: Separating Church and State

Here was a breakthrough, to what became the lasting solution to Protestantism's problem of church and state. Which is in charge? Neither! It is for each individual to follow personal choice in matters of religion. Where did this come from? It was an idea incubated in New England and transported back to the Old World with its prime mover, the English Christian statesman Roger Williams.

The search for the "true church" was also a search for the true relationship of church and state. The search culminated in the separation of the two, with individual liberty in matters of religion.

The next chapter describes how this happened.

2

The Invention of Democracy

This chapter is an account of how early democracy was developed, replacing Christendom as the guiding idea that legitimized the state.

The Path to Providence

Roger Williams arrived in Massachusetts in 1631, part of the second wave of immigrants into the Bay Company's project. Still a young man, he was an admired church minister and Cambridge graduate who had studied law as clerk to the great judge Sir Edward Coke. He refused a prestigious church position in Boston. He announced that Congregationalism should separate itself from the Church of England. He proceeded to launch a series of attacks which questioned the legitimacy of the Bay State.[1]

Its charter was, he explained, invalid, since it assumed the king of England had the right to dispose of land which actually belonged to the indigenous peoples. The proper course would be to negotiate with these owners for the purchase of land. Furthermore, he asserted that the civil magistrate did not have a legitimate right to enforce religious conformity.

In July 1635, Roger Williams went on trial in Boston, Massachusetts. The charge was promoting "diverse dangerous opinions."[2] One was that the civil courts had no business trying to compel worship of the true God, in conformity with the first four of the Ten Commandments. Another was that oaths

---

1. Roberts, *Subversive Puritan*, 60–61.
2. Barry, *Roger Williams*, 196.

in God's name should not be required of the "unregenerate"—people should not be required to profess faith in a God in whom they did not in fact believe.

Williams was sentenced to be transported back to England. There his views would be punishable with mutilation and life imprisonment. The ruling council decided to suspend action to give the young man time to settle his affairs at home and recover from illness. Then they learned that he was still preaching and teaching in Salem, against their express instructions. The council ordered he be arrested and deported back to England. In January 1636, fifteen soldiers arrived in Salem to arrest him. He was gone.

Tipped off by none other than the Bay governor, John Winthrop, Williams had fled. He took refuge among native American peoples, the Wampanoag and the Narragansett. He knew their languages and had studied their culture. With the support of the leading sachem (prince) of the Narragansett, he acquired rights to land at the confluence of two rivers. He called his new home Providence.

Others came. By 1640 there were some three hundred English settlers around the territory.[3] They needed civil order—systems to agree on and enforce criminal law, recognize land tenure, and manage such things as water, trade, hunting, and military defense. By what authority might they do this? English settlement in America was supposed to extend royal power by rivalling Catholic expansion. According to a plan prepared for Sir Walter Raleigh to present to Queen Elizabeth I:

> This western discovery will be greatly for the enlargement of the gospel of Christ whereunto the Princes of the reformed religion are chiefly bound amongst whom her Majesty is principal.[4]

Now come English settlers hostile to church establishment, with no English royal warrant. What should be the basis of the state? A series of local agreements tried to solve this problem. They make a fascinating collection, helpfully collated by Professor Lutz.[5]

The town of Providence was established with a simple compact signed by thirteen men in 1637 or, possibly, later:[6]

> We whose names are hereunder, desirous to inhabit in the town of Providence, do promise to subject ourselves in active and passive obedience to all such orders or agreements as shall be made for the

---

3. Adams, *Founding*, ch. 6.
4. Turner, "Colonial Religion," 3.
5. Lutz, *Colonial Origins*, 151–86.
6. For a full discussion of the dating issue and the role of Williams in the document, see Watson, "Dating [Part 1]" and "Dating [Part 2]," esp. 281–82.

public good of the body in an orderly way, by the major consent of present inhabitants, masters of families, incorporated together in a Towne fellowship, and others whom they shall admit unto them only in civil things.[7]

There is no oath or reference to God or king. The consent of inhabitants is sufficient. The scope of common action is confined to "civil things." Though Roger Williams was not among the signatories, the brief document reflects his principles.[8]

In 1638, the people of the town of Pocasset thought the basis was the laws of God:

> We whose names are underwritten do here solemnly in the presence of Jehovah incorporate ourselves into a Bodie Politick and as he shall help, will submit our persons, lives and estates unto our Lord Jesus Christ, the King of Kings and Lord of Lords and to all those perfect and most absolute laws of his given us in his holy word of truth, to be guided and judged thereby.[9]

Soon a group decided to withdraw from Pocasset and set up a new jurisdiction, which became Newport. Their founding document does not mention either God or king.[10] But the influential William Coddington is a prime figure in both—as judge of Pocasset, then as the first signatory of Newport.

A little later, Pocasset was renamed Portsmouth. A new compact of 1639 bound its people together in the name of King Charles, and pledged to enforce his laws.[11] Portsmouth and Newport shared Aquidneck Island, also known as Rhode Island. The two towns merged their governments in 1641. The officers bound themselves by oath before God.[12] Had Roger Williams been involved, he would surely have objected to this violation of religious liberty. However, they affirmed religious freedom: "It was further ordered that . . . none be accounted delinquent for doctrine."[13] They also articulated a new concept in American state formation: democracy.

> The Government which this Bodie Politick doth attend vnto in this Island, and the Jurisdiction thereof, in favour of our Prince

---

7. Lutz, *Colonial Origins*, 151.
8. Watson, "Dating [Part 1]," 171.
9. Lutz, *Colonial Origins*, 152.
10. Lutz, *Colonial Origins*, 154.
11. Lutz, *Colonial Origins*, 155.
12. Lutz, *Colonial Origins*, 160.
13. Lutz, *Colonial Origins*, 161.

is a democracie, or Poplar Government; that is to say, It is in the Powre of the Body of Freemen orderly assembled, or the major part of them, to make or constiue Just Lawes, by which they will be regulated, and to depute from among themselves such Ministers as shall see them faithfully executed between Man and Man.[14]

How could there be a democracy "in favor of our Prince"? The political thought of the time, developed by Jean Bodin,[15] identified "sovereignty" as being absolute rule vested in one of three models: monarchy, aristocracy, and democracy. Democracy, also called "popular government," meant a system where "the greater part of the people have authority to command not only each particular citizen as such, but the minority of the people as a body."[16] Bodin also distinguished between the mode of sovereignty and the mode of government. Thus, a democracy may be governed aristocratically (for example, in ancient Rome). A monarchy may be governed democratically—as, he said, was the case in England, France, and Spain.[17] The 1641 Aquidneck document seems to be thinking along these lines: the island is democratically governed but favoring its prince as sovereign ruler.

In 1642, in a land dispute, Massachusetts made an offer to "protect" part of the territory of Providence. Plymouth and Connecticut also showed interest in extending their power into the area of Providence and Rhode Island. In response, Portsmouth and Newport decided to seek a "patent" from England—a recognition of their separate jurisdiction, independent of the rest of New England. The mainland towns, including Providence, agreed to join this quest. Roger Williams was appointed to represent the claim. In the spring of 1643, he set off for London.[18]

London and *The Bloudy Tenent*

Roger Williams traveled to England from the port of what was then New Amsterdam (later New York). His ability in the Dutch language was helpful in using this route rather than going via Boston, where he faced likely arrest.

---

14. Lutz, *Colonial Origins*, 161.

15. Jean Bodin (1530–1596) is often considered the father of modern political thought. His theory of sovereignty responded to the decline of Catholic rule and the rise of the nation state. His major work, *Six Books*, appeared in 1576.

16. Bodin, *Six Books*, 73.

17. Tooley, introduction to *Six Books*, 24.

18. Barry, *Roger Williams*, 269–72.

He reached London in June 1643, with a book ready for publication. *A Key into the Language of America: Or an Help to the Language of the Natives in That Part of America, Called New-England* was the first published textbook on North American indigenous languages, with guidance on pronunciation. But it is more than that. It describes a culture with which the writer is deeply familiar. It depicts a people who have an organized society with literature, law, and property rights—important to defend his claim that the Narragansett were the owners of the land at Providence, and had the right to dispose of it as they chose. Its study of language, humanity, and culture caught the "pansophic" zeitgeist of rising opinion, well represented in Parliament. This idea saw understanding language as the key to accessing, and sharing, universal human knowledge. It was a book not just about using language but about "how to think about America."[19] It is a passionate claim for human equality.

The *Key* appeared within a few weeks of Williams's arrival in London. Soon there also appeared, on the London streets, copies of a letter from John Cotton, a prominent Massachusetts church minister. His letter—originally a private one to Williams—defended Williams's expulsion from the Bay territory. Cotton argued for true religion to be enforced in the interests of public order. Williams published a rebuttal. The *Key* and the dispute with Cotton enabled Williams to appear before Parliament as the victim of an attack initiated by Massachusetts, and a good friend for England in dealing with the New England native peoples.[20]

Roger Williams won his "patent" for self-government for "Providence-Plantations, in the Narraganset-Bay, in New-England." Now his claim to territorial government in Providence was valid under English as well as Narragansett law. In granting support, Parliament cited his project "to make a neerer neighborhood and society with that great body of Narragansets."[21]

That project for harmony with the native peoples of New England did not end well: but that is another story.[22]

While in London, Roger Williams wrote a book explaining his ideas rather more fully than he had to Parliament. *The Bloudy Tenent of Persecution for Cause of Conscience Discussed: And Mr Cotton's Letter Examined and Answered* appeared in the London bookshops in 1644. By then he had already

---

19. Field, "Key," 366.

20. It is also thought that a further pamphlet, condemning the Westminster Assembly of Divines (set up to look into alternative models of church-state relations) as having no Christian warrant for its existence, was Williams's work, but this appeared anonymously.

21. Warwick et al., "Patent for Providence Plantations."

22. Late in life, Williams led troops in war with the Narragansett. For more on this, see Fisher et al., *Reading*, ch. 11.

sailed west to bring home to America the precious patent for what later became the state of Rhode Island.

Williams's *Bloudy Tenent* is not an easy read for twenty-first-century eyes. It is "addressed to the faithful, without the slightest concession to any reader who had not been drilled in the discipline of Puritan disputation."[23] It is a conversation between two characters, named Peace and Truth. Much of it is concerned with refuting the idea that there is a biblical warrant for a theocracy to recreate Old Testament Israel for the modern age. Such a theocracy was the self-appointed mission of Massachusetts.

Williams explained why there is no authority in the Bible to attempt the reincarnation of Old Testament Israel. Ancient Israel, says Peace, is a "nonsuch, unparalleled, and unmatchable."[24] Truth confirms that its modern parallel is not a political kingdom but rather it is the church: that "holy mystical nation, the church of God, peculiar and called out to him out of every nation and country."[25] The state has no business involving itself in people's quest to join that "holy nation," nor in any aspect of their pursuit of faith:

> It is the will and command of God that, since the coming of his Son the Lord Jesus, a permission of the most Paganish, Jewish, Turkish or anti-Christian consciences and worships, be granted, to all men in all nations and countries.[26]

Today, all see that Williams was ahead of his time. But his shocking radicalism may not be obvious. In political thought prevailing in his day, the state's first duty was to enforce true religion. It was basic political common sense that "a church without a state may be conceivable, but a state without a church is not."[27] Religious "toleration" was known, but it meant pragmatic submission, an allowance of temporary leeway, taking account of the risks posed to state stability by attempting to enforce true religion against powerfully held opinion.[28] Williams's famous contemporary, Thomas Hobbes, saw that the state had a purpose above and beyond religious enforcement, but still thought that religious conformity was essential to civil order. To Williams, such enforcement was wrong in principle. Other bases for order were needed. Teresa Bejan, an American political theorist and Oxford professor, places Williams alongside Hobbes and John Locke as a political thinker of the seventeenth

23. Simpson, "How Democratic?," 56.
24. Williams, *Bloudy Tenent*, 278.
25. Williams, *Bloudy Tenent*, 277.
26. Williams, *Bloudy Tenent*, 2.
27. Figgis, *Thought*, 99.
28. Figgis, *Thought*, 94.

century. Using Williams's own phrase for his political philosophy, she entitles her book *Mere Civility*.

Williams needs to deal with a vital question that will be in the minds of his readers: If the purpose of government is not to promote true religion, what then is it for? What, in terms we use today, makes government *legitimate*? Agreeing that "civil government is an ordinance of God," Williams has Truth continue:

> But from this grant I infer . . . that the sovereign, original and foundation of civil power lies in the people . . . a people may erect and establish what form of government seems to them most meet for their civil condition. It is evident that such governments as are by them erected and established, have no more power, nor for no longer time, than the civil power, or people consenting and agreeing, shall betrust them with.[29]

So according to Roger Williams, government is legitimized by the consent of the people—not by enforcing God's law.

It was not a new thought. This idea of community sovereignty was proposed by Marsilius of Padua as early as 1324.[30] Like Williams three centuries later, Marsilius saw that God's commands must be accepted in people's hearts, by choice, not imposed by the state. The church should be ruled "from the bottom up" by "faithful human beings" though with the continuing advice and support of the pope.[31] Marsilius's preferred system of government was an elected "prince" with executive authority, applying laws based on broad community consensus. Today many recognize the architecture of later "democracy" in his writing—though, as a student of Aristotle, Marsilius would not have used that word in a way suggesting approval.

As a Puritan, Williams's first concern was for "soul liberty." While the "liberty of the subject" is sweet, "infinitely more sweet is that true soul liberty according to Christ Jesus."[32] Why therefore not accept the conventional wisdom of his day, that the state should establish the right church in order to enable all to seek the best kind of freedom, which is the liberation of the soul in the love of Christ?

---

29. Williams, *Bloudy Tenent*, 214–15.
30. Brett, introduction to *Defender*, xxii–xxiv.
31. Brett, introduction to *Defender*, xxx.
32. Williams, *Bloudy Tenent*, 294.

Williams responds that if the state is to promote one kind of liberty, then it has to promote *all* kinds of liberty, for it is "a branch of the same root to forbid what liketh not, as well as to enjoin what pleaseth."[33]

It is worth lingering a moment on this sentence. If the state decides to "enjoin what pleaseth" when it comes to matters of religion, then by the same logic it may "forbid what liketh not." Williams's experience was of persecution by a state that saw itself as creating a true Christian commonwealth. Williams saw that, if the state decides to support and promote "Christianity," then it must decide what constitutes "Christianity" for legal and policy purposes. This inevitably means that some who think differently may be excluded from that benefit. This argument is the same as was deployed 130 years later by James Madison, as he set out the case against church establishment in the new United States.[34]

Williams saw that the solution to this problem is a state with no religious affiliation—one whose duty is to the whole population, not to any one part of it. It does not matter whether or not that state is run by Christians:

> Now what kind of magistrate soever the people shall agree to set up, whether he receive Christianity before he be set in office, or whether he receive Christianity after, he receives no more power of magistracy than a magistrate that hath received no Christianity. For neither of them both can receive more than the commonweal, the body of people and civil state, as men, communicate unto them, and betrust them with.[35]

Return to Providence: The Process of State Formation

Parliament's patent authorized the Providence settlers to govern themselves "by whatever form . . . they shall find most suitable."[36] A series of meetings culminated in the "Acts and Orders" agreed in Portsmouth in May 1647. This constitution declared that:

> It is agreed, by this present Assembly thus incorporate, and by this present act declared, that the forme of Government established is democraticall; that is to say, a Government held by ye

---

33. Williams, *Bloudy Tenent*, 294.
34. Lambert, *Founding*, 232.
35. Williams, *Bloudy Tenent*, 341. "Magistrate" in seventeenth-century terms means any state official; the ruler is the "chief magistrate."
36. Warwick et al., "Patent for Providence Plantations."

free and voluntarie consent of all, or the greater parte of the free Inhabitants.

The constitution is designed to accommodate diversity and individual liberty in matters of faith:

> And now to the end that we may give, each to other, (notwithstanding our different consciences, touching the truth as it is in Jesus, whereof, upon the point we all make mention,) as good and hopeful assurance as we are able, touching each man's peaceable and quiett enjoyment of his lawfull right and Libertie, we doe agree vnto, and by the authoritie above said, Inact, establish, and confirme these orders following.[37]

One town was not named in the parliamentary patent and had not previously agreed a local compact. However, Warwick was a named town in the new Providence constitution. A few weeks after the combined Providence Plantations document was settled, Warwick followed the others in creating a local agreement. It was published by "the chiefe Sachems, Princes or Governours of the Nanhigansets" having "just cause of jealousy and suspicion of some of His Majesty's pretended subjects" (presumably a reference to Massachusetts). They put themselves under the protection of "Worthy and royal Prince, Charles, King of Great Britaine and Ireland" and appointed leading figures among the English settlers as their "commissioners."[38]

The Providence constitution names a government comprising a president and one assistant from each of the four towns of Providence, Portsmouth, Newport, and Warwick. Roger Williams is the assistant for Providence. The assembly also agreed:

> Forasmuch as Mr. Roger Williams hath taken great paines and expended much time in the obtayning of the Charter for this Province of Noble Lords and Governors; be it enacted and established, that in regard of his so great travaile, charges and good endeavours, we do freely give and grant to the said Roger Williams one hundred pounds,[39] to be levied out of the three townes, Vidg't: Fifty pounds out of Newport, thirtie pounds out of Portsmouth, and twentie pounds out of Providence, which rate is to be levied and paid in by the last of November next.[40]

---

37. Lutz, *Colonial Origins*, 172.
38. Lutz, *Colonial Origins*, 164–65.
39. Worth about £20,000 or $25,000 in 2024 spending power.
40. Lutz, *Colonial Origins*, 169.

Williams's investment in his expedition to London brought huge benefits for Rhode Island. The impact on England was also considerable.

London: The Anabaptist Response

When Williams boarded a ship bound for Boston, he carried his patent and a letter from Parliament requiring the Bay authorities to grant safe passage. He left *The Bloudy Tenent* for publication. It appeared in July 1644. Three weeks later Parliament ordered all copies to be found and burned. But its effect was great nonetheless.

In 1645 a prominent Calvinistic Anglican, Dr. Daniel Featley, published an address to Parliament identifying the "Anabaptists" as the most dangerous of the "Heretics and Schismatics," for they posed a threat to state as well as to church.[41] He called for them to be "most carefully looked unto, and severely punished, if not utterly exterminated and banished out of the Church and Kingdom."[42] Not only, complains Featley, do these Anabaptists "defile our rivers with their impure washings, and our pulpits with their false prophecies and fanatical enthusiasms" but furthermore "the presses sweat and groan under the weight of their blasphemies. For they print not only Anabaptism, from where they take their name; but also many other damnable doctrines, tending to carnal liberty.... Witness the book printed 1644, called the Bloudie Tenet."[43] Featley proceeds to quote Williams's words on the granting of religious liberty to all, the role of the state in religious matters and the wrongfulness of religious persecution.

Featley recognizes that Williams's book is not Anabaptism—but it is being produced by the same presses that publish Anabaptist teaching. He sees Roger Williams's teaching on political liberty as an evolution within the Anabaptist community, making it an even more dangerous threat to the established order. The response he calls for is for the Anabaptists to be "punished . . . exterminated . . . banished." That was no casual use of loose language. This violent persecution was what Anabaptists had endured, in state after state in Europe.

A group of churches identified as "Anabaptist" responded with their own address to Parliament, specifically in response to Dr. Featley. With this they published a revised statement of faith, which included one significant change of policy. Up to this point, they held the view normal among Anabaptists: the state is necessary to enforce order among nonbelievers, but it does not exist in

---

41. Featley, *Dippers Dip't*.
42. Featley, *Dippers Dip't*, ii.
43. Featley, *Dippers Dip't*, iii.

"the perfection of Christ." True Christians do not participate in its business. Now they introduced a new article reversing this position. They now held that it is lawful for a Christian to hold state office. The language of the declaration reflected Williams's imagery and principles.[44]

Members of these congregations were active participants in the army and government on Oliver Cromwell's side in the Civil War. The signatories of the revised statement of faith, published in 1646, included William Kiffen, who rose to the rank of lieutenant colonel under Cromwell and went on to serve as a prominent and well-connected member of the House of Commons.[45] Among others, Paul Hobson was a captain and later a major under Fairfax in the parliamentary forces. He served as deputy governor of Newcastle in 1648. Hanserd Knollys was a chaplain in Manchester's forces. Samuel Richardson, as well as being a writer of tracts promoting religious toleration and believers' baptism, was an advocate of soldiers' rights and a supporter of Cromwell.

The Puritan minister Richard Baxter of Kidderminster, shocked to hear of "swarms of Anabaptists in our armies," went to see for himself and found "a new face of things, which I never dreamed of . . . Independency and Anabaptistry were most prevalent."[46] The most shocking thing about this "new face" of the Civil War was this demand for freedom of religion in a state with a strictly civil remit.

So an element in English society adopted the ideas promoted by Roger Williams and entered the arena of active struggle for a different kind of state. Williams offered them a vision of a society where the state did not enforce or promote any religious conformity. Furthermore, he was actually testing this model in an English settlement, with the permission of the English Parliament!

These London "Anabaptists" were the first stirrings of the English "Particular" (or Calvinistic) Baptists—part of the "nonconformist" strain of English Christianity which long remained the core support of "tolerance" and the rise of liberalism, after Parliament finally took control of the monarchy in the late 1680s.

Dr. Featley characterized the London Anabaptists as "brewers' clerks" and "watermen," cooks and tailors, who "break into" the church and "snatch" holy orders. A rising class of skilled workers and small business people was challenging the remnants of medieval authority.

---

44. Lusk, "Reappraising," 22.

45. Kiffen's name is sometimes spelled "Kiffin." For more, see the series by Kreitzer, starting with *Part 1*.

46. Woodhouse, *Puritanism*, 384.

THE INVENTION OF DEMOCRACY

Williams and the Origins of Democratic Thought

Bernard Bailyn studied the thinking that led to the American Revolution. Along this path, he saw the footprints of England's war for religious freedom. The American Revolutionaries read the "radical publicists and opposition politicians in England" who "carried forward into the eighteenth century ... the peculiar strain of anti-authoritarianism bred in the upheaval of the English Civil War."[47] Roger Williams was an influence on this strain. There is evidence for this in Featley's attack on the "Anabaptists." In a lecture in 1936, a historian specializing in the American colonial period reported "130 references to Williams and his writing in the English writings of the civil war and commonwealth period."[48] A generation after Williams came the English "Glorious Revolution" when King James II was deposed, and the Act of Toleration gave freedom to Protestant dissenters. The key thinker associated with the period is John Locke, whose "Essay on Toleration" appeared in English in 1689, the same year as the act. It has sometimes been suggested that Williams was a direct influence on the later, famous Locke. One of Williams's more recent biographers, John Barry, speculates that Locke was "fully cognizant of and strongly influenced by" Williams.[49] A religious historian found:

> The parallels with the thought of Roger Williams ... are so close that it is not an entirely implausible conjecture to suggest that Locke's major contribution may have been to reduce the rambling, lengthy, and incoherent exposition of the New England "firebrand" to orderly, abbreviated, and coherent form.[50]

Unfortunately for these suppositions, there is no evidence to show that Locke ever read Williams. The link between them lies not in any personal passing of the philosophical flame, but in the breath that gave life to the Revolution of 1689. Williams himself was forgotten, but he had left the "body" of Christian dissenters with the "clothes" of democratic ideas that gave them their place in the political arena.

Williams's radicalism went well beyond that of Locke. Locke did not favor granting toleration to atheists "because they did not believe in the sacredness of oaths, which for Locke was important to the stability of society." Nor did he want freedom for Catholics, who might overturn the Protestant

---

47. Bailyn, *Ideological Origins*.
48. Wroth, *Roger Williams*, 17.
49. Barry, *Roger Williams*, 315.
50. Hudson, "John Locke," 28.

monarchy in favor of the pope.⁵¹ Williams insisted upon full freedom for all. Catholics, Quakers, Anabaptists, atheists, Muslims, and Narragansett spirit worshipers were all just as entitled to civil freedom as any brand of Protestant.

For many decades after his death, Williams was "viewed and treated as a fanatical heresiarch in religion, and a factious disturber of the state."⁵² Bancroft's ten-volume history of the United States, published from 1834 to 1874, revealed him to be "the first person in modern Christendom to establish civil government on liberty of conscience, the equality of opinion before the law."⁵³ Williams became hailed as a national hero. In the first half of the twentieth century, he was depicted as a prophet both of democracy and of modern "progressive" thinking. In 1927, a Pulitzer Prize–winning history proclaimed that "the gods . . . were pleased to have their jest with Roger Williams by sending him to earth before his time."⁵⁴ Vernon Parrington found Williams to be "primarily a political philosopher rather than a theologian"⁵⁵ and a "confirmed individualist" whose work prophesied America's liberal settlement.⁵⁶

The views of Parrington and his followers were demolished by a new generation of historians in the 1950s. Mauro Calamandrei showed that "rather than being a man of the Renaissance and the Enlightenment Roger Williams was a Puritan."⁵⁷ Alan Simpson dismissed him as a "passionate pilgrim" with "no vision of modern times."⁵⁸ Rising intellectuals found the key to understanding democracy either in secularization and the Enlightenment, or in class analysis and the material forces of history discovered by Marx.⁵⁹

So do we understand Williams as a pioneer of democracy and liberty— or as a Puritan stumbling around the margins of change?

Modern democracy's invention in Providence was not the product of Williams and his writing alone. He was a Puritan thinker who did not believe in Puritan rule. Providence gave refuge to all who took shelter from theocratic persecution, and Williams was sometimes at odds with his neighbors' values.⁶⁰ Nonetheless he placed his gifts at their service. His diplomacy, contacts, and intellect put him at the intersection of many forces—Puritans, the sachems,

51. Schwoerer, "Locke," 545–46.
52. Knowles, *Memoir*, ix.
53. Bancroft, *History*, 255.
54. Parrington, *Colonial Mind*, 62.
55. Parrington, *Colonial Mind*, 66.
56. Parrington, *Colonial Mind*, 72.
57. Calamandrei, "Neglected Aspects," 239.
58. Simpson, "How Democratic?," 67.
59. For example, in the work of Christopher Hill, starting with "English Civil War."
60. See for example the case of "Long Dick" in Murrin, "Things Fearful," 27.

the English Parliament, and the English radicals. This combination made possible the successful invention of "democracy" in Providence by its diverse community.

Roger Williams was a theologian first. Theologically, he found all civil interference in religion to be a violation of God's law. So the state must be adapted to this reality. Hobbes and Locke were political philosophers first. Their concern was for the political order to maintain itself. Religious freedom was, for them, something to be limited according to the needs of the state.

State Formation and Democracy After Christendom

In the establishment of Rhode Island, we see a deeply considered process of state formation. The settlers explore and test different bases for public authority. They discard ones that prove inadequate to the task. In a rapid series of experiments, they set themselves up under theocracy, monarchy, and democracy. "Democracy" is first proposed in the merger of Portsmouth and Newport, but in terms recognizable within Bodin's theory of sovereignty. Then Roger Williams returns from London. The whole body of settlers agrees on a new principle of sovereignty. Theirs is a "government held by consent." This concept of state legitimacy is set out in Williams's book of 1644, which he wrote in London, lingering long enough to ensure its publication there. Williams's book sets out his model of a state legitimized by consent. But it does not use the word "democracy" to describe this.

He now returns with English parliamentary approval for Providence and Rhode Island to organize their own government according to their own chosen principles. Williams has himself written the theory of a new form of state, legitimized by consent, and this was previously the basis of Providence town rule. The two towns on Rhode Island have called their system of majority rule "democracy."

Now the two ideas come together in the formula: *democracy, that is to say, held by consent*. In modern parlance, we can translate "held by" as "legitimized by." Democracy is a new theory of state legitimacy, developed out of the practical and theoretical search for a new basis for a state by people who seek to replace Christendom with a system that allows religious freedom. It is "democracy after Christendom."

3

Freedom and Slavery

This chapter continues the story of American democracy. For a moment, Evangelical Christianity flourished in a free democratic order. But the church split over slavery. We consider why civil war resulted, and how it sowed the seeds of today's crisis where "culture war" is waged against democracy.

Church and State in America: From Establishment to Separation

As the thirteen colonies entered the eighteenth century, most people lived under official church establishment.

There were with three exceptions. Rhode Island maintained its distinctive principled separation. New Jersey was a Dutch settlement ceded to the English king in 1664, with no religious affiliation specified in its charter. Pennsylvania was, in fact though not in principle, a Quaker state.[1]

Of the other ten, seven established the Church of England. Three in New England continued with Congregational establishment.

What establishment meant in practice varied from colony to colony and according to local circumstances. There were four general features. Attendance at church was required or at any rate expected. A parish system recognized a local minister, with no right for any other Christian teacher to cross the parish boundary without permission from the established church. The established church was supported from taxes. Religious tests sought to ensure that holders

---

1. Lambert, *Founding*, 102.

of public office, elected or otherwise, comply with the established order, however that was defined.

In the late 1730s, George Whitefield toured the American colonies with a series of evangelistic crusades calling on audiences—often huge gatherings—to be "born again."[2] The resulting "evangelical" movement swelled Baptist, Methodist, and Presbyterian congregations.[3] Some among the older churches were supportive of the rising Evangelicals. But many found themselves challenged by converts who refused to attend established churches and denied that their clergy were Christians at all. Itinerant evangelists disrespected parish boundaries and the rights of the established ministries to control them.

Evangelicals found themselves paying taxes for established churches, questioned about their nonattendance, and facing legal penalties for their Christian worship. Baptists were imprisoned. In one notorious case, an Anglican minister in Virginia entered a Baptist congregation and dragged the pastor out, to be publicly flogged by the sheriff. Evangelicals, with Baptists often leading, agitated for disestablishment and religious liberty. Thomas Jefferson and James Madison, though not themselves Evangelicals, were sympathetic to the Baptist case. They led the movement which eventually culminated in the Statute for Religious Freedom, passed in the Virginia legislature in 1786.

In 1774, the first Continental Congress met to pursue grievances against the British government. A group of Baptists and Quakers mounted an organized confrontation with the Massachusetts delegation. They demanded that Massachusetts end its oppression of dissenters, notably Baptists.[4] The main speaker against Massachusetts was the president of the newly formed Baptist college of Rhode Island—now Brown University.

The first shots of revolutionary war were fired in 1775. The second Continental Congress declared Independence in 1776. A government of the United States was created in the Articles of Confederation, ratified by all thirteen states in 1781. Peace with Britain was concluded in Paris in 1783.

The Anglican establishment was obviously anomalous in the revolutionary situation, and all seven states with this arrangement ended establishment. But that did not mean complete religious freedom on the lines of Rhode Island or Virginia. States kept religious tests for office, based on biblical, Protestant ascendancy.

2. Fitzgerald, *Evangelicals*, ch. 1.

3. In accordance with David Bebbington's analysis, the "evangelical" movement, initiated by Whitefield's crusades, is recognized by a central focus on the Bible and on the cross of Christ; personal conversion; and activism in social and community outreach. See Bebbington, *Evangelicalism*, 3. His characterization has become widely accepted. See for example Ligonier Updates, "Bebbington's Four Points."

4. Lambert, *Founding*, 225.

In 1785, the confederal Congress considered a proposal for developing the Northwest Territories.[5] It included provision for land set aside for whatever religious purpose was favored by a majority of local inhabitants—the first time the issue of religious establishment had come to Congress. The representatives debated various alternatives before agreeing to delete all reference to religion. It was the representative from Rhode Island who proposed this deletion.

In 1787 Congress worked intensively on a new constitution to replace the 1781 confederacy with a more powerful central authority. Should this recognize the Christian character of the new nation? There were voices in favor of some sort of explicit Christian expression. There were others who wanted to rule out church establishment altogether, not just at the new federal level but also within the thirteen states. This anti-establishment force was an alliance of Evangelicals, campaigning to remove all obstacles to complete religious freedom, and Deists and skeptics in the mold of Thomas Paine and Thomas Jefferson. The latter saw themselves as rationalists, questioning the truth of the Bible.

A third force wanted to protect established religion at the state level, though now they offered "tolerance" of evangelical dissent. This element included the three New England Congregational states. Before the Revolutionary War, the Quebec Act of 1774 greatly extended the province of Quebec along their borders, and came close to establishing Catholicism. This led the three states to resist any central establishment that might again threaten the "Congregational Way." So they too opposed federal establishment.

The first draft of the new US Constitution was silent on religion. Facing a clamor for religious freedom, Madison promised an early amendment to address this. The new Constitution was ratified by the thirteen states in 1789.

In 1791 the Bill of Rights made the promised amendments, meeting concerns raised in the state debates. The First Amendment provided that:

> Congress shall make no law respecting an establishment of religion or prohibiting the free exercise thereof; or abridging the freedom of speech, or of the press; or the right of the people peaceably to assemble, and to petition the Government for a redress of grievances.[6]

This contains the key principles of the religious settlement: the "Establishment Clause" and the "Free Exercise Clause." The amendment limited the powers of the new federal government. It did not touch the position in the states.

---

5. This is the area that eventually fell into the states of Ohio, Indiana, Illinois, Michigan, and Wisconsin.

6. National Archives, "Bill of Rights," art. 3.

The extension to the states came after the Civil War. In 1868, the Fourteenth Amendment affirmed the right of all US citizens to "equal protection":

> All persons born or naturalized in the United States, and subject to the jurisdiction thereof, are citizens of the United States and of the State wherein they reside. No State shall make or enforce any law which shall abridge the privileges or immunities of citizens of the United States; nor shall any State deprive any person of life, liberty, or property, without due process of law; nor deny to any person within its jurisdiction the equal protection of the laws.[7]

In the twentieth century, the US Supreme Court interpreted this to mean that the states themselves could not do anything to favor or support any particular expression of religion. They drew authority for this view from President Thomas Jefferson's letter to the Danbury Baptists, written in 1802. Jefferson was, as we have seen, known for his work to achieve such a separation in Virginia.

The Baptists of Danbury, Connecticut, wrote to congratulate their new president. They added a hope that his election would prefigure an end of religious establishment in New England: an establishment where their freedom of worship came from "favors granted" rather than "inalienable rights."[8] Jefferson responded, perhaps with more enthusiasm than accuracy, claiming that the First Amendment erected a "wall of separation between Church & State."[9]

The vision of the Danbury Baptists did come to pass. But this was not due to the leadership of religious skeptics like Jefferson. Rather, Christians may see the work of the Holy Spirit in advancing the work begun through Whitefield. As European migrants poured into America in the first decades of the nineteenth century, preachers attracted vast crowds at tent meetings.[10] Evangelical churches grew apace. The vestiges of church establishment fell away: Massachusetts was the last to end it, in 1833.

In 1800, the USA had grown from thirteen states to twenty, plus the District of Columbia (DC), which has its own local government but has never been a state. In 1850 there were thirty-one. In these fifty years the population quadrupled. The modern USA was taking shape. By mid-century a large proportion of the population of America, white and black, slave and free, was evangelical. It was, for the moment, a Christian people without a Christian state.

---

7. National Archives, "14th Amendment."
8. Danbury Baptist Association, "To Thomas Jefferson," para. 2.
9. Jefferson, "To Danbury Baptists," para. 2.
10. Fitzgerald, *Evangelicals*, ch. 1.

Democracy After Christendom
Christianity, Slavery, and the Civil War

Tocqueville's Prophecy

In his survey of the United States in 1831, the French observer Alexis de Tocqueville found that "equality of social conditions" was the "factor which generated all the others." The resulting democracy was inevitably, and to the alarm of many, on its way to Europe.[11] But he was deeply aware of the "wide gap . . . caused by prejudice and law" defying the equality of America's "three races."[12] So great was this gap, thought Tocqueville, that racial integration was impossible in a democracy, though it could be possible in a powerful monarchy. To expect a democracy to overcome racial prejudice—on the scale the author encountered in the USA—would be to expect a "whole nation" to "rise above itself."[13]

Tocqueville died in 1859, a little too soon to witness his assessment of America's racial future put to the test.

Evangelicalism and Slavery

Right from the early days of the Republic, the evangelical movement divided over slavery. Evangelicals preached to slaves, and Evangelical Christianity spread among the enslaved community.[14] Many Christians held slaveholding to be sinful. Believers should, therefore, endow their slaves with freedom. In 1780, the Methodists set a deadline of three years, after which no member could own slaves.[15] The South refused to accept this, and eventually the new rule was withdrawn. Similar disputes affected the Baptists. Later, the great evangelist Finney urged Christians to abandon the practice and free any slaves they held. At first, he resisted the increasing politicization of the issue. He

---

11. Tocqueville, *Democracy in America*, 11.

12. Tocqueville, *Democracy in America*, 376. Richard Resh, in "*Democracy in America* Reconsidered," thinks that Tocqueville justified slavery. I do not think this is a correct reading of Tocqueville's argument. It is one that Tocqueville himself denied. Tocqueville suggested that African slaves, stripped of their own culture and language, aspired to belong to the culture of the oppressor, which they admired more than they hated. By contrast, native Americans enjoyed the "nobility" of their own culture even as it was gradually eroded in "uneven struggle."

13. Tocqueville, *Democracy in America*, 418.

14. Mohamed et al., *Faith*, ch. 10.

15. Fitzgerald, *Evangelicals*, 50.

hoped that voluntary settlement could head off the mounting pressure for a federally imposed solution.[16]

In 1800, of the twenty states and DC, only four had no slaves. Of a population of 5.3 million, about 16 percent were black slaves.[17]

By 1850, out of a population of 23 million, about 13 percent were slaves. Fifteen states were without slaves. Almost all slaves were in the eleven states that became the Confederacy, and in three others that divided over the secession. So over the first half of the nineteenth century, the growth in the number of slaves more or less kept up with the rapid population growth—but became concentrated in the states identified with the South in the Civil War of 1861–1865.

Gradually two strands in Evangelical Christianity parted company over the question—both the Methodists and the Baptists formally split in the 1840s, into southern (pro-slaveholding) and northern (anti) wings. Whether a Christian could hold slaves was a vociferously debated question, with both sides gleaning support from Bible texts. The USA headed for what is often considered a war over the meaning of the Bible. As the Christian historian Mark Noll puts it:

> The Book that made the nation was destroying the nation; the nation that had taken to the Book was rescued not by the Book but by the force of arms.[18]

The Civil War *became* a war over the morality of slaveholding. It ended, after the Union victory, in the Thirteenth Amendment to the Constitution, making the practice illegal. However, the war's origins do not lie in this moral question as such. How then did it come about?

The Origins of the Civil War

The explanation is found in the USA's continued *expansion*. Congress had to decide whether new territories, as they developed and became states, would allow slaveholding or not. This was not just a question of the rights and wrongs of the practice—though this entered the debates—but of the distribution of power. Places in the electoral college, which chooses the president, and in the federal House of Representatives, were both based on the size of population. For this purpose, one slave counted as three-fifths of a free person. Of course,

---

16. Noll, *God and Race*, 32; Fitzgerald, *Evangelicals*, 47.
17. Author's analysis of published US census data.
18. Noll, *Civil War*, 8.

slaves did not vote. But the number of representatives elected to the house and to the college reflected all of the free, plus 60 percent of the enslaved, populations. The power of the votes cast was magnified by the presence of the nonvoting slaves.

Many white southerners did not own slaves. But they still needed to earn their income by trading or working freely in an economy that used ever-growing numbers of slaves. Power in the slave states lay with the owners of enslaved labor. As the US grew, this power could grow in the new slave territories, and the slave owners' power thus be more and more magnified at the federal level. This was the issue that caused the Civil War in the USA. It started in Kansas, after a decision to resolve the issue by a vote among the population triggered a violent struggle between pro- and anti-slavery forces for majority control in the new state.

America After Slavery

With the Union victory came the Thirteenth Amendment. Freed slaves became owners of property and participants in the democratic order. For a short while, former slaves voted and took office. The first Civil Rights Act passed Congress in 1866, carried by a Republican majority that overrode the veto of the Democrat President Andrew Johnson. The continued presence of the Union Army in the former Confederacy protected the new federally endowed rights against violence instigated by the former slaveholders. The faction representing the white majority, led by the former slaveholders, called themselves "Redeemer" Democrats: they wanted to "redeem" the old order.

The national Republicans—the party of Lincoln and the Union side in the Civil War—became divided. "Radical" Republicans supported keeping the army on the ground to complete the process of "Reconstruction" of the South. "Liberals" were uneasy with federal enforcement in the face of resistance at the state level. The presidential election of 1876 resulted in a disputed near tie, with the Democrats taking over half the popular vote. A deal put the Republican Rutherford B. Hayes in the White House, after he agreed to withdraw the Union Army from the South. Thus "Reconstruction" ended in 1877.

After that, federal legislation to secure black rights stalled in Congress or was not enforced by the courts. Ultimately the impediment was not just the power of the white South in the Democratic Party. It was also the reluctance of the northern white working class to commit to black equality.[19] In the old

---

19. Schlozman, *Movements*, 239.

South, through a mixture of legislative devices and organized violence, freed slaves and their descendants were denied the right to vote and hold office.

In the twentieth century, a network of "African American" leaders developed the strategy to regain the status first won in the 1860s: the status of free and equal citizens in a democracy. Networks in churches and universities deliberated over objectives and tactics to achieve these. Black troops served honorably in two world wars. Between the wars, black advisers worked in the administrations of Franklin Roosevelt, to ensure that the fruits of the "new deal" welfare programs reached the black population. In the election of 1948, the Democratic Party platform included a commitment to civil rights.[20] The Democrat President Harry Truman desegregated the armed forces in the same year.[21]

As a result of the shift of the national Democratic Party in favor of black equality, the party split. In 1948, white southern Democrats ran Strom Thurmond as candidate for president against Truman. Thurmond won four southern states, taking thirty-nine places in the electoral college.[22] Twenty years later, the Democrats in office carried through civil rights legislation. Southern Democrats again supported a dissident, pro-segregation candidate. This time George Wallace and his American Independent Party won 13 percent of the vote in the presidential election of 1968. He took forty-five votes in the electoral college by winning five southern states.[23]

The outcome was a brilliant maneuver with a lasting impact on American public life. We see this in the next chapter.

Slavery and the Roots of Culture War

Modern liberal democracy first arrived as the way to replace Christendom, and to achieve freedom of religion based on equal rights to self-government. In the early USA, the democratic culture was one where all had equal access to the Christian faith. But seeing this to its conclusion needed Christians to agree to abandon slaveholding. The church failed to see this to completion. The task of liberation passed to the state. The "culture war" is the legacy of the resulting struggle.

---

20. Democratic Party, "1948 Democratic Party Platform," paras. 82–86.

21. By executive order, signed July 26, 1948.

22. Thurmond's party was the States Rights Democratic Party. For the full results, see the American Presidency Project: Woolley and Peters, "1948."

23. Woolley and Peters, "1968."

4

Culture War

"Culture war" has divided US politics by religion and race, denying space for democracy "held by consent." Crucial to this has been the development of a white Christian voting bloc, brilliantly engineered in the 1970s. This chapter explains how this happened.

The legacy of the Civil War and civil rights left a substantial "body" available to be mobilized by political organizers. But, to use Isaiah Berlin's metaphor,[1] a "body" requires the "clothing" of ideas to give it direction and purpose.

Nationalism and racism are commonly suggested—but are these enough to explain how the movement was "clothed"?

"War to the Death"

In the late 1970s, a new movement arose in American democracy. From 1979 to 1989, it was organized as the "Moral Majority." Its leader was the evangelical Baptist pastor Jerry Falwell. It was a project to recruit and train pastors to lead a political movement. This movement would be organized in worship gatherings, with congregations mobilized to become a force in political campaigning. "Make them write those letters in church," Falwell told pastors. "It's all perfectly legal as long as you don't use the church for special meetings."[2] Later, Rev. Falwell was content to give his accomplish-

---

1. Berlin, "Two Concepts," 193.
2. Lienesch, "Conservatism," 408.

ment the name by which it is best known. "I spent the last 30 years forming the religious right," he said in 2006.³

At the heart of the religious right was an alliance of two forces: white Christians distressed at the rise of a liberal, secular state that no longer endorsed their perceived Christian cultural values; and "right-wing" politics wanting to enhance the role of the free market, reduce the scale of the state, and diminish the place of state welfare.

The strategy to achieve this alignment was brilliantly engineered by political organizers using new communications technologies—the mass televised broadcasting mastered by Christian evangelists, and computerized mailing lists used for political fundraising—to "flip" two key voting blocs from Democrat to Republican: white, evangelical Protestants, especially concentrated in the South; and, to a lesser extent, Catholics.⁴

It proved a formidably successful alliance, giving the world the Republican presidencies of George W. Bush (2001–2009) and Donald J. Trump (2017–2021, and then for a second term from 2025). But its first great triumph was the victory of Ronald Reagan. In 1980, Reagan defeated the sitting president and avowed evangelical Christian Jimmy Carter.⁵ Reagan won again in 1984 before—as constitutionally required—retiring from the presidency in 1989.

In 1991 the conservative commentator Midge Decter wrote:

> The two decisive Reagan elections bore testimony not so much to a wish for radical new policies as to an open declaration of war over the culture. And a culture war, as the liberals understood far better than did their conservative opponents, is a war to the death.
>
> For a culture war is not a battle over policy, though policy in many cases gives it expression; it is rather a battle about matters of the spirit.⁶

Reagan was succeeded by his vice president, George H. W. Bush, who served one term before losing to the Democrat Bill Clinton in 1992. This election is often remembered for the slogan displayed by Clinton's campaign manager James Carville, in his headquarters in Little Rock, Arkansas:

> It's the economy, stupid.⁷

---

3. Meachan, "Editor's Desk," para. 2.

4. Himmelstein, *To the Right*.

5. The election takes place in November with the commencement of the presidential term in the new calendar year. Thus, Reagan served until January 1989 but was not a candidate in the election in November 1988.

6. Decter, "Reagan," paras. 16–17.

7. Bennett, *Race*, 124.

Most commentators agreed that the economy swung the vote in favor of Clinton.

But four researchers, sifting through the data, found something more profound below the surface. "Economic questions," they said, "represent . . . transient forces that surge and decline" against a "cultural bedrock." This *cultural bedrock* was shifting:

> A new kind of party alignment is emerging: a difference between religious and nonreligious voters from all traditions. . . . In this context, evangelical Protestants . . . are a fulcrum on which both present and future party alignments rest.[8]

The 2020 presidential election showed the resilience of their analysis. Seven out of ten white, non-Hispanic churchgoers voted for the Republican candidate, President Donald Trump. This included well over eight out of ten white Evangelicals, and more than six out of ten Catholics. Of black churchgoers, nine out of ten voted for the Democrat, Joe Biden. Of atheists and agnostics of all races, the proportion voting for Biden was close to nine out of ten.[9] This represents a big shift of party identity over a few decades: in 1960, 60 percent of white Evangelicals, and 73 percent of Catholics, identified themselves as supporters of the Democrats.

So the cultural "war to the death" is fought on two fronts. One is the *religious* front—a battle over the place of Christianity in governing a "Christian nation." The other is *racial*, between white and black people.

This war is fought in and through democracy. Voting is a weapon in religious and racial struggle. In studying how it came about, we learn much about *how* democracy works.

It is also a war *against* democracy. As we saw earlier, democracy in America begins with the idea that the power of the state is legitimized by the consent of all, or most, of the population. Culture war defies this claim. Its triumph will be completed when that shared consent has become impossible.

The Republican governor of Florida, Ron de Santis, was, for a time, a contender for the presidency of the US. Speaking to students at a Christian college in Michigan, the governor misquoted the apostle Paul[10] in urging the students to "put on the full armor of God. Stand firm against the Left's schemes."[11] Governor de Santis was saying something that many Republican electors take to be true. The "left" is the "devil."

---

8. Kellstedt et al., "Religious Voting Blocs," 309.

9. Norty, "Most White."

10. "Put on the full armor of God, so that you can take your stand against the devil's schemes" (Eph 6:11).

11. Cabellos, "What Message?," para. 2.

Among Americans who count themselves supporters of one of the two main parties, four out of ten now regard the other side as "evil."[12] As Midge Decter saw, the "liberals" understand even more clearly than the "conservatives" that culture war is *war to the death*. The reaction of one side feeds cultural conflict at least as fiercely as the provocation of the other.

Two out of ten Americans think that violence is an acceptable way of gaining their side's political objectives.[13] This is in a land where four in ten households are armed, and half of the rest think they may be in future.[14]

For months before January 6, 2021, folk gathered in a series of events to hear why the American state was not legitimate.[15] Convinced of this, they went to the Capitol, where their elected federal representatives meet in the two chambers of Congress. The protestors erected gallows and sought political leaders who (they thought) deserved to die. Many displayed crosses and banners proclaiming themselves followers of Jesus. They huddled in prayer and read their Bibles together.

In those Bibles they could, if they looked, find the Roman governor Pontius Pilate asking Jesus Christ if he truly is the king of the Jews. Jesus answers that his kingdom is not of this earth—otherwise, his followers would be using force to prevent his crucifixion.[16] The New Testament injunctions to "submit to the governing authorities" seem clear.[17] How can some "Christians" contemplate the overthrow of the established order and its replacement with a "Christian" state?

The next section explains the technical tour de force that engineered a new alliance between white Christians and the free-market right.

We then examine the ideas that continue to power it. Racism and nationalism play a part, and these often feature in hostile critiques of the religious right.

The Right Gets Religion: Making the Religious Right

The great military organizer Dwight D. Eisenhower served as Republican president for most of the 1950s. During this time, a section of the Republican Party was unhappy with what it saw as the left-wing, pro-welfare stance of the mainstream party. They were roughly on the same page as the rising

---

12. Kleinfeld, "Rise," 167.
13. PRRI Staff, *Values*.
14. K. Schaeffer, "Key Facts."
15. Seidel, "Events."
16. John 18:36.
17. Rom 13:1; 1 Pet 2:13.

Thatcherites in Britain: admiring right-wing, free-market economists such as Von Mises and Hayek, favoring a smaller state and lower taxes, and critical of the welfare state as developed in America by President Franklin Delano Roosevelt's "New Deal." Their wing of the party succeeded in making Barry Goldwater the Republican nominee in the presidential election of 1964. Goldwater was trounced by Lyndon Baines Johnson. Johnson pushed through the long-awaited Civil Rights Act and expanded the welfare state through the "Great Society" program. Richard Nixon won for the Republicans in 1968 and 1972, but then resigned amid the disgrace of Watergate. His vice president, Gerald Ford, took over, and then chose Nelson Rockefeller to be *his* vice president. Rockefeller was the standard bearer of the liberal left in the Republican Party.

The free-market right needed a new strategy.

The key figure in finding this new strategy was the political consultant Richard Viguerie. He was skilled in the art of campaigning and fundraising through computerized mailing lists. He developed this first within an early right-wing movement, the Young Americans for Freedom, and then as part of the Goldwater campaign. Seeking a new way forward for the Republican right, he offered his services to George Wallace, to raise funds to pay off campaign debts.

This was not an obvious move for someone like Viguerie. Southern whites were far from favoring free-market, small-state economics. The white Christian nationalist movement, heavily supported in the South, promoted radical redistribution of wealth in the 1930s, while being virulently pro-segregation and anti-Semitic. Southern whites were key beneficiaries of the New Deal. Wallace's platform included expanded social security and protecting trade union rights.

Viguerie was familiar with raising money from middle-class, middle-income conservatives, traditional Republicans supporting the party of Lincoln and anti-slavery. Now he was addressing his mailshots to working-class, big-state racists. It was a journey of discovery, from which emerged the coalition of the "New Right." From his work with Wallace, Viguerie made an important finding. "Wallace supporters went to church."[18]

In 1976, the southern evangelical liberal Jimmy Carter defeated Gerald Ford and regained the presidency for the Democrats. But Viguerie, himself a Catholic, had found the key to the prospects for a revival of the American right. He knew that, with the correct strategy, the "next majority for growth for conservative ideology and philosophy is amongst evangelical people."[19]

---

18. Schlozman, *Movements*, 85.
19. Schlozman, *Movements*, 85.

His strategy achieved the white evangelical bloc vote, which has remained one key base in "culture war" politics ever since.

Viguerie is a great example of a key figure in American democracy: the "broker" whose career is assembling alliances of disparate groups that may deliver a majority to their clients.[20] This was not something invented on the right. Viguerie said that "all the New Right has done is copy the success of the Old Left."[21] The Democratic Party has always been a coalition of disparate interests. The Republicans, in developing cultural warfare, learned how to craft their own.

Nationalism and Racism

Any such alliance needs more than just its "body" formed of material interest. To return to Isaiah Berlin's metaphor, it needs also the "clothing" of ideas. Without these it is blind and directionless.

So the next question is: What are the *ideas* that give vision and direction to the body of white Christians who have been so ably marshalled into the "religious right"?

Christian Nationalism?

One widely heard explanation is "Christian nationalism." Lawyer Andrew Seidel explains this means:

> An identity built on the claim that America was founded as a Christian nation, that it was based on Judea-Christian principles, and, most importantly, that we have strayed from that foundation, from our godly roots.[22]

Andrew Whitehead and Samuel Perry describe churches where nationalist theology is preached and nurtured. Worship leaders, and their supporting large choirs, all wear military uniform. Congregations pledge allegiance to the US flag, the Christian "flag," and the Bible, in that order. They hear that Jesus laid down his life for the American nation.[23] The psychologist Dave Verhaagen defines this Christian nationalism as a "belief that the United States is a special

---

20. Schlozman, *Movements*, 35.
21. Schlozman, *Movements*, 81.
22. Seidel, "Evidence," 2.
23. Whitehead and Perry, *Taking America Back*, 1–2.

entity ordained by God for special historical purposes"—rooted, he suggests, in "narcissism."[24]

The British academics Roger Eatwell and Matthew Goodwin say:

> Nationalism refers to a belief that you are part of a group of people who share a common sense of history or project . . . it involves a strong desire to preserve national identity from radical change.[25]

So, for these writers, "nationalism" is a *cultural* movement celebrating, and seeking to preserve, a shared identity developed through a common history.

In his defense of Christian nationalism, Stephen Wolfe writes:

> A nation has no power in itself to bring anyone internally to true faith—to realize heavenly good in individuals. But nations have the power to ensure that outwardly the things of salvation—the preaching of the Word and the administration of the Sacraments—are available to all and that people are encouraged, even culturally expected, to partake and be saved unto eternal life.[26]

In this sense we may see a "Christian nation" as a *cultural union* where individual conversion to Christianity is encouraged and even expected. Preaching, worship, and other activities are open to all.

However, "nationalism" means *more* than just a loyalty to a culture that nurtures a particular identity. Let me illustrate this.

I live on an archipelago off the northwestern coast of Europe called the British Isles. Four nations live on our islands—the English, Scottish, Welsh, and Irish peoples. There are two states here. One nation, the Irish, is split across two states. The northeastern end of their island is a province of the United Kingdom of Great Britain and Northern Ireland. The rest of the island of Ireland is the territory of the Republic of Ireland. Some (though not a majority) in the "north" would prefer their territory to become part of the Republic: they are called "nationalists." Across the Irish Sea, and to the north of England, lies Scotland. Around half the population of Scotland support "nationalism." They wish to break up the UK and form a Scottish state. The Scots who disagree with their "nationalist" neighbors are still part of the Scottish nation. They are patriotic Scots, who share and celebrate a Scottish cultural identity. They just take a different view of the best relationship between nation and state. They wish Scotland to remain part of the United Kingdom, which is a *multinational* state.

---

24. Verhaagen, *White Evangelicals*, ch. 2.
25. Eatwell and Goodwin, *National Populism*, 78–79.
26. Wolfe, *Nationalism*, 15–16.

A "nation" may be a body of people with a shared cultural identity linked to their occupation of a particular piece of territory. It is, as Benedict Anderson says, an "imagined community."[27] It is a number of people who do not in fact know each other, but think they know each other through a number of features that they see themselves as sharing. These may include language, diet, dress, family practices, and religion. These cultural features make a shared community life.

A "nation" may also mean a body of people who are subject to the authority of a particular state. In this sense, we speak of the "United Nations Organization." Its members are not "nations" in the sense of being cultural unions; they are actually "states."[28]

Nationalism Defined

"Nationalism" means the *union* of these two *different* ideas of what "nation" means. "Nationalism" is a claim that the state should represent, and be based upon, a cultural union of the people under its authority.

In this sense Dr. Wolfe defends and promotes "Christian nationalism." Steeped in his study of late medieval and early modern thought, he talks of a Christian "prince" or "magistrate" to rule over this cultural union. The Christian *nation* must, he thinks, have a Christian *state*.

Democracy began in America through Roger Williams's realization that a Christian society should *not* have a Christian state. To put this in Dr. Wolfe's terms, Williams's idea was that a Christian nation would nurture a Christian culture but that it would *not* have a Christian state.

Dr. Wolfe is not alone in missing this vital point. Andrew Seidel writes that "religious nationalism" is based on a "demonstrably false" claim that "America was founded as a Christian nation." He proves this "falsehood" by quoting an international treaty made between the USA and Muslim powers in 1797, specifically this line:

> The Government of the United States is not, in any sense, founded on the Christian religion.[29]

This, he says, *proves* that the US was not then a Christian nation. Mr. Seidel assumes that "the Government" and "the nation" are the same thing. He then says that Thomas Jefferson made Virginia "the first state to separate

---

27. Anderson, *Imagined Communities*.

28. Maybe the "United Nations" should have been called the "United States," but that name was already taken.

29. Seidel, *Founding Myth*, 16.

government and religion" in 1785[30]—unaware, it seems, of Roger Williams and Rhode Island's much earlier model of separation. The First Amendment to the federal Constitution forbade establishing a religion. This was Roger Williams's solution to the problem of Christendom faced by the Protestant Reformation.

Earlier generations understood that, as a historian wrote in 1924:

> We are a Christian nation even though Christianity is not a feature of the American state.[31]

This seems to have been forgotten. Once, it was generally accepted that what enabled both Christianity and democracy to flourish in the United States was—in the words of a Lutheran minister—the "basic American principle that Church and State should be kept wholly separate."[32]

Now Whitehead and Perry identify a hallmark of Christian nationalism as *rejection* of the separation of church and state.[33] Representative Lauren Boebert is an officer of the Republican "Freedom Caucus" in the House of Representatives. She denounces the idea of separating church and state as "junk." This "junk," she thinks, resulted from Jefferson's "stupid letter" to the Danbury Baptists, rather than an accurate reading of the Bill of Rights. The actual constitutional intent, she says, was that:

> The church is supposed to direct the government. The government is not supposed to direct the church.[34]

Clearly, if "the church is supposed to direct the government" then the consent of all, or most, citizens applies only as long as they agree with this proposition. Democracy, in other words, is subordinate to something else: rule by Christians organized into "the church."

So American "Christian nationalism" is in part a belief in God's special purpose for the American people, disclosed in the foundation of the "nation." But it is not only that. It is also a claim about the relationship of nation and state—a claim about who should properly have control of the state and for what ends that state exists. We need to examine why and how some American believers have lost confidence in the separation of church and state, and now call for some sort of reunification.

---

30. Seidel, *Founding Myth*, 37.
31. Humphrey, *Nationalism and Religion*, 2.
32. Schoenfeld, "Separation," 662.
33. Whitehead and Perry, *Taking America Back*, 8–9.
34. Dress, "Boebert," paras. 1–2.

CULTURE WAR

"Racism" and Othering the Religious Right

Viguerie's strategy detached a historically racist but broadly left-wing white bloc from the Democratic Party and attached it instead to the Republican "right." So is "Christian nationalism" to be understood as really a racist movement? Is "Christian nationalism" better described as "white Christian nationalism"?

Introducing a study of the violent invasion of the Capitol on January 6, 2021, Amanda Tyler says:

> Throughout the report, the authors use the terms "Christian nationalism" and "white Christian nationalism," the latter term explicitly acknowledging the overlap of Christian nationalism with racism and white supremacy. The different contributors to the project use the terms with which they are most comfortable or that best reflect their research and areas of expertise.[35]

This is revealing. The authors' analysis is admittedly subjective. Is this sporadically violent challenge to American democracy essentially racist? It depends who's asking! "Different contributors" give an answer from their own comfort zone, rather than an objective study of the situation. The researchers find evidence of a church-led conspiracy against democracy. But their resulting analysis is based on the most "comfortable" positions from which to assault their target. They are, in the end, more interested in firing salvos in the culture war than in seeking to understand what is really going on.

This applies more widely to public discourse about the "religious right." Tony Keddie writes for "anyone who is fed up with the Republican Jesus."[36] Kristin Kobes Du Mez calls on misogyny to explain *How White Evangelicals Corrupted a Faith and Fractured a Nation.*[37] Random House made a late change in title before publishing Sarah Posner's *Unholy: Why White Evangelicals Worship at the Altar of Donald Trump.* Its original title, according to the author's agent's website, was *Alt-Bloc: The Religious Right's Unlikely Union with the Alt-Right, and How It Is Changing American Politics.* The publisher's blurb promised to solve a mystery:

> Why did so many Evangelicals turn out to vote for Donald Trump, a serial philanderer with questionable conservative credentials who seems to defy Christian values with his every utterance?[38]

---

35. Tyler, introduction to *Christian Nationalism.*
36. Keddie, *Republican Jesus,* 19.
37. Subtitle of Du Mez, *Jesus and John Wayne.*
38. https://www.penguinrandomhouse.com/books/605774/unholy-by-sarah-posner/.

There is merit in these books. But the marketing plays into the culture war, cultivating a sneer at the other side and denying space for the kind of discussion that is needed if democracy is to be retrieved. No doubt there is misogyny, idolatry and racism at work among the religious right—perhaps more than on the secular left—but, may I suggest, anyone who has not come across these vices on the "left" should have got out more.

The white religious vote for the Republican side has been consistent since first analyzed in the early 1990s—it is not something that arrived with Trump. To give the name "worship" to the act of voting for Donald Trump is merely an aggressive blow in the culture war. If Evangelicals had been interested in keeping one of their own in the White House, they would not have voted to evict Jimmy Carter.[39] Christians who voted for Trump did not, or at any rate did not need to, suppose that he has faith in Christ. They believed that he, rather than his opponent, would work in the secular domain to defend and promote their interests and causes.

"Nationalism" and "racism" are often offered as explanations of why the religious right movement has apparently succeeded in stirring cultural war. These do not function well as explanations. They are, rather, retaliatory strikes intended to bolster one side in the "war." We need to look elsewhere to discover the ideas that clothe the body that identifies itself as the "conservative" side in the culture war.

The Demand for a Christian State

American Christians once, generally, embraced the idea of a Christian nation *without* a Christian state. This meant they could enjoy a culture in which it was permissible, even preferable, for an individual to be "born again" as a believer. Christians accepted what Roger Williams and then the Evangelicals in English America had found: that this culture was best facilitated by a state that protects freedom of choice in matters of faith. This state does not favor any brand of Christianity or any other religious or anti-religious outlook. This is an element of what is known as the "liberal" state.

Cultural war demands the restoration of a "Christian" state. The idea of a "Christian" nation cannot alone justify or explain this demand.

---

39. Hart describes how President Carter invited leading Evangelicals to breakfast in 1980. His guests concluded they had a president who "confessed to be a Christian, but didn't understand how un-Christian his administration was." Hart, *From Billy Graham*, 97.

5

Education and the Rise of Theonomy

This chapter seeks to understand the underlying idea which gives the movement direction—the "clothing" for the "body," in Berlin's metaphor. "Nationalism" and "racism" do not suffice to explain the political success of the "Christian Right."

"Theonomy" is a better explanation. It means applying the Bible as civil law. This is a legitimizing theory for the state. It rivals democracy's consent theory.

A New Force Unleashed

Theonomy arose as a viable political doctrine in reaction to Supreme Court decisions which aimed, as Professor Davis explained, to "rid the country of a vast accumulation of state-initiated, organized, religiously-based intrusions into the public schools."[1] This was based on interpreting the First Amendment in a way that "transformed" the US Constitution and so "gave birth to the modern Establishment Clause in 1947."[2]

Professor Davis supports the legal arguments underpinning some, though not all, of these judgments. But two in particular "set off a firestorm" and "unleashed a new political force," when the "so-called religious right found a rallying point in supporting the rise of the Reagan administration. . . . Supreme Court decisions strongly separating prayer and public schools . . . played an important role in dividing the country politically along

---

1. Davis, "Religion," 42.
2. Feldman, "Transformation," 675.

religious lines."[3] In a moment we will examine these events, and the linkage between them.

First, though, let us clarify the role of the US Supreme Court.

Who Makes the Law?

The Congress of the United States of America comprises two houses: the House of Representatives and the Senate. This was modeled on the British Parliament, which also has two houses: the Commons and the Lords. These are "legislatures": one of their functions is to pass laws. They do this by approving written documents. The members of these assemblies are sometimes called "legislators." This word is a bit of a mouthful. The media often offers a simpler word to describe these members: they are called "lawmakers."

However, a "legislator" is not quite the same thing as a "lawmaker." Legislatures do not, ultimately, *make* the law: rather, they agree and issue the vital first draft. Their drafts are developed and molded into *laws* by the courts. Courts decide not just what the laws say, but what they mean. They apply laws to cases. This may be complex and challenging. Legislation—the writing that Parliament or Congress approves as "law"—is sometimes clear and easy to apply. Sometimes it is ambiguous and confusing. The courts must sort this out. Their decisions are "precedents" and become "case law." Disputes before courts become arguments about "points of law." As a general rule, appeals against decisions made in lower courts are made on these "points of law." Higher courts generally accept the facts confirmed by a lower court and consider whether the law was properly understood in the judgment made on those facts. Higher courts make decisions about what the law really means. These judgments become law. In this way, courts, not legislatures, make the law. This should not be controversial. It is simply what is meant by the "rule of law." The decisions of legislatures must always be subject to review by the law courts to ensure they are in keeping with the body of learned rules and procedures that make up the "law."

There is a significant difference here between the United Kingdom and the United States. In the United Kingdom, the ultimate power to change law lies with the House of Commons.[4] The Commons is "sovereign." So if

---

3. Davis, "Religion," 44.

4. Some may claim that the sovereign body of the UK is still the "Crown in Parliament," meaning that there are three elements that agree on legislation—Commons, Lords, and Monarch. This is a true description of the formal procedure. However, it is thoroughly established in law that Parliament is supreme over the Monarch, and has been since the seventeenth century. Under the Parliament Acts passed since 1911, the Commons can

legislators are unhappy with a court decision, their solution is to change the legislation. The courts may still find that the new legislation does not make sense. They may decide that the new law conflicts with fundamental rights that are laid down in other laws and even traditions. But the Commons is the "sovereign" body that has the right to change any law. So we expect to find a close resemblance between what legislators have decided and what the courts agree constitutes "law."

This is not so in the United States. Laws here must comply with the Constitution. If the courts decide a case based on what the Constitution says, Congress has no power to change it. The Constitution can be changed, but this is a complex matter involving approval by the states, now made close to impossible in the conditions of cultural war.[5] When it comes to the Constitution, Congress is the prisoner of the courts.

Under the federal Constitution, the final say on appeals lies with the Supreme Court of the United States, or SCOTUS for short. Its nine members take only a small fraction of the cases that people ask it to consider. SCOTUS judges decide what cases they take, and what they leave untouched. The members of SCOTUS serve until they resign or die. New members, like all the judges in the federal courts, are appointed by the president with the "advice and consent" of the Senate. In practice this means the president makes nominations, which are then approved or rejected by the Senate.

The "culture wars" are fought not just in elections, but also in the courts. Some controversial SCOTUS decisions have been central to these battles. A series of these concerned education.

Establishment and Education: Culture War Declared?

The USA has a famous system of public education—cost-free schools for all, run by the state at the local level. In the twentieth century, this enabled the proportion of Americans completing high school to grow from under 10 percent to over 80 percent in fifty years.[6]

After the Second World War, SCOTUS made a series of decisions about religion in public schools. These concerned how the "Establishment Clause" of the Constitution applied to state-funded, state-directed education. As we have seen, the First Amendment forbade Congress from establishing a religion.

---

overrule the Lords. So it is a fact of law and politics that the Commons is the sovereign body under the Constitution of the United Kingdom.

5. Wegman, "Constitution."
6. Putnam, *Upswing*, fig. 2.6.

After the Civil War, the Fourteenth Amendment said that states must honor the "equal protection of the laws" to which any US citizen is entitled. SCOTUS decided that this gave it jurisdiction over the cases of religious observance in schools.

In the state of New York, public education is controlled by "the oldest continuous policy making board of education in the world":[7] the Board of Regents appointed by the New York state legislature.[8] In 1951, the board, being "aware of the dire need . . . to pass on America's Moral and Spiritual Heritage to our youth" introduced a "spiritual and moral training program." This included recommending that schools have the following prayer recited at the start of the school day:

> Almighty God, we acknowledge our dependence upon Thee, and we beg Thy blessings upon us, our parents, our teachers and our Country.[9]

This was not a requirement. John F. Brosnan was a prominent Catholic lawyer elected as a regent in 1949, later serving as chancellor of the university and chair of the regents. He wrote in 1955:

> We have the power to mandate; we seldom do. Usually we only recommend, because we believe in the principle of home rule. If the people at the grassroots want good schools and good teachers, they can get them. If they don't, neither you nor I nor anyone else can force these good things upon them.
>
> We believe that moral and spiritual training in the schools is a sine qua non. Therefore we have been gravely concerned with our schools' drift away from our fundamental American Moral and Spiritual Ideals—Liberty under God, Respect for the Dignity and Rights of Each Individual and Devotion to Freedom.
>
> From the beginning of our deliberations, we were committed to the preservation of the American doctrine of the separation of church and state. We want no sectarianism nor any preference for any religious tenet in our public schools. But we believe that moral and spiritual training is shadow, not substance, if divorced from God.[10]

---

7. University of the State of New York, *Regents*, 11.

8. Though entitled the Board of Regents of the University of the State of New York, its responsibility extends to all public education in the state, presiding over both the university and the State Education Department.

9. Stone, "In Opposition," 823.

10. University of the State of New York, *Regents*, 14.

Education and the Rise of Theonomy

In line with the policy to "recommend" but not "mandate," it was for local school districts to take what they wished from the regents' guidance. In 1958, the district of Hendricks, in Long Island, decided to implement the "Regents' Prayer" in the schools under its authority. Here the school board oversaw seven schools—five elementary, one junior high, and one senior high—with a total of 5,400 students.

Five parents mounted a legal objection. They included two Jews (Mr. and Mrs. Engel), a Unitarian, an agnostic, and a supporter of the humanist Ethical Culture movement. These parents objected that the prayer violated the "Establishment Clause" of the Constitution.

The New York state courts dismissed the claim, having established that students could absent themselves from the prayer without incurring any penalty.

SCOTUS accepted an appeal. In 1962, it found for the claimants and overturned the state courts' decision. The Regents' Prayer, they decided, amounted to the state "establishing a religion." The case is *Engel v. Vitale*.

In the opinion for the court, Justice Black wrote:

> We think that the constitutional prohibition against laws respecting an establishment of religion must at least mean that, in this country, it is no part of the business of government to compose official prayers for any group of the American people to recite as a part of a religious program carried on by government. . . . There can be no doubt that New York's state prayer program officially establishes the religious beliefs embodied in the Regents' prayer.[11]

The school board's attorney argued:

> [The] men who put the country together have publicly and repeatedly recognized the existence of a Supreme Being, a God. . . . We are proceeding fully in the Court with the tradition and heritage which has been handed down to us . . . in the Declaration of Independence, we have four references to the Creator, to the Supreme Being who gave us our unalienable rights. We can't rewrite history now. Those words are emblazoned in that document, and they will always be with us.[12]

Justice Black responded:

---

11. Engel v. Vitale, 370 U.S. 421 (1962), 425–30.

12. Engel v. Vitale, 370 U.S. 421 (1962), oral argument, Apr. 3, 1962, pt. 1, https://www.oyez.org/cases/1961/468.

> It is a matter of history that this very practice of establishing governmentally composed prayers for religious services was one of the reasons which caused many of our early colonists to leave England and seek religious freedom in America.... It was doubtless largely due to men who believed this that there grew up a sentiment that caused men to leave the cross-currents of officially established state religions and religious persecution in Europe and come to this country filled with the hope that they could find a place in which they could pray when they pleased to the God of their faith in the language they chose.... [The] best example of the sort of men who came to this country for precisely that reason is Roger Williams.[13]

These two statements—the school board's attorney's and Justice Black's reply—are not necessarily contradictory. The USA developed—eventually—as a Christian people without a Christian state. That said, Justice Black offered a false reading of America's history. There were not "many" early colonists who thought as Roger Williams did on the matter of religious freedom. The court suggested that the prohibition of establishment, implemented in the First Amendment, was meant to prevent religious persecution. Even tokenistic religious acts in schools risked opening the way to the return of persecution. As Professor Davis pointed out, the court needed only to look across the Atlantic to see, in the United Kingdom, a place with both an established church and religious observance in schools—but no more apparent risk of religious persecution than in the US. The argument that prayer or Bible reading in schools opened the way to renewed persecution, of the kind endured in early modern Europe, was absurd.[14]

Professor Davis finds "irony" in the fact that these decisions, made with the intention of bridging social division, resulted in the opposite outcome: radical confrontation. Would it not have been better for these matters to be settled "through the democratic process" rather than "someone in a black robe" telling people that their ideas were unconstitutional? His example of democratic settlement concerns a dispute in his home state of Kansas over the teaching of evolutionary science in school.[15]

However, had the issue of school prayer been referred to the democratic process, the outcome would not have been in doubt: polls consistently found

---

13. Engel v. Vitale, 370 U.S. (1962), at 421, 425, 434, including note 20.
14. Davis, "Religion," 43–44.
15. Davis, "Religion," 45–53.

Education and the Rise of Theonomy

around three-quarters of the population in favor of praying in the public schools.[16]

The court struggled to find reasoning to support its position on school religion. Eventually it hit on *equality* as the basis for its judgments. The "equal protection of the laws" meant that no student may feel diminished by not taking part in communal religious observance. The "Establishment Clause" was thus transformed "from protector of liberty to guarantor of equality."[17] This new doctrine interpreted the First Amendment (in the words of Justice Clark, writing the opinion in *Schempp*)[18] as a "Command . . . that the Government maintain strict neutrality, neither aiding nor opposing religion." The fact that a "majority of those affected" consented made no difference: they still could not forego their First Amendment "right to free exercise of religion," which, SCOTUS found, required state neutrality.

The new doctrine enunciated in these rulings was one that replaced democratic consent with new principles for state legitimacy: individualism, equality, and neutrality. The state's job was to protect each individual's right to equal inclusion, and to remain neutral between competing demands on individual loyalty.

The heart of the matter here is the purpose and control of education. The regents were appointed to manage *education*. Their remit extended only to what went on in that sphere. There is no need for the state to have any responsibility for education: it could be left as a matter for the family and private endeavor. However, tax-funded education is an engine of equality and social development. It aims to ensure that all are equipped to enter the labor market and contribute, as producers, to a modern economy.

Is that all it is? Clearly not. Education shapes culture: what goes into education is what is thought necessary for culture to thrive. In the USA, this has meant shaping a diverse community for citizenship. That is why the school day usually starts with the pledge of allegiance to the flag. To British eyes, this is weirdly idolatrous. But we can make sense of it if we understand America as a land for immigrants, to be transformed, rapidly, into a body of citizens, while having a deep attachment to an ancestral identity. They remain "Italian Americans" or "Irish Americans" or even "African Americans" while becoming and remaining "American." How?

---

16. Gallup, "People Favor Prayers."
17. Feldman, "Transformation," 678.
18. School District of Abington Township, Pennsylvania v. Schempp, 374 U.S. 203 (1963). This case, considered a little later than Engel, found that a Bible reading at the start of the school day violated the Establishment Clause.

The New York school authorities said that their job is to transmit American cultural heritage, and this includes monotheism. To understand what this means requires some practical experience of how speaking to one God looks and feels: otherwise it is "shadow, not substance." The regents are accused of "Protestant indoctrination,"[19] but the chancellor was a Catholic, and the prayer was designed to be shared by any monotheist believer. We can, however, relate the regents' case to Stephen Wolfe's account of Protestant national culture: one where a Christian culture does not make Christians, but it can be one where coming to personal "saving" knowledge of Christ is acceptable, even perhaps expected. For this to be "substance" then some experience of how prayer looks and feels is not necessarily inappropriate provision.

SCOTUS held that the law against church establishment required the state to be "neutral" in religion. The state does not endorse or favor any particular religious view. But can education be neutral? Surely not. Education is based on the point of view considered authoritative in a culture. Of course, students must also learn to think critically about what they are taught: a good teacher exposes the assumptions behind the dominant wisdom and encourages intelligent questioning of these. But "neutrality" is never a sensible aspiration in education.

It may or may not have been wise for the regents to recommend praying as part of the school day, or to go as far as actually writing the words of a recommended prayer. But it was not SCOTUS' job to review that matter. SCOTUS had to decide whether this recommendation amounted to "establishing a religion" in violation of the First Amendment, to the extent that it should overturn the New York regents' advice.

It would be futile to suggest here that the judgment be reversed, or that (as Ronald Reagan promised, but did not deliver) the Constitution be amended to permit religious observance in schools. We cannot turn back the clock of history. It is no longer likely that a majority of parents would see themselves as "Christian." Any action now to restore "Christianity" in the public schoolroom would be understood in the context of the culture wars, as an action in those wars, arousing a response from the other side.

But I think we may reasonably infer that SCOTUS, in its judgments on school religion, ignited the culture wars. Recognizing this would be a step in resolving the wars and preparing a way for the settlement that is essential if democracy is to be restored.

---

19. Davis, "Religion," 44.

Education and the Rise of Theonomy

Men in Black Robes

So who were the "men in black robes" who launched the SCOTUS assault on school religion? These lawyers were, unsurprisingly for the times, all white men, born in the last two decades of the nineteenth century. But they were also working politicians.

Hugo Black wrote the majority opinion in the 1962 *Engel* case. Black was from a poor, rural, Baptist home in small-town Alabama. When appointed to SCOTUS in 1937, he had been a US senator from his state for ten years. He was a leading advocate of Roosevelt's New Deal and of protecting and expanding labor rights. He was also a former member of the Ku Klux Klan, a notoriously violent, racist, anti-Semitic, and anti-Catholic organization dedicated to protecting white Protestant ascendancy in the South. Without winning Klan support, he would not have become a senator.[20] He was a qualified and seasoned lawyer, but his only judicial experience was a short period as a part-time police court judge in Birmingham, Alabama. Tom Clark, who wrote the court's opinion in *Schempp*, had been attorney general in the wartime government: in this role, he had overseen the locking up of all Americans of Japanese descent. Justice Jackson, also a former attorney general, had been chief prosecutor at Nuremburg when the defeated leaders of Nazi Germany were put on trial.[21] Another justice had been the key legal adviser to the Roosevelt administration in its banking and monetary reforms.

So these men in black robes were not dispassionate observers simply applying the law to the changing American landscape. They were drivers and shapers of America as it emerged from 1945 as the world's preeminent power. They were not merely interpreting the Constitution. They were constituting America itself, to prepare it for its new mastery of a world where fascism was defeated and European imperialism was terminally diminished. Now only Communism posed any serious challenge to the new American era.

This was largely the same court that, in 1953, banished the doctrine of "separate but equal" segregated education and required the racial integration of the public schools. These white men in black robes were deeply aware of America's racism. Some had built their careers on its appeasement. Now their task was to reshape American culture to fit the needs of the new American world-state.

---

20. According to the *Encyclopedia of Alabama*, Black's victory in the 1926 Democratic primary was "one of the greatest upsets in the state's political history," achieved after "Black courted Klan support by visiting all of the state's 148 Klan chapters." Hébert, "Ku Klux Klan."

21. For more on the impact on international law of this case, see Sands, *East West Street*.

Ostensibly SCOTUS' rulings on religion and race were both aimed at creating harmony out of diversity. Ironically, Professor Davis notes, the religious findings had the opposite effect. This is not surprising, considering that some version of monotheistic religion was a point of unity between the main races of postwar America—white, black, Hispanic, and Jewish. In overcoming what Professor Davis called "Protestant indoctrination," the judges were in fact unpicking an obvious way to knit people together.

Prayer as Public Ritual

I used to be a member of a local council, the lowest level of elected public body, in my English village. A senior Conservative member decided to move a motion that we should pray before the start of the meeting—something that was once common but has gradually drifted out of everyday local politics. He said this would restore "formality" to our proceedings.

In a secret ballot, I voted against the proposal. Group prayer is for believers, not for mixed groups in public ceremony. But the proposal passed. At first an Anglican minister, who was a member of our council, read prayers aloud from a printed card. Later I became chair of the council. I prayed as I normally would, not from a script but speaking to God, naturally, from my heart.

The local Anglican bishop visited. He asked me if it was true, as he had heard, that I "prayed like an Evangelical" at council meetings. Indeed I do, I said, because I am one!

Had there been another vote on the matter, I would still have voted against. Prayer as public ritual at formal government meetings is a hangover from Christendom. It pretends that all are Christians. But the members wished to have prayer, and then they elected me as chair. I showed them what (in my experience) prayer is.

Praying at the schools in Hendricks was not the same as prayer at my council meetings. The Board of Regents wished to transmit cultural values to a new generation. It was not my job, as a council leader, to transmit cultural values to my members. If my Conservative fellow councilor wanted a way to confer more formality on our council proceedings, then we could have devised a ritual more relevant to the secular proceedings of local administration.

Education and the Rise of Theonomy

Enter Rushdoony

SCOTUS did not deny America's Christian heritage, affirming that "we are a religious people."[22] Both sides offered a simplified understanding of what this meant for public life. However, the SCOTUS opinion was, by some distance, further from the truth than was that of the educators. The fundamental question of what this meant for education was not asked.

There was a logical conclusion to be drawn. Consider the following three propositions. Education should communicate culture. Monotheistic performance belongs as part of American culture. The "neutral" state must not provide monotheistic performance in schools. From these it follows that someone else—not the state—should be running the schools.

One man, Rousas John Rushdoony, stood ready to seize the time. His ideas on biblical government became the foundation of the religious right.[23] The education controversy opened the way for his radical doctrine to enter mainstream politics.

Rushdoony was a Presbyterian missionary working with Native American people in the Duck Valley Reservation in Nevada. Public education was, he found, a central force in their disempowerment and oppression. Why, and what was to be done? Pursuing this led him to homeschooling, then largely forbidden or discouraged by the state authorities. He fought a series of legal cases on this. In 1970, he succeeded in overturning the Texas Education Agency's total ban on homeschooling. He showed the falsehood of the agency's claim to provide a consistent standard of education to all parts of the community.[24] He became a leader and mentor of a movement claiming for families the right and opportunity to educate children in a Christian framework, both in Christian private schools and in the home. This movement must be rated as a successful insurgency against state power.

The Christian education movement rose in parallel with the racial integration of public (state) schools. In ruling circles in federal America, there was a tendency to presume that the real purpose of Christian private schools was to maintain racial segregation.[25] In a move begun under President Nixon, the Internal Revenue Service (IRS) investigated whether private schools were in fact practicing racial exclusion. The IRS approach was to presume that the private schools were discriminatory: they had to prove otherwise to keep their

---

22. From Justice Douglas's opinion for the six to three majority in Zorach v. Clauson (1952).
23. Ingersoll, *Reconstruction*, 3.
24. McVicar, *Christian Reconstruction*, 2.
25. Freedman, "Religious Right," 238.

tax-exempt status. The rising religious right managed to hold President Carter to "blame" for this IRS policy. Outrage at apparent state suppression of Christian private education was a "turning point" in the effort to capture the white South for the Republicans.[26] Ronald Reagan, as presidential candidate, promised action to reverse it. Rushdoony worked for Reagan's election, expecting to secure this support for Christian schools. When Reagan reneged on this pledge, Rushdoony withdrew from the circle of Christian advisors gathered around the new regime in the White House.

His place as intellectual counsel to the religious right passed to a more popular, less complex thinker. Francis Schaeffer was, like Rushdoony, a Presbyterian missionary, concerned about the damaging effects of modern Western civilization on more vulnerable people. Among his achievements was a famous retreat providing refuge and care for victims.[27] He wrote commentaries on art and culture from an evangelical Christian perspective. He came to see abortion, legalized in the 1972 *Roe v. Wade* SCOTUS judgment, as signifier of the West's dark embrace of death. This stand against abortion brought him new, Catholic admirers and cash. Ronald Reagan's presidency, he proclaimed in his *Christian Manifesto*, offered a window for Christians to regain the West.[28] Jerry Falwell distributed over sixty thousand copies of the book through his Old-Time Gospel Hour broadcasts.[29]

Theonomy and the Religious Right

The Coming of Theonomy

Rushdoony developed a Christian political philosophy that denied the legitimacy of the democratic state. A Christian society must be one based on observing God's law, as found in the Bible. The only proper role for the state was as a "ministry of justice" enforcing God's law. In his 1974 book *Institutes of Christian Law* he distilled from the Bible a complete account of what civil law should comprise. All law is religious in origin, he argued; any change in law is a change in religion. A pluralistic society, with tolerance toward diverse religious persuasions, is actually polytheism.

Rushdoony and his followers gave a name to the system they expected to be installed once Christians had taken control of the social order, in a process

---

26. This was the view of Paul Weyrich, a key figure in the strategy. Freedman, "Religious Right," 236.

27. L'Abri.

28. F. Schaeffer, *Christian Manifesto*, 73.

29. Schlozman, *Movements*, 106.

they called "Reconstruction." It would be "theonomy," meaning "God's law." In accordance with the Old Testament commandments, worship of false gods would attract the death penalty.

Schaeffer presented a softer face of Christian authority. Pluralism and religious liberty were commended. However, he affirmed biblical law as the basis for the legitimacy of the state. Schaeffer was the widely admired inspiration for the first generation of religious-right politicians.[30]

Rushdoony gathered around him a small group of dedicated thinkers and writers who promoted his philosophy under the rubric of "Christian Reconstruction." His most flamboyant follower married his daughter. Later in Rushdoony's life, Gary North broke the heart of his father-in-law when he set up a new branch of the Reconstructionist movement in Texas. Here, in a church, he stored weapons in readiness for armed struggle. Rushdoony was horrified beyond measure. He broke off all communication with his son-in-law.[31]

For Rushdoony, the modern democratic state is "Moloch," the satanic, false god demanding idolatrous worship. His "ministry of justice" is not a different legitimizing principle for a renewed state. Rushdoony's idea was closer to the Marxist one of the withering away of the state. Once converted Christians understand their true calling, there is no need for a state, except to enforce God's law against a minority of unbelievers and dissidents. He did not think Christians had any mission to overthrow the state by force.

Schaeffer calls on Christians to remodel the state as an instrument to enforce submission to God's law. Civil disobedience is justified, even mandatory, in this quest. "We are at war," he wrote. "There does come a time when force, even physical violence, is appropriate."[32] The modern state, in its refusal to be subordinate to the law of God, is a "tyranny." It is worse than the states that persecuted the Reformers.[33] Much of the *Manifesto* is a call for civil disobedience in the "war" against the state that rejects the final authority of God. This, he accepts, may become a campaign of violence to overturn the state. Sometimes "force in a defensive posture is appropriate. This was the situation of the American Revolution."[34]

---

30. Lusk, *Jesus Candidate*, 13.
31. McVicar, *Christian Reconstruction*, ch. 6.
32. F. Schaeffer, *Christian Manifesto*, 130–31. Schaeffer used the term "civil disobedience" when in fact he described armed struggle. He did not recognize what Martin Luther King Jr. and Mahatma Gandhi meant by "civil disobedience," i.e., nonviolent action designed to provoke state violence and thus expose state injustice.
33. F. Schaeffer, *Christian Manifesto*, 101–2.
34. F. Schaeffer, *Christian Manifesto*, 117.

Racism, Nationalism, and Theonomy

Modern democracy is threatened by "cultural warfare." This warfare denies the possibility of rule by consent. It demands that people identify with one side or the other in struggle for control of culture and state.

Clearly *race* has played a large part in defining the identities that are at war with each other. America is still undoing the legacy of slavery and the Civil War. We may describe this in terms of "racism." But we need to be clear what this means. In normal usage, when we say that someone is "racist," we refer to feelings, attitudes, and behavior toward others. Such racist *feelings* shape identity and what Professor Berlin called the "body"—that driver of history called the physical, material, or natural force. But the body is directionless unless it wears the clothing of ideas.

Racism may provide such clothing, in the form of the *idea* that one race is naturally superior, so entitled to rule. This racist *idea* prevailed in the early part of the twentieth century, drawing strength from Darwin and providing legitimacy for the European empires. It served the needs of the white South in post-Reconstruction USA. But it could not survive the outcome of the Second World War, with the full horror of state-sponsored racial hierarchy laid bare in the Nazi death camps.

Attributing culture war to "Christian nationalism" begs its own question. A "nation" may be the whole populace served by a state, or it may be a cultural union. "Nationalism" is an idea that brings these two together. It claims that the state must serve a cultural union, so that those outside the cultural union are, at best, less entitled to the protection of the state, and to a voice in its affairs. At worst, "nationalism" may explode into destructive, state-sponsored violence against the cultural "other." American Christian culture flourished with "separation of church and state." The question is: How did a large body of Christians come to reject this, and to call instead for a new union of church and state?

An important part of the answer is *theonomy*. It is theonomy, invented in the modern era by Rushdoony, that provides the driving force for religious right political thinking.

The evangelical theologian Wayne Grudem says that he rejects theonomy because he rejects the philosophy proposed by Rushdoony. He means he rejects the idea that all civil law should be derived from the Old Testament. However, Grudem continues that Christians should "persuade others that the moral standards found in the Bible are correct and should be used in human government."[35] After all, Grudem says:

---

35. Grudem, *Politics*, 169.

> [The] laws against murder are based on a moral conviction that murder is wrong. The laws against stealing are based on the moral conviction that stealing is wrong. Laws against polygamy and incest are based on the moral conviction that those things are wrong. Laws against sexual harassment, or adults having sex with minors, are based on convictions that those things are wrong.[36]

He infers from this that abortion should be illegal because it is wrong. He also suggests that allowing it to be legal makes it impossible to argue that it is wrong.

Grudem's argument merges *three different* frameworks for judging and regulating human behavior: the civil law, which concerns actions to be penalized by the courts; moral assessments of what makes conduct virtuous; and God's law, as found in the Bible. Grudem says that Christians should work to bring these together into a single system to be "used in human government."

Christians observe God's law out of love for God. This foundation does not exist for nonbelievers. It cannot be instilled by legislation. Grudem's argument amounts to proposing that Christians, who obey God's law out of love, should use civil law to make others conform to its practical outworking. This line of argument is, I suggest, the essence of theonomy. It is now the core position of the religious right. Inevitably it invites others to find other bases for law, and thus other foundations for state legitimacy. Here is cultural war: the "war to the death" over the nature and purpose of the state.

This is not to say that racism and nationalism do not matter. Many people identify as whites, or as members of the "true" American Christian people, or both, and feel that they share collective interests with others in this group. They may think their material or other interests will be better met by policies sympathetic to white, racial nationalism. A large number seem ready to celebrate the idea that Americans, or maybe just white Americans, are a new version of "God's chosen people": that the European settlement of America was God's "most significant attempt" at forming a "new Israel."[37]

The idea that Americans (or British, or any other people group) have a special status in God's new kingdom flies in the face of the New Testament. In the body of Christ:

> There is neither Jew nor Gentile, neither slave nor free, nor is there male and female, for you are all one in Christ Jesus.[38]

---

36. Grudem, *Politics*, 168.
37. Peter Marshall and Manuel, *Light and Glory*, 21.
38. Gal 3:28.

God calls the church to be a body that transcends differences of nation, culture, gender, and social status, and brings together his people from all cultural and national settings. Reflecting this in practice is challenging. Of course, actually existing church gatherings are always constrained by the cultural affinities that help people enjoy each other's company. The challenge is always to question this, to refuse to settle for this as how things must be, to seek out ways to give expression to the truth of gospel freedom reflected in the unity of believers across culture. Martin Luther King Jr. lamented that eleven a.m. on Sunday was the most segregated hour in America.[39] He was not condemning the church, but he was wanting it to ask itself questions.

Stephen Wolfe belongs to the "Reformed" Christian tendency. Being "Reformed" would usually suggest a resort to the Bible as the first source of God's word. His idea of the "Christian nation" as one where culture and institutions facilitate belief in Christ is helpful. But he bases his "Christian nationalism" on this argument: humans create localized settlements and then reproduce successive generations, so that over time people acquire loyalty to their ancestral culture. This is not a biblical argument. It is based on "natural law"—the idea that observing and analyzing material reality gives an insight into the mind of God.

Surprisingly, Dr. Wolfe does not mention the account in Genesis of the tower of Babel (Babylon). God dispersed people into nations in order to frustrate human attempts to create a powerful unified culture that would set its own goals.[40] God then calls out a people over whom he will rule. He gives this people his law to keep and uphold. With the coming of Christ, all now can join God's people. This new people, living under God but free of the restrictions of race and nationality, is entrusted with the task of building God's kingdom.

The Guiding Idea: Theonomy

The key guiding idea of the religious right is *theonomy*. This calls on Christians to establish God's law in the government of the state. This is not nationalist: it can apply to any people in any state. Nor is it racist. However, like nationalism and racism, theonomy flies in the face of the obvious meaning of the Bible. Christians are called to obey God out of love for him, not to earn God's favor by obeying him. The obedience compelled by theonomy can only be loveless conformity. Theonomy says the state is legitimized by Christian values. This calls out opposing values, leading to the cultural "war to the death."

---

39. Speaking on *Meet the Press*, Apr. 17, 1960. M. King, "Most Segregated."
40. Gen 11:1–9.

Education and the Rise of Theonomy

In England, for the first time in maybe a thousand years, the people who call themselves "Christians" are in a minority. America is fast approaching the same situation. The emerging majority claims to have "no religion." Many Christians see theonomy and cultural war as proper ways to call society back to a righteous path. Many fear that liberal democracy cannot survive the transition out of the majority "Christian" society in which it was established.

6

Politics and the State

Democracy is a *political* system. But what does that mean? If we want to think effectively about democracy and its alternatives, then we have to be clear about what we are referring to when we use the word "politics."

This chapter argues that the study of "politics" concerns the relationship of citizens and the state. By "the state" we mean a social institution that successfully claims a monopoly of the use of physical force in a geographical territory. It then proposes that the Bible offers a view of politics that helps us understand the modern situation. We can derive a biblical theory of the state that helps us understand the Christian role in modern democracy.

This chapter is in two parts. The first part answers the questions "What is politics?" and "What is the state?" The second part examines politics and the state in the Bible.

What Is Politics?

A "Political Gospel"?

"The gospel is a political gospel," writes the eminent Christian thinker Stanley Hauerwas:

> Christians are engaged in politics, but it is a politics of the kingdom that reveals the insufficiency of all politics based on coercion and . . . finds the true source of power in servanthood.[1]

In similar vein, a pastor writes:

---

1. Hauerwas, *Peaceable Kingdom*, 100.

> The church is political. . . . To the extent that a church regularly discerns how to live socially, economically and morally, together under his [Christ's] authority, by definition it is a politics.[2]

"Everything in the church is political," explains Jonathan Leeman:

> The church's political nature begins with its own life—with its preaching, evangelism, member oversight and discipline.[3]

"Jesus was political," a prominent Christian teacher told one of Britain's biggest yearly Christian gatherings in 2022:

> Jesus spoke about a model which illustrated what is leadership and what is authority—and what is politics if not these things?[4]

The theologian Luke Bretherton defines politics as "the ongoing process through which to maintain commonality . . . in pursuit of shared temporal goods."[5]

These all depict "politics" as a property to be found in *all* human relationships, wherever they require leadership, power, or organization in common endeavor. Christians in their church communities can then model how to do these as Christ expects. This is "politics." To be "political" is to *be* the church. Christians do not *have* a social ethic, says Hauerwas. They *are* the social ethic.[6]

These thoughts are beautiful and inspired by a godly mindset. Sadly, they are also misleading. They draw our attention away from what "politics" really is. Power, leadership, and authority are relevant in politics, but they are also relevant in every aspect of human conduct—in the many ways that people make their livings, carry on their family life, or create and destroy the conditions of happiness. Are these all "politics"? Or does "politics" refer to something more specific?

This widespread problem is not confined to Christian thinking. Professor Lane opens her book about classical thought with these words:

> Politics is a spectrum of the possibilities of power. It defines relations among humans and the purposes they pursue.[7]

---

2. Fitch, *Church*, 144.

3. Leeman, *Political Church*, 52.

4. Dr. James Robson speaking at the Keswick Convention on July 17, 2022. Keswick Ministries, "James Robson," 58:15. Dr. Robson is now principal of Oak Hill College, a conservative evangelical seminary in the UK serving both independent and Anglican ministries.

5. Bretherton, *Politics*, 35. Luke Bretherton is now Regius Professor of Moral and Pastoral Theology at Christ Church, Oxford.

6. Hauerwas, *Peaceable Kingdom*, 99.

7. Lane, *Birth*, 3.

So Professor Lane's initial thought is to define politics as concerning *all* power in *all* human relationships. Likewise, Professor Sir Bernard Crick defined politics as "the activity by which differing interests within a given unit of rule are conciliated by giving them a share in power in proportion to their importance to the welfare and the survival of the whole community."[8]

So we see there are many ways of defining "politics." These can have useful insights, but they fail to tell us what distinguishes "politics" from other forms of human social organization. Power in relationships, conciliation, and violence are all ways in which human beings seek to achieve their objectives in relating to their neighbors—are these always "politics"? I think most people would answer no. When we talk of "politics" we mean something more specific.

Weber and the Monopoly of Force

Max Weber faced this question in a famous lecture, given in 1919, foreseeing how "politics" would develop in the emergent democratic world. Yes, he said, maybe we can speak of "politics" as a general feature in our economic, social, and family existence. But primarily "politics" means "the leadership, or the influencing of the leadership, of a *political* association, hence today, of a *state*."[9] A state, he continues, is a "human community that (successfully) claims the *monopoly of the legitimate use of physical force* within a given territory."[10] Weber here gives us a definition both of "politics" and of the "state." He explains how we tell the "state" apart from other social arrangements, such as families, commercial enterprises, or trade unions.

It does not tell us what the state *should* be or what we should expect the state to *do*. In philosophical jargon, Weber gives us a *positive* theory of the state, not a *normative* theory. Normative ideas are essential. But before we can get to normative ideas about the state, we need the positive idea, so we know what we mean when we talk of the state. Otherwise we risk assigning tasks and values to the state that do not properly belong to it, but belong to something else.

Weber does not mean that *only* the state will use force. He says that, according to his theory, "the state is considered the sole source of the 'right' to use violence."[11] There is always a right for citizens to use force in specific circumstances, including self-defense. What force is included in the scope of "self-defense" may vary between times and places. For example, Europeans

---

8. Crick, *Defence*, 21.
9. Weber, "Politics," 77; emphasis in original.
10. Weber, "Politics," 78; emphasis in original.
11. Weber, "Politics," 78.

are commonly shocked at how liberally the USA lets private citizens possess and carry firearms. However, this is for "traditionally lawful" purposes such as self-defense.[12] An individual who poses a threat to others may be denied the right to a firearm.[13] It would not be right to suppose that the US Constitution permits the use of firearms beyond the state-specified right to use violence.

Weber also makes it clear that he does not mean that the state is defined by its *use* of force.[14] He means that if there were no human organizations ready to use force, then the state would not exist.[15] The point about the state is not just that it can use force, but that it can prevent others doing so. This may be by using its own force to suppress a threat posed by others. That may extend to "warfare." But a successful state persuades others to choose not to use force to achieve their ends. This is the essence of the activity we call "politics." It is about how people are persuaded to support the institution we call the state.

Not all human communities have a state. It is possible to be a thriving human society without the institution of a state. It is possible to discuss what form "politics" takes in "stateless" societies. The definition could be extended to say that "politics" is broadly about how social power modifies formally constituted authority.[16] For the purposes of this book, "politics" is about how social power creates and directs *the state*. The state is a humanly created institution that successfully claims a monopoly of the use of force across territory.

The State in the Bible

"There Is No Political Theory in the Bible"

The political philosopher Michael Walzer suggests that "there is no political theory in the Bible. Political theory is a Greek invention."[17] The ancient Greek philosophers were concerned with politics as an activity that would foster human virtue. They asked: What makes for a *good* community? The Bible does

---

12. District of Columbia v. Heller, 554 U.S. 570 (2008).
13. United States v. Rahimi, 602 U.S. (2024).
14. A leading early twentieth-century anthropologist defined "political organization" as "that aspect of the total organization which is concerned with the control and regulation of the use of physical force." Radcliffe-Brown, preface to *African Political Systems*, xxxiii. It was an unfortunate error to infer this from Weber.
15. I do not think he is correct about that. Even if there were no one prepared to use force, it would still be necessary for society to share the cost of "public goods," i.e., products where the cost cannot be recovered by a charge imposed only on users.
16. In this sense people talk of "office politics."
17. Walzer, *In God's Shadow*, xii.

not see virtue as an achievement of the state. Virtue, the good life, is achieved by communion with the mind of God. But this does not mean that political theory is not there, in the Bible. We just need to look.

Three episodes in the Bible help us understand politics. The first is in the book of Deuteronomy, when God gives instructions to his nation, Israel, on the appointment of a king. The second comes later, when Israel attempts to appoint a king. The third is Paul's famous instruction in the book of Romans, to "submit" to the "powers that be."

The State in Deuteronomy

The fifth book of the Old Testament offers a record of Moses' legacy to the Hebrew tribes. Moses has led them out of slavery at the hands of the Egyptian state. They have come through the desert, to the edge of the lands lying across the river Jordan—the destination promised by God.

At a recorded time and date, forty years into their migration, Moses "proclaimed to the Israelites all that the Lord had commanded him concerning them."[18]

Israel learns about a time to come: a moment to appoint a king.

> When you enter the land the Lord your God is giving you and have taken possession of it and settled in it, and you say, "Let us set a king over us like all the nations around us," be sure to appoint over you a king the Lord your God chooses. He must be from among your fellow Israelites. Do not place a foreigner over you, one who is not an Israelite. The king, moreover, must not acquire great numbers of horses for himself or make the people return to Egypt to get more of them, for the Lord has told you, "You are not to go back that way again." He must not take many wives, or his heart will be led astray. He must not accumulate large amounts of silver and gold.

> When he takes the throne of his kingdom, he is to write for himself on a scroll a copy of this law, taken from that of the Levitical priests. It is to be with him, and he is to read it all the days of his life so that he may learn to revere the Lord his God and follow carefully all the words of this law and these decrees and not consider himself better than his fellow Israelites and turn from the law to the right or to the left. Then he and his descendants will reign a long time over his kingdom in Israel. (Deut 17:14–20)

18. Deut 1:3.

"Let us set a king over us like all the nations around us." But there is a surprise. This king will rule without great military power ("great numbers of horses") personal wealth ("silver and gold"), and multiple wives. Here are the usual ways by which ancient kings exercise internal control: armies to suppress, money to bribe, and marriages to make dependent families in the various parts of their kingdom. How, we may ask, can a king rule without these resources?

The text offers two answers to this question—one of principle, another of practice. In principle, and in the answer on the face of the text, the king rules with the authority of God. He is God's choice. But this cannot conclude the examination. After all, most political power is justified by the "mandate of heaven." In the words of the anthropologist Georges Balandier, "Statesmen are kinsmen of the gods."[19] How are people to know who has this mandate? The text says that the king will be a submissive student of God's law, a law he can both read and write, so "his heart is not lifted above his brethren." This king accepts the same rules as the rest of society. He does not lift himself above them. This will be one measure of God's endorsement. It is useful only if the rest of society knows these rules and is able to judge the king's service against this measure. In terms of practical politics, without the resources of overwhelming force, bribery, and polygamy, the king can rule only with the *consent* of the population. This consent is based on their assessment that the king has God's mandate to rule, which can be tested by his submission to the written law of God: so this is *informed* consent.

Michael Walzer identifies three things that mean the proposed system is an "almost democracy."[20] Two of these are just mentioned—consent and the rule of law. The third one is the place of the prophets. They come from all parts of Hebrew society, often the humblest, and often appear in the Old Testament as critics of the king. One example is Nathan, who uses a story to bring King David to face his guilt for using his office to take a man's wife, and then his life.[21]

But why would this "almost democracy" have use for a king? Israel's sophisticated existing system of social authority is described in Deut 1:13–16. Tribal chiefs head structures with leadership over thousands, hundreds, fifties, and tens, supported by tribal officers. Judges are appointed to settle disputes. This structure served Israel well in migrating across the desert. It will continue to do so in the promised land.

The text gives two clues about what a king would add. First, the people would decide to appoint a king when they "possess and dwell in" the territory

---

19. Balandier, *Political Anthropology*, 99.
20. Walzer, *In God's Shadow*, 200–201.
21. 2 Sam 12.

God has given them. A king (or queen) is a ruler of *somewhere*. Monarchy is rule over *territory*. This is not just temporary possession of territory. It is (at any rate in principle) permanent—it is able to reproduce itself over time.

Second, having a king will mean they have a ruler "like all the nations around." Clearly this king is not to be "like" other kings in many significant ways. This king rules in submission to God's law, without recourse to force, money, or multiple marriages. But Israel will give itself a system of territorial rule that mirrors that of its neighbors.

With kingship comes a system of rule: the system we call the "state." A state is a particular kind of social institution, with control over defined territory. It does not exist alone. It exists in relation to other states. It is part of a system of states with formal arrangements for relations between states. A state claims allegiance of all who dwell within its claimed territory, and the right to use force to compel submission. When it gave itself a king, Israel would be forming a state—something it did not have (or need) before.

Why monarchy? A state may be a system with no royal family. Monarchy, however, provides a simple means for a state to continue its existence by nurturing and reproducing the structures and human resources that make a state happen. A monarch is a sufficient, though not a necessary, condition for the presence of a state. In general, where we see "king" in the scriptures, we find a state. The exception is "King" Jesus, whose kingdom is not of (or "from") this world, and so is not a state.[22] States are, very much, of this world!

The coming of a state is not the same thing as the coming of "government" or "governance." Families, tribes, and other ways for societies to organize themselves all have "governance." This means they have authoritative systems for making decisions, with rules and procedures for carrying these out and enforcing them.

A state is a social institution with an exclusive claim over territory. It has a government which oversees the business of the state. It should not and need not abolish the forms of governance that social groups within that territory operate for themselves, including the conduct of family life. In our time this extends to the conduct of unions, economic units, associations, churches, and so on. The state does not abolish judges, whose independence is protected under the doctrine of the "rule of law." If the state does abolish, or incorporate, these various forms of social provision, then its project becomes "totalitarian." Under totalitarian rule, the state must represent the "totality" of society.

---

22. John 18:36.

Politics and the State

The First King: Gideon

The book of Judges is the history of Israel in the second half of the second millennium before Christ. It depicts a dispersed and troubled community ruled by a succession of short-lived "judges" who give temporary respite from incursion by pagan tribes. There is one attempt to establish order under a monarch, which we describe here. This fails. With no king, the clans make war on each other.[23]

In Judg 8:22–27, we read:

> The Israelites said to Gideon, "Rule over us—you, your son and your grandson—because you have saved us from the hand of Midian."
>
> But Gideon told them, "I will not rule over you, nor will my son rule over you. The Lord will rule over you." And he said, "I do have one request, that each of you give me an earring from your share of the plunder." (It was the custom of the Ishmaelites to wear gold earrings.)
>
> They answered, "We'll be glad to give them." So they spread out a garment, and each of them threw a ring from his plunder onto it. The weight of the gold rings he asked for came to seventeen hundred shekels, not counting the ornaments, the pendants and the purple garments worn by the kings of Midian or the chains that were on their camels' necks. Gideon made the gold into an ephod, which he placed in Ophrah, his town. All Israel prostituted themselves by worshiping it there, and it became a snare to Gideon and his family.

Israel is asking Gideon to become king. If he agrees, he will found a ruling household where authority will pass to the next in line among the male members of the family. Gideon is the first person to be invited to become king of Israel.[24]

The background to this, described in Judg 8:2–9, is that Gideon has used military power to conquer a defined territory over which he exercises control. In the border towns of Succoth and Penuel, he demands support for his troops. When this is denied, he returns to destroy the opposition and demolish the tower that dominates a strategic route into his territory. Elsewhere he uses charm and praise to assuage the wounded pride of those whose military support he has decided he does not need. By a mix of force and politics, he has built the basis for a state to exist—he is able to win the loyalty of the tribes who

---

23. Judg 21.

24. Some commentators miss this and take Saul (considered in the next section) as the first king. See for example Parker et al., "King." Michael Walzer sees the offer to Gideon as being the offer of monarchy, but takes Gideon's refusal at face value: Walzer, *In God's Shadow*, 54. The most recent authoritative evangelical commentary on Judges agrees that Gideon is the first "judge" to be offered the position of monarch. See Boda and Conway, *Judges*, 393.

occupy the land, to project force across the territory and control its borders, and to enforce submission when necessary. By asking him to become king, Israel is asking him to consolidate the state that he has started to build.

When a delegation offers him the throne, Gideon refuses on the grounds that God should rule. He then requests gold to make an ephod to be kept in his home city. He succeeds in this request. An ephod is a garment, usually elaborately designed, used by priests, and others in suitable authority, when coming before God. In other references to ephods in the Old Testament there is no indicated disapproval of such dress. However, in this case: "All Israel prostituted themselves by worshiping it there, and it became a snare to Gideon and his family."[25]

The implication is that it became an idol. It may be that it was treated as an oracle, for Gideon to exercise rule while being, apparently, a channel for the direct rule of God. However this worked, clearly Gideon was claiming to be setting up a theocracy. But what he actually brought about was idolatry. During his life there was peace. The new state was successful. But then it all broke down. It was assumed that Gideon's sons would take over, but Gideon left no arrangements for an orderly succession. By not appointing a prince to take his place on death, he failed to secure the continuity of the state.

State Failure: Fire Out of the Thorn

The outcome is described in Judg 9:1–21. Gideon has a son by a concubine. He is "Abimelek," which means "son of a king." This name is perhaps given to him by his mother's family. After Gideon's death he visits his maternal uncles to ask if they would prefer "all seventy" of Gideon's sons to rule over them or "just one" who is their relative. The community in Shechem uses temple money to pay "reckless scoundrels"[26] to join Abimelek in murdering the other sons of Gideon. One young prince escapes. His name is Jotham. When he learns of the massacre of his brothers, he climbs Mount Gerizim and shouts out a parable aimed at the perpetrators.

In Jotham's fable, the trees ask the olive, the fig, and vine to become king. They refuse, because they serve the community better with their fruit. Then the thornbush agrees, warning that he will offer shelter provided they act in truth—but otherwise, he will catch fire and burn them all up, along with the finest products of civilization ("the cedars of Lebanon").

---

25. Judg 8:27.
26. Judg 9:4.

Jotham then applies the story to the current position. He asks if the new dominant party has acted "in truth" toward Gideon and his house. If not, they will be burned up.

Clearly Gideon's supposed refusal of the throne is qualified by the facts that he continued to rule, albeit via the harlotry of the ephod, and that his sons are expected to succeed him. There is continuity between Gideon and Abimelek: if the son is a thornbush, so is the father. Jotham is not talking about a choice between father and son, between good and bad tree, but about whether the people are looking after their thornbush "in truth."

The political meaning of this parable is not always appreciated. But it was recognized by the founding editor of a long-established journal; Joseph Addison wrote of Jotham's fable in the *Spectator* in 1711:

> Fables were the first pieces of Wit that made their appearance in the World, and have been still highly valued, not only in times of the greatest Simplicity, but among the most polite Ages of Mankind. Jotham's Fable of the Trees is the oldest that is extant, and as beautiful as any which have been made since that time.[27]

The olive, the fig, and the vine refuse the throne because they would be sacrificing their fruitful calling as providers of nourishment. But, contrary to what is often said,[28] the thornbush is not a useless tree. Its benefit to the community is a boundary surrounding land, which can then be protected. The line of thorn, projecting painful force, will keep out intruding beasts and thieves. It will keep domestic animals and prisoners within its enclosure. The boundary hedge of thorn does not replace the productive trees: it protects them. But in hot, dry conditions the thornbush can catch fire from the sun's warming rays. Its burning can destroy all it encloses. People who plant thornbush must keep it trimmed and watered. Otherwise, it may destroy not just itself, but also the good things it encloses.

The thornbush depicts the state. It is a tree specializing in the task of compulsion, protection, and border control. Among the trees, it has a monopoly of force. It should be maintained "in truth": with a correct understanding of its function and handling. Otherwise, it will destroy all it is supposed to protect. People can live without the thorn, but it is useful to protect the other trees, allowing them to flourish and focus on their tasks. Jotham notes that the rebels have carried out a massacre of the princes, and this does them no credit. But this is not the main reason for doubting Abimelek's prospects for success.

---

27. Morley, *Spectator*, Sept. 29, 1711.
28. Poole, *Commentary*, 1:477; Henry, *Commentary*, 255–56; Bruce, "Judges," 266.

The real problem is whether his clan has really understood what they have done in making him king. Have they understood what the state actually is?

As it turns out, they have not. As the history continues, we see the "scoundrels" enrich themselves by highway robbery. Abimelek attempts to bring his gangs under control. He dies in the process.[29] Israel becomes what we call a "failed state." Who is responsible? The blame does not lie solely with the clans of Shechem. Gideon had the honor and glory of rule, behind his ephod, but did not want the responsibility of a "succession plan" for a sustainable state. Theocracy was his excuse for not respecting the "truth" of the state.

In our own time we see the price of failing to cultivate thorns "in truth." International powers conquered Iraq in 2003, resulting in the capture and death of the dictator Saddam Hussein. They attacked Libya in 2011, resulting in the death of the dictator Muammar Gaddafi. But destroying the thornbush did not, as the external powers apparently supposed, result in the flourishing of fruit trees. Rather the result was fire that engulfed those they attacked, and singed cities around the world.

Some societies benefit from thorns so neatly manicured and well watered that their combustibility gets forgotten. It is important to make their keepers aware of the dangers of a return to the wild. Those who live in Addison's "polite ages" may so fail to see their thorny nature that they confuse thorns with fruit trees and treat them as a source of wine, oil, and figs. These good things become possible not *despite* the thorn, but *with the aid* of its carefully cultivated protection.

The Trouble with Saul: Violent Dictatorship in 1 Samuel 8–11

Samuel is the last of the "judges" of Israel. In his old age, a delegation of clan leaders demands that he "appoint a king to lead us, such as all the other nations have." Unhappy at this, the old judge turns to God for help. God tells him to warn the people of the burden the king will impose: control over their land, money, and families amounting to enslavement. Still they make their demand.

> We want a king over us. Then we will be like all the other nations,
> with a king to lead us and to go out before us and fight our battles.

Give them their king, God tells Samuel.[30]

The story follows, in 1 Sam 9–10, of the new king's arrival at the throne. Saul is a tall, handsome young man from a distinguished household in the

---

29. Judg 9:53–54.
30. 1 Sam 8:19–22.

clan of Benjamin. When a herd of donkeys goes missing, Saul sets off on a long search for them. He is ready to give up, when his servant tells him there is a "seer" who will help. The servant even offers his own money to pay the necessary consultation fee to the "seer." Looking for the "seer," the search party gets directions from some young women fetching water. This "seer" is Samuel, whom God has advised of his forthcoming meeting with the chosen ruler. Samuel meets and feeds Saul, and then pours oil on his head to anoint him king. Part of the verification to Saul of his God-given mission is that he will meet "prophets" and be filled with spiritual gifts. To the surprise of onlookers, Saul joins the prophets. He worships God. When he returns to his family, all he has to say about these events is that Samuel told him the donkeys had been found. He says nothing about his kingship. Samuel summons the tribes of Israel to a gathering to choose the king. He does not reveal that this man has already been identified. An elaborate lottery is held to find this person, who turns out to be Saul. When they look for him, with God's help, they find him hiding in the luggage stores. The crowd celebrates their new king, but many are skeptical. Samuel makes an official record of the "regulations of the kingship." Saul goes home with a small team of "valiant men whose hearts God had touched."[31]

The culmination of this story comes in chapter 11. News arrives of a disaster in the city of Jabesh Gilead, a city on the east bank of the Jordan. The Ammonites, regular enemies of Israel, threaten an atrocity as the humiliating price of a peace treaty. Saul was back on his farm. But when he heard the news,

> the Spirit of God came powerfully upon him, and he burned with anger. He took a pair of oxen, cut them into pieces, and sent the pieces by messengers throughout Israel, proclaiming, "This is what will be done to the oxen of anyone who does not follow Saul and Samuel." Then the terror of the Lord fell on the people, and they came out together as one. (1 Sam 11:6–7)

A third of a million men are mustered[32] and the Ammonites duly routed. Only now do the people agree to accept Saul as king.[33]

In blessing their revived monarchy, Samuel has warned of what to fear: this seems to contradict the positive view of monarchy in Deut 17. However, once convinced of Saul's unsuitability, Samuel, at some personal risk, follows God's lead to anoint David as replacement. So the text does not suggest that Samuel opposes monarchy as an institution.

31. 1 Sam 10:26.
32. In other words, a large number. We do not need to take this as an accurate count.
33. 1 Sam 11:15.

The old judge's rupture with Saul comes when the king usurps Samuel's role in making offerings to God.[34] Later, nearing the end of his life and power, Saul approaches a witch in a bid to get advice from the dead Samuel.[35] After being anointed king, he does not announce the fact even to his own close family.[36] He is not transparent and so cannot be held accountable for his submission to the law. After conferring the throne on Saul, Samuel writes down the "regulations" for the monarchy, as required in Deut 17. But if Saul makes his own copy to keep and consult, as is also required, it is not mentioned. Quite possibly the warrior-farmer Saul is not literate. Anyway, he shows no interest in submitting to God's laws for the ruler.

The story of Saul's rise to power climaxes when he hears the plight of Jabesh Gilead. He rips up an ox and sends a messenger to brandish the bits around the territory. This symbolizes the violence he will bring on his subjects if they fail to follow him. The people rally enthusiastically, the Ammonites are vanquished, and national honor is restored.

This moment tells us about politics. The people are still, like earlier Hebrew generations, *capable* of war-fighting and defending their security. Earlier generations followed directions without question. But now people need more than orders alone. They have to be threatened. People want the benefit of the security possible from collective action in self-defense. But they are not willing to pay the price in terms of disruption, with the risks of injury and death. They want to be "free riders"—to enjoy the fruits of collective action without bearing any cost. Saul changes the calculus. He names the price you pay if you do not join this action. He measures the price carefully. He threatens not human life, but that of cattle. Presumably his team of "brave men" can project enough force to raid cattle. This is what the people meant when they told Samuel to find a "king to lead us, such as all the other nations have": someone who would meet the external threat with what Balandier calls the "double aspect of power . . . directed both inwards and outwards." The violence directed *inward* offers assurance that it can also be directed *outward*, promoting unity and cohesion in the face of external threats. Politics is necessary to "defend society against its own weaknesses," against the "entropy" that threatens disorder when the moment of automatic obedience to rules has passed. Coercion alone is never enough. "All the mechanisms that help to maintain or recreate internal cooperation must be considered," including ritual and ceremony.[37]

---

34. 1 Sam 13:6–13.
35. 1 Sam 28.
36. 1 Sam 10:16.
37. Balandier, *Political Anthropology*, 35–36.

Politics and the State

Submission: Romans 13:1–7

A millennium after the age of Jotham and Saul, Paul writes to Christians in Rome. Here, the local church sits in the capital of the great international state system we know as the Roman Empire. The benefits of civilization are accompanied by phenomenal state violence. The new Jesus movement is acutely aware of the injustice accompanying that violence. The church worships Jesus Christ. His earthly life ended in public execution on a state charge of political rebellion, pronounced when state authorities were forced to rule on accusations made by the religious authorities. The apostle James was among those who died in a wave of political persecution.[38] Christian leaders disobeyed rulers' instructions not to preach about the life, death, and resurrection of their Lord: they would obey God rather than man.[39]

Paul sends the Roman church these words on politics:

> Let everyone be subject to the governing authorities, for there is no authority except that which God has established. The authorities that exist have been established by God. Consequently, whoever rebels against the authority is rebelling against what God has instituted, and those who do so will bring judgment on themselves. For rulers hold no terror for those who do right, but for those who do wrong. Do you want to be free from fear of the one in authority? Then do what is right and you will be commended. For the one in authority is God's servant for your good. But if you do wrong, be afraid, for rulers do not bear the sword for no reason. They are God's servants, agents of wrath to bring punishment on the wrongdoer. Therefore, it is necessary to submit to the authorities, not only because of possible punishment but also as a matter of conscience. This is also why you pay taxes, for the authorities are God's servants, who give their full time to governing. Give to everyone what you owe them: If you owe taxes, pay taxes; if revenue, then revenue; if respect, then respect; if honor, then honor. (Rom 13:1–7)

How could Paul possibly say that only wrongdoers could suffer at the hands of the state, and that doing the right thing would bring approval from the pagan, violent regime in charge of the government of Rome? What could he mean?

It cannot, I think, make sense to take this remark out of context and treat it as a free-standing piece of political philosophy—to suggest that the voice of the government is the voice of God, and its commands are always right. Paul

---

38. Acts 12:2.
39. Acts 5:29.

and his readers knew full well that the state was capable of being terrifying to those who do right.

One suggested explanation comes from the religious right. It is that Paul means Christians should submit to the state only insofar as it applies God's law. On this argument, Christians have a duty to change the state to make it conform to the "theonomic" model.[40] But there is no evidence in the New Testament of this intention. It seems to contradict the plain meaning of what Paul is saying.

We can make sense of Paul's words if we look at the context. The chapter breaks in our English translations are not in the original Greek text. Immediately before his words on "submission" to the state, Paul has quoted from the Old Testament book of Proverbs:

> If your enemy is hungry, feed him; if he is thirsty, give him a drink. For in so doing you will heap coals of fire on his head. (Rom 12:20, quoting Prov 15:21–22)

Elsewhere in his writing, Paul urges Christians to have the same mindset as Jesus:

> Who, being in very nature God, did not consider equality with God something to be used to his own advantage; rather, he made himself nothing by taking the very nature of a servant. (Phil 2:6–7)

Clearly Christ was not *nothing*. But he "made himself nothing" in order to fulfill his God-given purpose.

The people of Christ, Paul says, are "not to be overcome by evil, but overcome evil with good."[41] This offers a general principle in relations with those who are not part of the body of Christ. From here, he turns to the question of dealing with the state. His words should be taken in this context. Paul suggests that Christians are to "make themselves nothing" in framing their relations with the ruling authorities. He is talking about the *mindset*, the assumptions they carry in their heads when dealing with them. It is about the role the Roman church is to play in handling relations with a state compelling obedience through awesome levels of force.

Most people would think it smart not to resist. There is, anyway, Paul says, no mandate for the emergent Christian communities to resist the state. It is a lawful institution, which does not bear the sword "in vain"—it is liable to be used. In dealing with the state, the church is to bring a presumption, a mindset, that these authorities are "established by God."

40. F. Schaeffer, *Christian Manifesto*, 92.
41. Rom 12:21.

Paul calls for more than nonresistance. He asks for willing, positive, and voluntary *submission*. This does not necessarily mean obedience. Christians may *submit* to the state's punishment even if they do not *obey* an instruction, if such obedience is to deny their faith. Furthermore, the church itself is (in human terms) a voluntary, self-regulating association joined by choice by those who believe in Christ.

The picture emerges of Christians as an *uncompelled* people. They are in the church because they choose to be. There is no *point* in the state trying to compel them. In most matters, Christians do not need to be compelled because they submit as a matter of choice. In a few matters, to do with speaking of Christ, they *cannot* be compelled. Force, in relation to Christians in society, becomes irrelevant. This illustrates what Paul has in mind when he speaks of "overcoming evil with good."

"Submission" does not mean being passive or ineffective. It means that there is a distinctively Christian way of having an effect: by putting others' interests first, by loving enemies, by becoming "nothing."

"Democracy" means that the people rule. In a democracy, we, the citizens, are the "governing authorities." For this to work, there must be some citizens who are ready to express views about how governing should work in practice. Submission, in conditions of democracy, requires participation. To participate in politics while honoring Christ is to act in the interest of others in the wider community—putting ourselves last. It also requires that we show love for each other, even when opposing each other in our political stance. Then everyone will know that we are Christ's disciples.[42]

This does not mean that Christians (or anyone else) should be silent on matters that may be seen as distinctive, and controversial, concerns. When Roger Williams called for a new kind of state, not enforcing religious uniformity, he said he was calling for "mere civility." This does not mean "politeness." Williams was not polite. He "could be obnoxious." The test of "civility" is not civil peace and quiet. Its "crux" is the right and ability of all to oppose what they cannot approve.[43] We return later to the question of freedom of religion and speech.

Why the State?

Human beings need to be in reliable groups in order to survive and flourish. These groups have "government," meaning formal means to make and

---

42. John 13:35.
43. Bejan, *Mere Civility*, 65–69.

enforce decisions. But this is not the same as having a "state." Why then are there "states"? What are the things that can be accomplished when there is an institution with a monopoly of force across territory? In other words, what is the state *for*?

The state's functions can be listed under five headings. It provides for orderly *external relations*: normally this means relations with other states outside its own borders. It secures *internal order* within its borders. It procures what economic theory calls *public goods*. This does not mean "things that are good for the public." It means things whose benefits cannot be confined to those who contribute to their cost. The state is also likely, in modern conditions, to have two further functions. One is to issue *money*. The other is to support citizens' consumption of *private goods* in order to secure a level of equal access to the minimum requirements of participation in society. "Private goods" (also called "excludable goods") means things that can be provided only to those who pay (or labor) for them. These state-funded "private goods" are likely to include education and health care. This heading also includes a level of income to enable access to the means of life for those unable to achieve that through labor or other sources of money.

The State and Justice

All societies have some notion of "justice." People generally know when they are being treated unfairly, though different parties to a relationship may view this differently. All cultures have some means of recognizing this and encouraging just or fair behavior. All societies have some "law." That includes conduct that incurs a penalty imposed by the whole community, and procedures for settling disputes between parties. The people who issue rulings may be called "judges." Whether their rulings are accepted and acted upon is a matter of the consent they enjoy from society, in particular its dominant elements. None of this requires the existence of a state.

However, the coming of a state changes the working of law and enforcement.[44] The state has a monopoly of the use of physical force, so cannot permit physical law enforcement without state authority. We may think of two examples in the New Testament. In one, Jesus is asked to confirm that a woman caught in the act of adultery should be stoned to death. He suggests that a man without sin should throw the first stone. The accusers slink off, ashamed.[45]

---

44. It is a mistake to see the defining purpose of the state as being "justice," as Jonathan Chaplin proposes (see Chaplin, "Reframing," 592–93; *Faith*, ch. 1).

45. John 8:3–9.

The assumption seems to be that justice may be executed on the spot by the witnesses, with the authority of a suitably qualified judge. Here, Jesus, as a religious teacher, is that judge. Later, Jesus is himself convicted on a charge of blasphemy. The religious authorities bring him to the Roman governor. They cannot carry out the death penalty on their own authority.[46] In this instance, the state has brought this punishment within the scope of its own monopoly of force.

The State's Legitimacy

Max Weber defined the state as the social institution which succeeds in claiming a *"monopoly of the legitimate use of physical force."* The philosopher Thomas Nagel explains that the word "legitimacy" refers to "the history of attempts to discover a way of justifying coercively imposed political and social institutions to the people who have to live under them, and at the same time to discover what those institutions must be like if such justification is to be possible."[47] Nagel says that states are "imposed." "Legitimacy" justifies a state's form and adapts its arrangements to fit that justification—in a process Weber called "legitimation." Nagel adds that justification is not the same as persuasion. A reasonable justification may fail to persuade the unreasonable, and people may still be persuaded even if no such justification is offered.

Professor Seymour Martin Lipset defined legitimacy as "the capacity of the system to engender and maintain the belief that the existing political institutions are the most appropriate ones for the society."[48]

Thus, in the standard account, legitimacy is something an existing state apparatus fits to its equipment to perpetuate its existence. Weber and Lipset were political sociologists. For them, the state is first of all explained sociologically. It takes its shape from social forces. It then uses legitimation to justify and reproduce itself. The "system" comes first. "Legitimacy" is invented by this system to secure itself by nonviolent means.

Providence Plantations declared itself "held by consent." I have argued that this asserted the *legitimacy* of the new state. It was drawing on the work of Roger Williams. Williams, in *The Bloudy Tenent*, proposed a form of state that did not, at that point, exist. Nothing like it had been "imposed." It was not a theory retrofitted onto a "system" to secure itself. Williams was designing a *replacement* for an existing form of state. The existing state was legitimized

---

46. John 18:31.
47. Nagel, "Legitimacy," 218.
48. Lipset, "Conflict," 52.

by God's law. The replacement envisaged by Williams, legitimized by popular consent, took shape in 1647.

The settlers knew they needed a state. We saw earlier the functional reasons a state may be practically necessary, and the three prime considerations all received attention when they met in Portsmouth.[49]

The *legitimacy* of the state does not derive from what it does and how well it performs. It is an idea about the wider purpose it serves. That purpose, in Williams's day, meant the protection of the true religion and church, in order to conform society to the will of God. "Legitimacy" refers to a meaning for the state that goes beyond its day-to-day functions. It is a *transcendental* purpose.

Today such legitimizing or transcendental purpose may be to promote God's will in terms of a religion, such as Islam. It may be nationalism, meaning that the state exists to promote the security and survival of a particular cultural inheritance.[50] It may be Marxism: the fulfillment of a historical-material path discovered by Marx and fulfilled through the political power of the rising industrial working class. These principles may be found together and form a "blend."

For example, Vietnam is a Communist one-party state. Marxism plays a part in affirming the legitimacy of the state. But so do nationalism and Buddhism. Elections allow choice among approved party candidates who compete for votes. It thus has certain features of a "democracy" and a large measure of support and consent. But the Vietnamese state is not "held by" consent. Fundamentally it is "held by" an idea of the future of humankind derived from Marxism. But it appeals also to the many Vietnamese for whom honoring ancestors and preserving their distinctive culture are what legitimize the state.

An artfully managed state may hold together varying ideas of legitimacy. Sometimes these competing notions may need to be held in balance at some distance to each other. Arrangements to allow this are called "consociational" (rather than "associational").[51] One case is Switzerland.[52] Consociationalism enabled diverse religious and national affiliations to establish a successful state. Autonomous cantons rotated positions in a central executive in order to provide for mutual defense in the face of predatory empires. Less successfully, the consociationalism of Lebanon accommodates diverse interpretations of Islamic legitimacy, along with versions of Christianity. In Northern Ireland, consociationalism secures the co-operation of Protestant unionism and Catholic nationalism in power sharing.

---

49. These are external relations, internal order, and public goods. See p. 87.
50. For more on the definition of "nationalism," see pp. 49–51 and 67.
51. Dahl, *Democracy*, 192.
52. Switzerland's direct democracy is considered further on p. 99.

Ideas of legitimacy may co-exist. They may clash and make it impossible to hold a successful state. For example, in the USA, nationalism and theonomy are claims about legitimacy that threaten to erode democracy. The state is the body with a monopoly of legitimate force. Those who dispute the legitimacy of the state may be encouraged to consider the use of force, on the part of themselves or others, inspired by alternative claims to legitimacy. Those who rioted in Washington, DC, on January 6, 2021, included some who held to alternative accounts of state legitimacy. They thought these claims justified force against the illegitimate entity that had just confirmed Joe Biden as the elected president in accordance with democratic procedures.

Christianity and the State

The state is a human institution exercising a monopoly in the use of physical force across a defined territory. It has three core functions: external relations, internal order, and provision of public goods. It has acquired two additional functions in modern conditions: provision of private goods for the purpose of social welfare, and issuance of money.

People can and do live without the state. It is not intrinsic to the human condition. It is neither the sole nor a superior means of human governance. However, the Bible permits and authorizes the establishment of states.

There is no mandate for Christians to refuse to submit to the state or to seek to change it by force. Nor is there a mandate for Christians to establish a theocratic state. Theocracy is idolatry. The state does *not* convey a privileged word of God. There is no authority for a state that enforces biblical law or is legitimized by God's *specific* approval.

The state is useful but also dangerous. The thornbush of the state, if not watchfully managed, may catch fire and destroy all it is supposed to protect. We need to take care that it does not intrude on other forms of human government. We need to hold it accountable. These are not duties that can safely be performed only by the institutions of the state itself. They must be the task of "civil society."

7

Democracy in Public

"If we wish to keep 'democracy,' then we must understand what it is."[1] Democracy is government "by the people," at two levels. At the *personal* level, democracy means equal rights to individual self-government. This includes legally protected rights to free expression and free association.

This chapter considers the *public* level—the level of the state, where decisions are binding on all. One hundred fifty-three million people voted in the 2024 US presidential election. Almost fifty million citizens of the UK are registered to vote, and over seventeen million in Australia. They are said to enjoy "voice and vote to shape public life"[2]—but what does this actually mean? How can it amount to "government by the people"?

The standard answer goes like this. "Democracy" may be "direct" or "indirect." The "direct" version means citizens gather to make decisions themselves. The "indirect" alternative means that voters choose their representatives in "elections." These representatives govern and pass laws, reflecting choices made by voters. This works if elections are "free and fair." This means that all citizens enjoy an equal right to vote. All must have a right to offer themselves for elected office. There is freedom of speech and association. A variety of sources of information help voters with their assessments.[3]

This chapter examines these models and their limitations. It returns to "consent" theory to consider how it applies to the constitutional mechanisms of public democracy.

---

1. Sartori, *Revisited*, 17.
2. Alexander and Welzel, "Measuring Effective Democracy," 272.
3. Dahl, *Democracy*, 85–86.

Democracy in Public

What Are Constitutions For?

Sheldon Wolin observed the change that took place in Eastern Europe in the transition from Communist authority to democracy. While the old regime was still in government, large numbers of people took part in all sorts of discussions about the arrangements to replace that regime. Democracy was happening in "civil society." But afterward, when the new way of running the state was in place, "a different politics began to take shape . . . of organized parties, professional politicians and economic interest groups."[4] A democratic constitution, he suggests, may be a contradiction in terms. Its representative structures may enlarge "democracy" but also leave it "diminished in order to smooth the way for . . . the effective organization of the power to govern."[5] This should not surprise us. A state needs a government—that is to say, a known location for making decisions about what the state apparatus will do. A "constitution" confers the legal power to become "government." Government does not secure democracy: civil society does. The democracy of civil society does not arise from the constitution—that is, from the legal authority conferred upon the government of the state. It arises from the private rights of expression and association. Government may, and to some extent always does, suppress the impulses of civil society. Actors in civil society need to be adept at knowing how to counter this tendency.

Government becomes government through the medium of the constitution. Government usually has little incentive to change the constitution. The democratic enthusiasm that drives the process of crafting a constitution will rarely be something government is ready to promote.

To become "the Government" is highly attractive to some people. To be "in Government" appears to be to enjoy power and glamor[6] as well the ability to make decisions that may be beneficial to oneself, one's community, and the wider population of the land and even the planet. The constitution is the means to access that position. Those competing for government will look to find the best route through the constitution. Their vehicle to carry them on this route is the "political party"—or, rather, the faction or movement generated with the party. Actors seeking to control, or become, "the Government" will design a movement to capture dominance within a party. Donald Trump created "MAGA" (Make America Great Again) as a brand within the Republican Party. He built it on the "religious right" designed by previous generations of power brokers, working with religious activists. Tony Blair was the leading

---

4. Wolin, "Norm," 30.
5. Wolin, "Norm," 33.
6. Politics being "show business for ugly people" (aphorism of unknown origin).

public face of "New Labour," designed to free the UK Labour Party from its historic socialist project.

Political parties are not like clans that reproduce genetic material from generation to generation. They are holding pens for shifting groups of people. Joining a party is a strategy chosen by individuals and those who capture their loyalty in order to win a route to government for the people and causes they favor. An alternative strategy may result in a newly minted party, such as the one that carries President Macron in France, or the various iterations of the party led by Nigel Farage in the UK.[7]

Parties solicit votes in order to make their way to government. This means being "efficient" in getting votes in the right places. For example, the UK Labour Party gained fewer votes in the general election of 2024 than it did in the previous one, in 2019. But 2019 produced its worst election result since 1935. In 2024 it won two-thirds of the seats in the Commons, giving it one of the best results ever achieved by a UK political party. Specific factors explain this, notably the unpopularity of the Conservative government and the rise of a rival on the "right" of politics.[8] But it still takes an "efficient" strategy to maximize the benefits of such an opportunity by "targeting" the votes needed to turn the currency of votes into the money that buys office. This is the smart work of political strategy. Any such strategy exploits the constitution in order to maximize advantage for the chosen project or people.

"The People Decide"

Professor Albert Weale defines democracy as a system where "important public discussion of questions of law and policy depends, directly or indirectly upon public opinion formally expressed by citizens of the community, the vast bulk of whom have equal political rights."[9] In a recent contribution, Manville and Ober say that democracy means "collective self-governance by citizens."[10] Citizens exercise "active and ultimately authoritative participation in making important decisions."[11] The authors accept that this model of democracy has never been "fully realized."[12]

---

7. The "UK Independence Party," the "Brexit Party," and currently the "Reform Party."

8. "Reform" took 14 percent of the votes but won only 5 seats out of 650 in the House of Commons.

9. Weale, *Democracy*, 14.

10. Manville and Ober, *Bargain*, 18.

11. Manville and Ober, *Bargain*, 21.

12. Manville and Ober, *Bargain*, 22.

Democracy in Public

Giovanni Sartori was scathing about defining democracy in this way, with all citizens acting with equal capacity to make or at least to approve decisions.

> The state of inattention, non-interest, sub-information, perceptive distortion, and, finally, plain ignorance of the average citizen never ceases to surprise the observer.[13]

Generally, he says, research finds that:

> The ordinary citizen has little interest in politics, that citizen participation is minimal if not subliminal, and that in many respects and instances the public has no opinion but, rather, inarticulate feelings made up of moods and drifts of sentiment.[14]

In our day, two outstanding US politicians appealed to these "feelings made up of moods and drifts." Speaking in his campaign for the Democratic Party nomination, Barack Obama said:

> Change will not come if we wait for some other person or if we wait for some other time. We are the ones we've been waiting for. We are the change that we seek.[15]

Speaking to the Conservative Political Action conference on March 4, 2023, Donald Trump said:

> For those wronged and betrayed, I am your retribution. I am your retribution.[16]

Obama and Trump both succeeded in finding routes into the consciousness of bodies of people. As Sartori suggested, voters collect around an attitude to the world and to fellow citizens, rather than around a specific set of "decisions."

So can we sensibly suggest that the voters make or approve "decisions"?

Consider one example. It concerns one of the most consequential decisions taken by democratic governments in recent years: to invade Iraq in 2003. How did this come about?

In 2001, the newly elected President George W. Bush appointed Condoleezza Rice as national security advisor. Dr. Rice was a Russian-speaking expert on relations with the former Soviet Union. She had little interest in, or knowledge of, international terrorism. When the White House head of

---

13. Sartori, *Revisited*, 103.
14. Sartori, *Revisited*, 44.
15. Obama, "Super Tuesday," para. 25. In Chicago, on Feb. 5, 2008.
16. Trump, "Trump Speaks," 1:25.

counterterrorism presented evidence that an organization called Al Qaeda had a squad in the US preparing a major attack, the response was to disregard the advice and demote the official concerned.[17] This played a substantial role in enabling the 9/11 attacks to succeed in bringing down the Twin Towers in New York. This in turn led to prolonged American wars in Afghanistan and Iraq. It was a decision reflecting poor knowledge of how rival government agencies had competing objectives in making assessments of threat. President Bush and Dr. Rice made decisions without knowing the consequences of their choices or the nature of the information they would be considering.

As he took his country into war, President Bush sought to justify his action to skeptical Americans. A sincere Christian, he urged them that the task of bringing democracy to Iraq was a divinely appointed mission:

> The liberty we prize is not America's gift to the world, it is God's gift to humanity.[18]

At the same time, the UK prime minister, Tony Blair, was at the height of his power over government and party. He decided to commit my country to joining the American invasion of Iraq. According to the well-connected English journalist Matthew d'Ancona, Blair wanted "to make his mark, to free himself from the constraints of focus groups and polling, and actually participate in history." Blair explained that he would

> show through what we do in Iraq after liberation that we have indeed made the condition of people better—we made it more free, we made it more prosperous, we made it more just, we protected their rights—and let that stand as an example of how in fact the best motivations of people from our religion and the best motivations of people from the Muslim religion are in the same line of tradition.[19]

This interview is remembered for a remark by Blair's famous communications director. Alastair Campbell intervened in the conversation to warn: "We don't do God." This is often quoted to show, perhaps lament, that the Christian faith plays no part in British politics.[20] But in fact, as he led his country into war, Blair was indeed "doing God." Campbell's famous dismissal is a case of what media operators call the "dead cat" strategy. If it is necessary to distract attention from what is really happening, throw in a dead cat. Journalists will write

17. Wright, *Looming Tower*, 335.
18. Domke and Coe, *God Strategy*, 8.
19. Margolick, "Blair's Big Gamble," para. 30.
20. See for example Carey and Carey, *We Don't Do God*.

about the dead cat, not what is really going on. Campbell was not affirming that "we don't do God." He was, successfully, distracting attention from the fact that his boss was doing exactly that.

For Tony Blair, the relationship with George W. Bush and Iraq was his moment to "free himself from the constraints of focus groups and polls"—in other words, to break *out* of the limitations imposed up him by the decisions of citizens.

Before they can gain this freedom, democratic politicians make commitments in order to be elected. These may not reflect a realistic understanding of the facts and responsibilities faced when taking office. They are a poor preparation for the most important decisions that government must make, especially in response to the unexpected. It is unrealistic to say that voters "make decisions" through the medium of elections. Governments make decisions in response to interpretation of current conditions and information. They will be concerned about whether the results will be as expected and, if so, will be viewed favorably next time they face election.

"The People Appoint"

Professor Grayling's definition may be better.

> [Democracy is] a political system in which the people appoint a government and instruct it to legislate and administer on their behalf, protecting and enhancing their interests by responsible and informed action.[21]

If making a job "appointment," you may be surprised to be offered a short list of two candidates—one sixteen years past normal retirement age, the other removed from the same position four years previously. You will recognize this picture of the US presidential election of 2024, up to the moment that President Biden withdrew his bid for reappointment. The distinguished Democrat campaigner James Carville then urged the party to conduct a concentrated period of meetings and votes to involve the public, or at any rate party supporters, in the selection of the new candidate.[22] This advice was not taken. Vice President Harris was ushered in to fill the vacancy, formally endorsed at the party convention with no opposition. Of course, at the actual general election, there were other candidates to vote for apart from former President Trump or Vice President Harris, but no one outside these two would have

---

21. Grayling, *Good State*, conclusion.
22. Carville, "Democrats."

any chance of success.[23] So, is Professor Grayling right to define democracy as being where "the people appoint a government"?

In a sense a democratic election is an "appointment." But it is one where the choice of candidates does not meet the standard of fairness and open competition expected when "appointing" someone in, for example, a modern business environment. In public elections, many agents intervene in the "appointment" process to limit the choices offered to voters. The candidates themselves are deeply involved in these interventions. This is not a secret. It involves access to decision-makers in political parties and in the worlds of media and money.

In the USA, around a quarter of voters take part in "primary" elections that select candidates to proceed to the final vote. These voters are often, though not always, state-registered supporters of the party in question. "Primaries" in the USA rose in importance in the latter part of the twentieth century, resulting from earlier efforts to make the process of candidate selection more open and "democratic." These provide a way for large numbers to have a say in filtering candidates and gaining more leverage over the "appointment." But they also increase the power of relatively small numbers of activists, and of those with means to reach and persuade potential voters to turn out. They embed the two-party duopoly in a state-sponsored system of election management. To exercise their vote, electors must first identify themselves, and even be registered by the state, as supporters of one of the established parties.

Does "democracy" reside in these procedures to sift potential officeholders and then make an "appointment"? If so, what makes the USA or the UK more "democratic" than, say, Russia or Iran, where elections take place among candidates previously sifted for loyalty to the Kremlin or to the Office of the Supreme Leader? We can refer to the private sphere of liberty to speak and assemble, and to everyone's resulting right and ability to challenge and question the controlling authorities. But in its *public* aspect, is democracy no more than inevitably flawed procedures revolving around periodic elections?

Minimalism

These obvious limitations lead theorists and advocates in different directions, as they search for the true meaning of "democracy." One option is "minimalism." Minimalism proposes that, as long as there is some means to remove

---

23. Of the 153 million votes cast, 150 million were for Trump or Harris. The rest were for the Greens, the Libertarians, or for Robert Kennedy, who had already withdrawn from the race, but too late for his candidacy to be removed from the ballot in many states. Numerous others put their names forward in some states.

a government nonviolently, with some public involvement, we can talk of "democracy." This is not because people will necessarily manage to replace a government with a better one making better decisions. Just the prospect of removal will cause government to adjust itself to public expectations.[24] Minimalism sets a low bar for our expectations of democracy—helpful perhaps in containing expectations, but a weak defense in addressing the claims of rival versions of "legitimacy."

At the opposite end of the scale from "minimalism" are solutions aiming at "direct democracy." This contrasts with so-called "indirect" systems where voters "govern" through elected representatives. "Direct democracy" refers to arrangements for "collective self-government" to occur through citizens acting themselves.

Direct Democracy

Athens

The word "democracy" comes to us from ancient Greek. In the city-state of Athens, citizens gathered to take decisions. This did not mean *all* subjects of Athenian rule: it meant a small minority comprising free males of Athenian descent. Within this racial elite, "democracy" meant giving power to the poor rather than to the wealthy and aristocrats. Mass meetings of all these Athenians could happen. However, the main decision-making bodies were chosen by lot. "Election" meant choosing men with skills required for a task, such as commanding military forces. General policymaking was a duty of any Athenian, so could be carried out by any cross section of them. The "crucial moment" in its development came when the "restored democracy rejected a proposal to limit the franchise to property owners" but, at the same time, refused to extend citizenship to slaves who had been active in that restoration.[25]

Modern public democracy delegates decision-making to elected representatives. If we think that "people rule" should mean people decide, then modern "indirect" democracy is a sham. The alternative is Athens-inspired "direct" democracy—though now using Lincoln's definition of the "people." This enables decision-making in principle by the whole population. But how can the vast numbers of citizens of a modern state actually make decisions?

---

24. Przeworski, "Minimalist Democracy," 45.
25. Wolin, "Norm," 43.

Democracy After Christendom

The Swiss Model and Its American Progeny

The Swiss Republic developed as a "consociational" democracy, designed to balance the rival interests of Protestant and Catholic areas and urban and rural communities.[26] Much power lies with twenty-eight cantons. The cantons appoint a federal executive who works by consensus.

At the heart of Swiss democracy is "direct" decision-making through initiatives and referenda. Citizens may put forward proposals for approval in a referendum. First a proposal needs to be endorsed by at least one hundred thousand Swiss voters.[27] Civil servants advise and support those leading in offering proposals. Any new law may be challenged in a referendum. In the first seventeen years of the present century, over 150 proposals were considered by referendum, covering a range of topics including transport, environment, and health care. Swiss vote, on average, four times a year, using scheduled dates booked many years in advance. This system provides a "brake" (stopping legislation) and a "gas pedal" (driving innovation). It offers opportunity for agenda setting and encourages careful consultation ahead of government decisions, recognizing the chance of a future referendum.

Despite low participation in elections of federal officials, around 90 percent of Swiss take part in votes of one kind or another. Advocates stress the difference between the Swiss "referendum" system and that of a "plebiscite." A "plebiscite" is a one-off vote on a government proposal. A "referendum" is citizen led, and part of a habitual system, integrated into democratic life. Thus, the UK Brexit vote was not a referendum: it was a plebiscite.[28]

Does this difference in wording matter? It does. The point about what the Swiss call "referendum" is that is embedded, as a regular feature, into their way of doing democracy. It is initiated by the people. Civil servants support the process. The UK's Brexit "referendum" was a "plebiscite" organized from above. It was a novelty, a one-off called on the mistaken assumption that the campaigners for a "no" vote would "win." Once having "lost" the vote, the prime minister resigned, leaving behind no plan to implement Brexit. There was no contingency planning for the eventuality of a "yes" result.[29]

The "Swiss model" entered American democracy, especially through the work of John W. Sullivan. In the USA, Sullivan wrote:

---

26. The term "consociational" is explained on p. 89.
27. This number was raised from fifty thousand in 1977.
28. Kaufmann, *Modern Direct Democracy*, 16–27.
29. The UK's most senior civil servant, Sir Jeremy Heywood, told a subsequent parliamentary inquiry that "there had been no formal contingency planning for a Leave vote, as the government's official position had been to remain in the EU." BBC, "Brexit," para. 6.

The county, state, and federal governments are not democracies. In form, they are quasi-oligarchies composed of representatives and executives; but in fact they are frequently complete oligarchies, composed in part of unending rings of politicians that directly control the law and the offices, and in part of the permanent plutocracy, who purchase legislation through the politicians.[30]

Seeking a solution, Sullivan examined, and promoted, direct democracy on Swiss lines. This became established in parts of the USA, known as the "Oregon system." It exists in some form in many US towns and states, most notably in California as well as in Oregon. There are differing levels of support required for initiatives and for scope to impede the work of the elected legislature. It does not exist at all at the federal level. It can be expensive, both to pilot through legal and constitutional barriers and to submit ideas to voters. Thus, it faces one of the objections Sullivan made in 1892: serving the interest of big money. It is a system that "at its most dubious" nurtures "poorly designed policies, obscene amounts of money, highly technical measures, unanticipated consequences and confused voters."[31] It works better if proposals are simple, with consequences well considered, and which can be judged by the experience of voters and offered for the process at moderate cost.

Deliberative Democracy

"Deliberative democracy" challenges us to reject "vote and voice" as sufficient to define democracy in the public sphere. Rather, democracy should mean "a process of open discussion leading to an agreed judgement on policy."[32] Deliberative democracy agrees that democracy means rule by the people, and this means the people make decisions. It says that electing officials on the basis of rival programs does not meet this expectation. People can, and should, make decisions on the basis of shared reflection. Deliberative democracy is fundamentally about "reason-giving."[33] It imagines a grand conversation in which everyone hears information and arguments. A common view arises, based on what is reasonable.

Such conversations are not likely to arise in practice. No one has the time, inclination, or capacity to consider all information about everything under consideration by the state. Most of us have very little of any of these.

---

30. Sullivan, *Direct Legislation*, 12–13.
31. Ellis, *Delusions*, 2.
32. D. Miller, "Deliberative Democracy," 54.
33. Guttmann and Thompson, *Why Deliberative?*, 3.

Therefore "direct democracy makes room for many other forms of decision making," including bargaining between members of elite circles.[34] However, decisions made in these ways should always be justified in a deliberative process. Large-scale deliberation, even if possible, may not add value to what these other forms achieve. It may make things worse. Daniel Bell draws attention to the possibility that exposing and discussing reasons for decisions "intensifies disagreement" and "increases the risk that things may go drastically wrong."[35]

Deliberation by Sortition: "Lottocracy"

Citizens' juries and citizens' assemblies are terms used for a process for deliberation in small, representative groups. The only difference is that "juries" are smaller than "assemblies." Groups are selected to be statistically representative of the population as a whole. They then conduct several days considering an issue. They look at evidence and arguments with guidance from a moderator. They reach a conclusion in the form of a policy recommendation.

The selection process is to send an invitation to join to a randomly selected cross section of the population. Volunteers may be offered payment to compensate for their time.[36] Typically, between 2 and 5 percent of those invited will agree to join.[37] Among these, a further randomized selection takes place, this time to achieve balanced representation according to such factors as age, sex, race, and disability. The arguments for this process are that it enables deliberation and removes the bias found among political elites toward high income and other social privilege.

"Sortition" is the technical term for selecting decision-makers by this random method. The Oregon-based nonprofit Healthy Democracy is one of the USA's foremost advocates and service providers for this system. It calls the decision-making bodies "lottery-selected panels." Cristina Lafont uses a handy shorthand: "lottocracy." In the world of marketing, randomly selected, representative panels are used for researching consumer preference. They are usually called "focus groups."

---

34. Guttmann and Thompson, *Why Deliberative?*, 3.

35. Bell, "Democratic Deliberation," 73.

36. Chwalisz and Česnulaitytė in "What Is 'Successful'?" report that payment occurs in 57 percent of cases. Harrison in "Can Citizens' Assemblies Help?," reports that participants in Belgium's G1000 citizens' assemblies receive eighty-two euros per day. The UK charity Involve suggests a payment of seventy pounds per day. These figures are roughly in line with the UK statutory minimum wage.

37. Gąsiorowska, "Sortition," 3.

Democracy in Public

The basic proposition behind "lottocracy" is that a "mini-public" is a feasible substitute for the impossible ideal of full public involvement in a deliberative process. Noelle McAfee is, like Lafont, a philosopher following the German pioneer of the deliberative public sphere, Jürgen Habermas. She judges deliberative processes, using juries and polls, to have been successful in such cases as developing an energy strategy for Texas. But, like Lafont, she questions the basic logic. "Lottocracy" is a "shortcut" that expects the "larger public to uncritically defer to what a sample has decided—and there is simply no compelling reason that this larger public would or should do so . . . deferring to them would violate the larger public's political task of authoring laws themselves." The lottocracy shortcut exemplifies "well-meaning theories" that "fall short of the deeply democratic ideal of full participation in collective self-governance."[38]

From the other side of the debate, lottocracy threatens the "indirect" model of democratic rule through elected officials. In February 2024, the London *Times* published excerpts of a forthcoming biography of Sir Keir Starmer, leader of the Labour Party and expected to become prime minister, as he did five months later. Starmer's chief of staff was Sue Gray, previously a senior civil servant. She was recruited by Labour to help ready the party leadership for government, a move that attracted Conservative objections.[39] The *Times*' rival, the Conservative-supporting *Daily Telegraph*, found from the excerpts that Gray had plans to "bypass" civil servants by using citizens' assemblies. The *Telegraph* quoted Luke Akehurst as saying:

> Citizens' assemblies are a stupid idea. . . . We already have elected politicians who are put there by the public to take tough decisions. It is an abdication of responsibility to farm these out to potentially unrepresentative panels of people with no specific knowledge or accountability.[40]

The *Telegraph*'s parliamentary sketch writer wrote that all this confirmed that Labour was "the stupid party."[41]

Luke Akehurst is a former member of Labour's National Executive Committee and a professional political campaigner and influencer. He became Member of Parliament for North Durham in the general election that took

---

38. McAfee, review of *Democracy Without Shortcuts*.

39. Sue Gray served as chief of staff to the prime minister after Labour's election victory on July 4, 2024. She resigned on Oct. 6, 2024, following perceived political errors by the new government. Her replacement, Morgan McSweeney, was, like Akehurst, a political organizer from the Labour "right."

40. Gutteridge, "Labour Backtracks."

41. Grant, "Labour Has Confirmed."

place on July 4, 2024. For a number of years before that, he played a critical role in organizing so-called "Blairite" party members to regain control of the party from the left. As the *Telegraph* quote shows, Akehurst sees deliberative democracy as a rival to his project of governing the UK from Labour's center and center right, via "elected politicians put there by the public."

In fact, few seriously think that deliberative processes may *replace* elected politicians. The process is almost always advisory.[42] Devotees of deliberative theory think they are exploring an Athenian model to replace representative systems. But this is not a realistic picture. The real question is whether government can use deliberative processes to strengthen decision-making. Generally advocates of "sortition" see it as an advisory tool, making recommendations to government.[43]

An exception is the UK Sortition Foundation, which is campaigning for a citizens' assembly to replace the House of Lords and thus become the UK's second legislative house. It proposes that members serve for two years and are paid the same as members of the House of Commons.

Assembly-Size Decision-Making

Sartori explained that:

> When the term "demokratia" was conceived, the people concerned were the demos of a Greek *polis*, a small, tightly knit community operating on the spot as a collective deciding body.[44]

This community could comprise up to five thousand people. Medieval "democracies" in Italian city-states were of this kind of scale. Modern society nurtures "megapolis—the political city that has lost all proportion."[45]

So can modern democracy restore "polis" on the "assembly scale"? One way may be to make decisions at a level small enough to enable all those affected to participate. For example, residents may form co-operatives to design and manage housing and neighborhood assets. This is a way of "building democracy"[46] or "bringing democracy home."[47] Residents enjoy "active and

---

42. Chwalisz and Česnulaitytė, "What Is 'Successful'?"
43. McKee and Pannell, "Citizens' Assemblies."
44. Sartori, *Revisited*, 25.
45. Sartori, *Revisited*, 25.
46. Towers, *Building*; Co-Operative Development, *Building*.
47. Bliss, *Bringing*.

democratic citizenship."[48] In the middle of the twentieth century, Saul Alinsky founded the "community organizing" movement in Chicago. He wrote that "citizen participation is the animating spirit and force" of a democracy concerned with the "ongoing pursuit of the common good by *all* of the people." Alinsky italicizes the word "all."[49] Such a vision of participative mass democracy at the local level is an exciting one for democratic politicians, whether on the "left" or the "right." President Barack Obama learned his political craft in Alinsky's Chicago movement. Successive UK governments since the 1990s have sought ways to transfer power to a variety of neighborhood-level institutions and initiatives.[50]

Little Hitlers?

Assembly-scale democracy is not immune from familiar political problems. Promoters of co-operative management acknowledge vulnerability to control by small groups. They talk of a "little Hitler" syndrome marked by "oligarchy, corruption, favouritism, lack of accountability, secretiveness and failure to declare conflicts of interest, and apathy."[51] The solution is external regulation, but this requires the resources of a willing and capable state. Judgments by the state may be bypassed by astute political activists claiming to implement local democracy. For example, consider the case of a small neighborhood action group in an English city. A heroic "tribal leader" inspired by a "vision for a self-regenerating community" won support from the highest level of state, government, and church to establish a tightly governed "independent micro-state" running multiple public services and economic ventures. Unable to manage debts or meet commercial standards, the project succumbed to "takeover and asset-stripping" with access through the tribal leader's exiled son. Members remain with lovely homes in streets named after the founding heroes.[52]

More tragically, a London co-operative managed ten thousand homes on behalf of tenants, five thousand of whom were members. The elected leaders ignored the pleas of a hundred residents for an investigation into their concerns over fire safety. Seventy-two people died in the ensuing conflagration.[53]

---

48. Bliss, *Bringing*, 16.

49. Alinsky, *Rules*, xxv; emphasis in original.

50. The literature on this is vast. For a useful survey at the height of the Blair government, see Hilder, *Seeing the Wood*. The Cameron government drew inspiration from Norman, *Big Society*. For current news, one source (among many) is www.localtrust.org.uk.

51. Bliss, *Bringing*, 52.

52. Thompson, *Reconstructing*, ch. 8.

53. Booth, "Grenfell."

My point here is not to decry "civil society" initiatives that represent and serve community purposes. Many are admirable.[54] The point is that "assembly"-scale local democracy is open to the same risks that afflict all political organizations. These stem from poor skills in "governance" and low accountability to stakeholders—members, customers, and funders. The other side of this picture is that skills that work well at the small scale can be transferred to the larger. It was impressive to learn about one front-runner for his party's nomination for the US presidency in 2020. Pete Buttigieg was mayor of South Bend, Indiana, home to about a hundred thousand people. Mr. Buttigieg was twice elected as mayor, winning around ten thousand votes. In the UK, it is inconceivable for a politician of this rank to run for our kingdom's highest executive office. Procedures would not allow it, and anyway he or she would not be considered to have relevant expertise.

Palaver

But does "assembly"-scale democracy need leaders to govern? Surely with "no boss" people can make decisions as a group? Calling on insights from anthropology, Marxism, and personal experience, the Congolese philosopher Ernest Wamba-dia-Wamba presented the African clan "palaver" as "democracy" meaning "a free collective and individual exercise of free speech by everyone and by the whole community. It is a complete freeing, allowed by the democratizing community, of one's whole body, its senses, its gestures, etc., so that no aspect of bodily creativity is fixed or blocked." In *palaver* everyone may converse and be heard until frustrations are removed and differences resolved. A key role is played by *Nzonzi* who facilitate discussion and "surmount every obstacle to clarification."[55] The palaver revives, celebrates, and confirms the unity of the community. Professor Wamba rejected postcolonial rulers' claims to be practicing an "African" one-party version of "democracy" by calling on traditional rule by consensus. This tradition does not allow the suppression of free speech. On the contrary, he says, it is characterized by free speech.

The distinguished Ghanaian professor Kwasi Wiredu described this traditional African system as "consensual democracy." He contrasted this with "majoritarian" systems, which are "in principle based on 'consent' without consensus."[56]

54. By way of declaring an interest, I add that I have spent much of my working life promoting such initiatives.
55. Wamba-dia-Wamba, "Experiences," 17.
56. Wiredu, "Democracy and Consensus," 59.

The traditional "palaver" presupposed that a settled decision to be agreed by all was possible and necessary. It was mandated by the ancestors, whose will was channeled through the living leaders. Consensus rediscovers the "organic unity of the community." "In the clan there must be no individualism."[57]

Modern neighborhoods rarely offer the possibility for such "organic unity." Extended family networks located around a shared economic life used to be common in towns built around a mine or one manufacturing works, but these are disappearing. Instead shared residential assets—roads, paths, shops, bus stops, playgrounds—serve people who belong to, and shift around, diverse social networks. Individualism is the order of the day. This does not mean that people lose all sense of mutuality. But it does mean that the individual is a moral agent, freed to make choices about what is "good." Christianity has spent centuries on a process Larry Siedentop called "inventing the individual." Christian thought was the "foundation for the individual as moral agent and primary social role." This "took centuries" as Christianity's "moral intuitions had to be worked out against prejudices and practises sometimes as old as the social division of labor." It "involved fierce controversy, frequent back-tracking and frustration."[58] The individual cannot now be uninvented and returned to the box marked "organic unity."

The modern individual accesses a vast range of ways to meet needs. For Saul Alinsky, organizing the community meant disrupting these in order to arouse the thirst for mass participation. He described finding a key healthcare need that could be met easily by private agreement. He organized a militant confrontation with the provider, in order to create the illusion that mass political action was necessary. "The disruption of the present organization is the first step towards community organization."[59]

There is, of course, always more to be done to enable neighborhoods to work better and human needs to be better met. Modern democracy should enable people to do this through free association led by individual choice. It should also enable the power of the state to be deployed to provide public goods. Organization at the local or "assembly" level calls for time and skill to be devoted to decision-making. Those who actually do this, in any one situation, are almost always a small minority.

---

57. Wamba-dia-Wamba, "Experiences," 8.
58. Siedentop, *Inventing*, 355.
59. Alinsky, *Rules*, 116.

The Dangerous Myth of Collective Self-Government

There is a basic problem revealed in the literature on "democracy" just reviewed. It lies in the definition of "citizenship" as comprising "active and ultimately authoritative participation in making important decisions."[60] Everyone who asserts this then agrees that it does not happen. If we follow Lincoln's definition, then the word "citizens" means all those subject to the authority of the state—excluding children, possibly also criminals, and some limited categories of immigrant. It is unreal to suppose that mass participation ever happens. It is simply inconceivable that anything more than a small, largely professional, minority engages with all the detail of state policy. It may be said to be an ideal. But it is a dangerous one, for three reasons. It is *elitist*—it privileges the few who are thought to be the true "citizens" and marginalizes the rest. It promotes a *false* and incredible idea of what democracy is. This brings democracy itself into disrepute. It is *unintelligent*—it leads to the routine assumption that those who are alleged to "participate" are those with the right answers to problems. The multiple complexities of the modern state and its massive spending programs require original and critical thinking if there is to be innovation. The circle of those thought to be the true "citizens" may well be those with the strongest interest in excluding innovative thinking.

This does not mean that public participation in state decision-making does not happen or is not important. Hardly anyone can be said meaningfully to participate in *all* decisions. But large numbers do participate in *some* of them. This happens in and through civil society. This is founded on the rights to associate and to communicate.

"Held by Consent"

Models of democracy based on mass participation and collective decision-making are deceptive. May we revive the definition of democracy, in its public dimension, as a system "held by consent"—the definition first made in 1647?

Objections to Consent Theory

Objecting to defining democracy as a state "held by consent," Professor Grayling quotes two Virginians from the time of the American Revolution. George Mason wrote that "all power is derived from the people." Thomas Jefferson

---

60. Manville and Ober, *Bargain*, 21.

wrote of "governments deriving their just powers from the consent of the people." Professor Grayling finds a "highly significant difference" between these positions. Mason's is a "bottom-up," and Jefferson's a "top-down," formulation. Jefferson's approach offers a picture of the citizens as "passive."[61] Similarly, Professor Weale suggests that, if "consent" is enough to "hold" the state, then people may consent to a regime that is the opposite of democratic, such as the one endorsed in *Leviathan* by Thomas Hobbes—an absolute monarchy or tyranny from which there is no escape.[62]

These professors have not read Williams. They meet "consent" in the work of the American Revolutionaries, created more than a century after Williams's time. These bore the marks of Williams's ideas, as they filtered through the seventeenth-century English revolutions, and then the radicals who took them forward. If we look at Williams's words, we see that Mason's and Jefferson's formulations have the same root: the true and original source of legitimacy is popular sovereignty and *therefore* government is held by consent. This consent cannot just be given once and never revoked, as Hobbes imagines.[63]

Consent Theory Revisited

All civil government, according to Hobbes and Locke, has its origins in consent. However, for a system to be "held by consent," it must be renewed. *Renewable* consent is what grants the legitimacy explained by Williams, and then defined by the Providence planters as "democracy."

It is a legitimizing theory of the state: that is to say, it is a story that explains the moral basis of state power. When first made, it replaced "Christendom" as the basis of state legitimacy. Its rivals now include expressions of theocracy and theonomy (the state exists to advance the will of God or to implement God's law) and nationalism (the state exists to protect and advance the interest of a particular culture).

Consent theory says that power properly belongs to individuals, who may surrender or transfer this only voluntarily. The democratic state protects individual self-determination as far as possible. This includes protecting arrangements made voluntarily for mutual ends. Compulsion for public purposes is

---

61. Grayling, *Good State*, ch. 1.
62. Weale, *Democracy*, 79.
63. Hobbes, *Leviathan*, 18.1: "Subjects Cannot Change the Forme of Government." According to Hobbes, the state (or "civitas" or "commonwealth") is first formed by covenant to which all consent, but thereafter all legitimate power (or "sovereignty") transfers irrevocably to the monarch.

legitimated by consent of most of the population. This requires that reasonable justification for such compulsion is offered and interrogated.

Consent is sometimes confused with "consensus." In a book about consent theory, Professor Partridge said that "'consent' and 'consensus' are not sharply separable concepts."[64]

However, the two words mean different things. "Consensus" refers to agreement on a decision. If consent theory is really another term for consensus theory, then we are back to decision-making as the defining democratic activity. It is possible and healthy for citizens to consent to a democratic state and to disagree with each other on decisions made by that state.

Consent, as a legitimizing principle, invites me as a citizen to consider what kind of state attracts my consent. But, importantly, it requires me to consider what attracts (or repels) the consent of others. My consent legitimizes the state only if, for the most part, my fellow citizens share the same view.

Many Christians think that the state is legitimized by enforcing the will or law of God. When the great majority of our fellow citizens professed, sincerely or not, to be Christian, then arguments based on this principle could be broadly accepted as reasonable. Now a majority (in the UK) or a substantial and growing minority (in the USA) deny the truth of Christianity. It is no longer possible to cling *both* to a political position based on legitimacy by consent *and* to one based on legitimacy by enforcing God's laws. Christians must of course assert the right to live by God's law as a voluntary choice, and to speak freely and distinctively about God's call to humanity. But this is now within a framework of consent where equal rights are extended to all. Demonstrating this is to display the truth of the Christian gospel.

A Better Myth?

One of the problems of discussing "democracy" is the multitude of definitions in use. To investigate all 3,539 usages collected by Dr. Gagnon would take up more time than anyone is likely to find worth spending.[65]

The most common idea is that democracy consists in collective decision-making by citizens. I have argued that this is a myth, and a dangerous one—it is unrealistic, elitist, and may work against making good decisions. People do of course make decisions as individual and groups, and influence state decisions through the rights to associate and communicate. Democracy includes ways to hold the state to account for the decisions it makes.

---

64. Partridge, *Consent*, 139.
65. Gagnon, "Database, at 3,539."

However, to define democracy as collective decision-making is to lay a false trail. The proposal in this book is to define democracy as a system legitimized by consent. It may be objected that "consent" theory is also a myth. But "consent" makes better myth. It is a reasonable aspiration for a democratic state to seek the consent of all, or most, citizens for its renewal. If this consent is withheld for long by more than a small minority, then democracy falters.

8

Democracy's Crisis of Trust

There is a well-reported "crisis of trust" in the democracies of the US and the UK. Two-thirds of Americans think their democracy is not working, and only a quarter think the federal government is to be trusted.[1] "Trust in Britain's system of government is at a record low" finds the think tank Demos.[2] Only around a third of UK citizens think they enjoy a well-functioning democracy.

In 2022, a report claimed, incorrectly, that 60 percent of British adults aged under thirty-five wanted to replace democracy with an authoritarian system.[3] Commentators seized on this, one thinking it time to restore "love" and "gratitude" for the "blessings that liberal democracies have bestowed."[4] Another, after humorously suggesting raising the voting age to fifty-five, lamented that the "only institution that can take on the forces that threaten democracy is our democratically elected government."[5]

Democracy is not working—but "only" the government can fix it. If so, democracy is in trouble. The government is the *product* of how democracy is currently organized. Even if the government is able to see what is wrong, it would be an act of self-sacrifice to change it.

---

1. Donaldson et al., *Trust*.

2. Goss et al., *Trustwatch*.

3. Stanley et al., *Kids*. This reported finding was based on answers to one question in a survey, but contradicted by other responses.

4. Syed, "Loss of Faith," paras. 4, 11.

5. Taylor, "Give the Young," paras. 7, 13.

Democracy's Crisis of Trust

If democracy is to reinvent itself for a new generation, then the creative work will not take place in government. It will take place in civil society, in the way that Sheldon Wolin saw happening in post-Communist Eastern Europe.[6]

We next consider the problems of the representative system of democracy in the USA and the UK, the possible solutions, and strategies for implementation.

What Are Elections For?

Democracy is a system of rule "held by consent." It is not *defined* by processes of collective self-government featuring public decision-making. Its definition *includes* the right and means to pursue collective decision-making via civil society.

So does this mean elections are not important for a democracy? It does not. Elections are, first, the occasion for the renewal of the "terms and conditions" on which people consent to the transfer of their personal sovereignty to the state. This may lead to the withdrawal of democratic consent, and its substitution with an alternative legitimizing principle. This does not mean the end of the state. It means that gradually it will cease to be "held by consent" and instead be "held" by an alternative such as theonomy or nationalism. Elections are, second, one means (though not the only one) for the debates happening in civil society to be transmitted into the realm of state decision-making.

For these things to happen elections need to be "free." We now return to Dahl and the standard conditions for "procedural" democracy—not with the thought that these procedures *define* democracy, but with the aim of renewing consent and keeping open the channels of communication between civil society and the state. Elections must be competitive—competition for votes should force candidates to adjust to electors' "terms and conditions" for consent. They must seek to confer equal rights on electors: this will never be absolute, but barriers to equality need to be identified, challenged, and removed as far as possible. They should be free in the sense of open to all to offer themselves as candidates: again, this will be far from absolute, but major obstacles need to be challenged.

The outcome of an election is a government. It is essential for that government to be competent. The distinguished scholar Larry Diamond says that poor performance is a major source of democratic failure.[7] Typical democratic theory emphasizes the role of government as being to raise the "decisions"

---

6. See p. 92.
7. Diamond, "Performance."

of the electorate to the level of state authority. However, if those decisions are incompetently conceived or executed, the effect is to persuade people to seek another legitimation for the state. People may consent to incompetent rule as a correctable exception, but they do not consent to government that is systematically incompetent. Barriers to competence also need to be challenged.

Who Votes?

To vote in elections in the US or the UK, it is first necessary to register with the authorities. Of US adults who could register, between a quarter and a third do not.[8] The corresponding figure in the UK is about one in eight.[9] More than half of US adults say they have never been asked to register.[10] In the UK, local authorities (district councils) are required, once a year, to contact everyone who could register and invite them to sign up. Councils also have rarely used power to levy penalties on those who refuse to register. Of those who register in the US, more than nine out of ten go on to vote in a presidential election.[11] In the UK, this figure was six out of ten in the parliamentary election of 2024 (66 percent was achieved in 2019).[12] So, in the UK, about half of all those who *could* vote actually do so. This proportion is higher in the US. To win control of government in the UK a party needs between 35 and 40 percent of the vote, which means having the support of under 20 percent of all potential voters. The corresponding figure to win a US presidential election would normally be higher, at about 30 percent.

Why do so many Americans not register to vote? The USA has a dark past of measures to deter registration. This history sometimes leads to a

---

8. The US Census Bureau publishes voter registration statistics every two years. In Nov. 2022, 69 percent of US citizens were registered to vote. In Nov. 2024 (at the time of the presidential election) this proportion stood at 73 percent.

9. Precise figures for the UK are not easy to establish as registration is by district-level local authorities, and eligibility differs according to types of election. British, Irish, Commonwealth, and some EU citizens with a home in a district are eligible to vote in local government elections. EU citizens are not eligible to vote in parliamentary elections. According to the Electoral Commission, 87 percent of UK and Irish citizens were registered to vote in 2022 (Explore the Data). Other measures vary slightly from this proportion.

10. Creek and Ueyama, *Why*, 3.

11. According to data published at Woolley and Peters, "Voter Turnout," there were 158,481,688 votes cast in 2020 out of 168,308,000 registered voters. The corresponding figure in 2024 was 154,308,000 cast out of 173,854,000. So 94 percent of those registered to vote actually did so in the 2020 presidential election. The corresponding proportion in 2024 was nearly 89 percent.

12. Sturge, "2024 General Election."

supposition that such "suppression" is to blame.[13] However, research shows that many make a *choice* not to become a voter. The unregistered are twice as likely than those registered to "dislike politics" and to say that voting "has little to do with the way real decisions are made."[14] These assessments are not unreasonable.

We have seen that in the Swiss "direct" model, referenda raise the level of participation. To become part of "democracy," this needs to be embedded in the political culture, with support in both framing and implementing resolutions. Civil society initiatives are another arena for democratic engagement. Voting for elected officials is an important expression of democracy, but it is not the only one, and staying away from it may be a rational response to its limitations and pretensions. That said, to preserve and reinvent democracy, we need to examine and be ready to overcome barriers to free, equal, and effective exercise of the vote.

Australia makes both registration (called enrollment) and voting compulsory for all citizens. The ballot itself is secret, so there is no way of checking who has complied with the law by reaching a booth, ballot paper in hand, and actually recording a vote. Compulsory voting is popular with Australians,[15] generally seen as confirming an equal obligation to perform a civic duty, with elections a moment of good-humored rejoicing.[16] It avoids the need for parties to devote energy to "getting out the vote." Like Swiss referenda, the compulsory vote "works" as an accepted and regular feature of Australian political culture. It may not translate into a different, more voluntaristic, culture.

Whose Vote Counts?

American democracy is "narrowing the battlefield." Choices made by ever-fewer voters are significant for the outcome of elections. Campaign strategy has moved from "wholesale campaigning" in the 1950s to "microtargeting" in the present century. Using modern research techniques and online advertising, campaigners target small groups of voters located where their votes have maximum leverage.[17]

---

13. For example, in Frum, *Trumpocracy*, 126–27.
14. Creek and Ueyama, *Why*, 4.
15. Evans, *Compulsory Voting*, 9.
16. Vinayaka, "Compulsion."
17. Shaw et al., *Battleground*.

The Electoral College

The presidency of the US is the most prestigious elected office in the democratic world. Under the Constitution, he or she is chosen by an "electoral college" comprising delegates from the member states, plus a few from Washington, DC.[18] Electoral college delegates are elected by voters and, usually, pledged to support a particular candidate as president. The authors of the Constitution, working at the end of the eighteenth century, thought the college would lead to wise and independent-minded people deliberating over the best qualified appointment. They thought they were placing a buffer between the expression of popular will and the appointment of the head of state. But it turns out that the college is just how voters elect their president. States can make their own arrangements, but in almost all cases a slate of college members is elected on a winner-takes-all, first-past-the-post system. Most states are "safe" for either Republican or Democrat representation. In a close election, a small number of voters in a few states decide the outcome. It is possible for a candidate to win the electoral college, and thus the presidency, without a lead in the "popular vote" among the voting public. This occurred in 2000 and 2016.

This system has often been contested through numerous attempts to make amendments. It has been proposed to use districts within states, rather than whole states, to elect the college. Some of the "founding fathers" who wrote the Constitution expected this to happen.[19] This would potentially empower many more voters to have a say in the election. Maine and Nebraska are states that work this way.

It would be straightforward to elect a US president through the popular vote alone, with no "college," and enable all voters to have an equal say.

Redistricting and Gerrymandering

The president heads the "executive" arm of government. Congress, comprising the two chambers of the Senate and House of Representatives, is the "legislature." Congress is elected separately from the president. There are two senators from each state. The house is elected by districts, which are redrawn after each census. The district maps are created by each state. The creation of these new maps is called "redistricting." This creates scope for "gerrymandering" whereby the ruling party seeks to maximize its own advantage in drawing boundaries.

For example, North Carolina is a state with a roughly equal balance of party support. Prior to 2024, this balance was reflected in the representatives

---

18. Though no woman has yet held the office.
19. Kefauver, "College," 196.

returned to the federal Congress. The Republican-controlled state government then redrew boundaries. The 2024 election was fought on the new map. Two point seven million Republican votes earned the party 10 seats, while 2.6 million Democrat votes earned them 4. This result came as no surprise—it was just as forecast by the campaign group Common Cause, drawing on a tool called Dave's Redistricting App.[20] Common Cause said that the new map was "incredibly disproportionate and will greatly favor Republicans."[21] Unless redistricting demonstrates racial bias, there is no federal law or institution that can challenge it. The important point for democracy is not so much that of fairness between parties, but rather those of competition and the equal weight of votes. Of 435 house seats, only 27 were "toss-ups" and a further 16 were rated "lean." This means that 9 seats out of every 10 were "safe"—compared with 6 out of 10 at the end of the 1990s.[22] This narrows the "battleground" where parties compete for votes.

Some states have independent "redistricting" commissions responsible for the boundaries. These independently drawn maps account for many competitive seats.[23] In states that allow it, a citizens' initiative may amend the state constitution to make an independent commission responsible for redistricting. Such a proposal passed in Utah, but the state legislature found reasons not to carry out the mandate from the voters.[24] An appeal to the state Supreme Court successfully challenged the legislature's decision, though the matter is not resolved at the time of writing.[25]

An initiative in Ohio was put before voters in 2024. It proposed an independent redistricting commission, including one-third membership from each of the main parties and one-third independents. The text to be considered by voters ran to over a thousand words. It included a sentence describing the proposal as being to establish a "taxpayer-funded commission of appointees required to gerrymander the boundaries of state legislative and congressional districts to favor either of the two largest political parties in the state of Ohio, according to a formula based on partisan outcomes as the dominant factor." This wording was created by Republicans, and opposed by Democrats, on both the board that agrees ballot measure wording and the Ohio Supreme

20. https://davesredistricting.org/.
21. Common Cause North Carolina, "DRA," para. 15.
22. Li and Feliz, "Competitive Districts."
23. According to Li and Feliz, "Competitive Districts," of the twenty-seven "toss-up" districts, ten were drawn by party-controlled legislatures, thirteen by commissions, and four by courts.
24. Durham, *Amici Curiae Common Cause*.
25. McKellar, "Utah."

Court.[26] Asking voters to agree to stop "gerrymandering" by authorizing a "gerrymander" sounds like something from a satire by George Orwell or Tom Wolfe. However, the proposed brief to the commission was to draw a map that would achieve the outcome described: to reflect Ohio voters' party choices in the balance of representatives elected to the house. The aim was to maintain the two-party "duopoly"—provided neither could gain a disproportionate lead over the other.

Ohio voters rejected the proposal.

Money Talks—in Favor of Incumbents

In most countries, the law restricts the amount of money that may be spent in promoting a candidate or party at elections. This was so in the US until 2010. The federal Supreme Court then found that this restricted free speech. Unlimited money can be spent, unless it is pledged in a way that opens the system to charges of corruption.[27] Huge amounts of money now flow to support campaigns. In congressional races, most of this supports incumbents. For example, in 2021 and 2022, candidates for the House of Representatives raised a total of US$1.9 billion—an average of just under US$600,000 per candidate. Incumbents standing for reelection raised an average of US$2.8 million; challengers to incumbents an average of US$300,000.[28] Incumbents, it seems, are better placed to attract donors and represent a better investment than challengers.

In Australia, the state refunds election expenses for all candidates gaining over 4 percent of the vote in elections. In the 2022 parliamentary elections the total paid out amounted to A$75,876,944,[29] equivalent to about US$50 million. The intention of this system, introduced in 1984, was to reduce recourse to private donations. However, funding by corporations, trade unions, lobby groups, and individuals remains a feature of Australian democracy.

Alternative Voting Systems

Could a federal system override local arrangements in the US? FairVote is an organization campaigning for a "Fair Representation Act" to be passed by the federal Congress. This would require all members of the House of Representatives to be elected in independently mapped districts using a system called "ranked

26. Balmert, "Why?"
27. Citizens United v. FEC, 558 U.S. 310 (2010).
28. Open Secrets, "Incumbent Advantage."
29. Australian Election Commission, *Disclosure*, 9.

choice voting" (RCV) or "instant runoff." The UK calls it the "alternative vote" system. Under RCV, voters express a preference for their choice of candidate, making a choice of first, second, third, and so on. The usual outcome of RCV is that one candidate gains more than half of all votes, after transferring losers' votes to the next preference. RCV is gradually entering into some municipal and primary elections in the US. RCV makes elections more competitive by enabling minority or new parties or candidates to attract voters who may fear "wasting" their vote on a candidate with low prospect of victory.

Australia uses RCV. It enabled the breakthrough into Parliament of a loose coalition of independent members known as the "Teals" in 2022.[30]

FairVote proposes that US representatives be elected in multimember districts. This would open the way to FairVote's "gold standard" for elections: "proportional ranked choice voting," also called the "single transferable vote" (STV). This sets a target proportion of votes cast to qualify a candidate for election, after which "surplus" second choices are transferred until all places are filled.[31] This is one route to "proportional representation" (PR). PR means that the makeup of the resulting assembly reflects the balance of votes for parties standing in the election. RCV alone is not "proportional."

The UK's "Westminster Model"

The United Kingdom is the home of the "Westminster model" of public democracy. This means that voters elect an assembly to be the legislature. A majority in that assembly decides on the appointment of a governing "executive." The elected assembly typically has two chambers.

The contrasting American model holds a separate election of a governing executive. There is a "separation of powers" between the legislative assembly and the executive.

In both systems, there is a further function that falls on the elected assembly: monitoring the performance of the executive and holding it to account. We may call this function "scrutiny."

The United Kingdom is, in principle, ruled by "the Monarch in Parliament"—the Monarch appoints a government, and the two chambers of Parliament are responsible for legislation and scrutiny. However, the legal and political reality is that the House of Commons is the sovereign body.[32] It

---

30. Wahlquist, "Teal."
31. FairVote, "Proportional RCV." For a useful (and understandable!) summary of various voting systems, see UK Parliament, "Voting Systems."
32. For more on the sovereignty of the Commons, see p. 55, n. 4.

comprises (in 2024) 650 members, each representing one constituency. The average registered electorate per constituency in 2024 was about 74,000. Constituency maps are drawn by the "Boundary Commission."

Elections are on the "first-past-the-post" principle: the candidate with the leading number of votes is elected, regardless of whether they have a majority of all votes cast. A government requires a majority in the House of Commons: the leader of this majority becomes prime minister. Typically, people vote for a party that they prefer to become the government. This means, in practical reality, that they vote for (or against) a leader who is candidate for prime minister. The Monarch invites the leader of whichever party is sure of a Commons majority to become prime minister. The largest party outside the governing majority becomes the Opposition, and the "Leader of the Opposition" challenges the prime minister in the House of Commons. The House of Commons is the key body for agreeing legislation. The "upper" House of Lords can revise and delay legislation but may be overruled by the Commons. Though once it represented the aristocracy, nowadays the Lords consists of people appointed for life by a prime minister or, sometimes, by a Leader of the Opposition. Many are retired Commons politicians.

There is a beautiful simplicity about the UK system. Voters make one mark on one piece of paper. As a result, within a few hours of the end of polling, they have chosen a prime minister, an opposition leader, and a legislature, all rolled together in one small chamber. Its merits are a cause of self-admiration by the British political elite. William Waldegrave was Margaret Thatcher's last appointment to a cabinet.[33] Writing in 2015, he contrasted UK democracy favorably with the systems of France or the USA, where "the separation of powers is a recipe for paralysis . . . in our great crises, we know who matters and where he or she is to be found: standing at the despatch box[34] in the House of Commons."[35]

What's Wrong with British Democracy?

However, it is now widely accepted that action is needed to address deep public disaffection with the state of democracy in the UK.[36]

---

33. Now Lord Waldegrave.

34. From where, in the center of the chamber, government ministers make statements and answer questions.

35. Waldegrave, *Weather*, 198.

36. Renwick et al., *Future*, 90.

Many studies examine this problem. But their solutions are only marginal changes to the current arrangements.[37] They do not address its real problem. What is really wrong with democracy in my homeland?

Party Power

The Oona King Story

Oona King was just twenty-nine years old when, in 1997, she became the Labour Member of Parliament for a constituency in East London. In November 1998 she was in the House of Commons when she got a note telling her to go "immediately" to the office of the prime minister, Tony Blair. As Blair watched, Alistair Campbell said they needed her help. They wanted her to write a personal attack on Ken Livingstone. Livingstone was a left-wing Labour politician who wanted to be the first holder of the new, powerful post of mayor of London. Blair and his communications director, Alistair Campbell, wanted to stop him. King was reluctant. She explained:

> "I don't go in for personal attacks. It's not my style. And the other thing is, I don't agree with the strategy. We're alienating everyone, and Ken's going to win. Surely that's not what you want."

This did not go down well.

"Why me?" she asked. Campbell explained why her support mattered:

> "You're an ethnic minority MP,[38] you're held in high regard by the black community, and this election has a London electorate that's 40 per cent ethnic minority. We need you to get the message across."

The meeting ended with this exchange between Campbell and King:

> "Look, this is a direct request from the Prime Minister. Is your answer yes or no?"

> "I know it's the end of my political career, but the answer is no."

---

37. For example, Goss et al., *Trustwatch*; Hazell and Riddell, *Trust*.
38. King was the daughter of an African American civil rights leader and an English Jew. She served a mainly Muslim constituency.

"It's not the end of your political career, Oona. Just the next five years. You can go now."[39]

King left the House of Commons in 2010. Now, Lady King works for Uber, as Chief Economic Opportunities Officer. Ken Livingstone ran as an Independent for mayor of London. He won. The Labour candidate came third. Livingstone served as mayor for eight years.

Oona King might have had a remarkable political career had it not been cut short that day in Tony Blair's office. Her response showed both her accurate political judgment and her integrity. The demand to betray both of these came from the "prime minister." But this was not about government policy or national security, the sorts of things that concern "prime ministers." It was about internal party management. It should have been called a "direct request from your party leader."

Why Is the System in Disrepute?

This little story takes us to the heart of why UK democracy is in disrepute. Once, party leaders were elected by the Commons. Now all parties turn this decision over to the party members. Individual party members make up tiny, shifting groups of self-selected people.[40] Once taking office, the new leader captures control of the party machine. In this capacity he or she uses that power to suppress opposition from within the party and assert his or her own control. When Campbell told King that her career was over "for five years" he was referring to her prospects of applying her considerable talents in ministerial office.[41] But the destructive power of the party-leader-cum-prime minister is even greater. An unfaithful Member of Parliament might "lose the Whip." This means that he or she cannot run for Parliament as a party representative. Of course they can continue as an Independent. However, when people vote, and put a mark against the individual, they are really voting for the party as government. Above all they are voting for the leader as would-be prime minister. By removing the Whip, a leader is terminating the career of the member. In October 2019, twenty-one Conservative Members of Parliament lost the Whip when they defied Boris Johnson by voting for the European Union (Withdrawal) (No. 2) Act. Some ran as Independents in the election a few

---

39. O. King, *House Music*, 114–15.

40. Four hundred ninety thousand people voted in the 2020 Labour leadership election. Ninety-five thousand people voted in the 2024 Conservative leadership election. These numbers equate respectively to about 1 and 0.2 percent of the UK electorate.

41. King remained in the Commons until 2010 but was never a government minister.

weeks later, but none of these won. Early in the 2024 Parliament, seven Labour MPs lost the Whip for voting against the government on a welfare measure. This was a temporary suspension, to be reviewed. If the Whip is not restored, then they will not be able to stand as Labour candidates in the next election.

In the House of Commons, the real business of members takes place in small meetings and offices. They examine concerns raised among the approximately one hundred thousand people they each represent.[42] They meet in committees, research ideas and interrogate ministers and their teams of officials. Much of this is collaborative, working across parties. As they work, they are interrupted by the drone of bells. This noise tells them to stop what they are doing and come as fast as possible, running if necessary, to the "division lobby" where they vote as the Whips instruct. This activity is absurd. The voting could easily be done online, with minimum disruption to the real work. But the droning bells, and the lining up to be counted, remind members of their true masters—not the people, but the Whips, and behind them, the party system.

What Is to Be Done?

The long-standing Electoral Reform Society campaigns for more "proportional" elections.[43] Members would be elected by single transferable vote (STV) in multimember constituencies. This would make the outcome of elections more closely mirror the voters' choice of governing party. But it would lose the personal connection between one MP and their constituents. In terms of the House of Commons, it would risk making a bad situation much worse. After Brexit, when there was no majority for any one model of future relations with Europe, the House spent months voting over what to do while the government was helpless to resolve things. The only thing agreed was to delay a decision. The Commons alone is not capable of governing. The result of PR would be either minority government or coalitions. The only recent example of a Westminster Coalition was that between the Conservatives and the Liberal Democrats, from 2010 to 2015. It resulted in the near wipeout of the minor partner in the 2015 election. This experience warns of the perils of this arrangement.

Meanwhile, the House of Lords is democratically indefensible. But an elected Lords would challenge the power and privilege of the Commons, and leave prime ministers with nowhere to send discarded colleagues.

After Brexit and the resulting Commons debacle, a group called Tortoise Media invited proposals on how to sort out UK democracy. One suggestion

---

42. Including children and others not registered to vote.
43. https://www.electoral-reform.org.uk/.

was for a written constitution. There is a myth that the UK does not have one. But when Boris Johnson, as prime minister, tried to use the "royal prerogative" to suspend Parliament for a few days in 2019, the Supreme Court did not find it too difficult to locate the relevant law and overrule him.[44] There is no single document with "the Constitution." However, this absence is a minor issue. The fundamental problem is the concentration of all branches of government in one chamber, controlled by tiny party leadership groups.

Many recognize the need for "reform" of the UK Constitution. But solutions can be disappointing. For example, the Institute for Government and a unit from the University of Cambridge agree that the "UK's constitution has been tested to its limits and found in urgent need of reform." The proposed solutions are led by "a new Parliamentary Committee on the Constitution" with an "independent Office of the Constitution." A "new category of constitutional acts" will "formally recognise the importance of key pieces of legislation" with "more extensive scrutiny" by Parliament. The "role and . . . capacity of the civil service to give constitutional advice" is strengthened with a "permanent centre for constitutional expertise within the Cabinet Office." This is to be topped off with integrated "public engagement—though citizens' juries and assemblies—into the processes of constitutional change."[45] This is not a response to any "urgent need for reform" in a system "tested to its limits." It is an effort to defend the "system" by giving an appearance of "reform."

What form might a more radical solution take? When they reach the polling station, voters wish to elect a prime minister. We could elect a prime minister directly. But this would generate a power struggle between the executive and Parliament. We could elect a small replacement for the House of Lords, on a proportional and regional basis. The elected Upper House should appoint a prime minister to serve for a set term. There would need to be clearly specified powers to each house, keeping the existing strengths of the Commons as a legislative and scrutiny assembly. The current House of Lords includes many experts who contribute wisdom to deliberation, and such "associate membership" could be retained.

Any strategy to amend a constitution faces the problem of how it is to be implemented. A government produced by the current system is unlikely to foster a change that may have produced a different result. In 2010 the UK Liberal Democrats promised a "more proportional" voting system with a preference for the single transferable vote for a smaller House of Commons.[46] When they negotiated a coalition with the Conservatives, they agreed a referendum

---

44. Judgment in case number CO/3385/2019, Sept. 11, 2019.
45. Sargeant et al., *Review*.
46. Liberal Democrats, *Manifesto 2010*, 87–88.

on a change to ranked choice voting (known in the UK as the alternative vote). This system gives more opportunity for minority parties to attract support, but it is not proportional. The Liberal Democrats in power did not use the opportunity to press the case for PR. The proposal was lost in a referendum, with little campaigning in its favor.

If "civil society" groups are to frame a "reinvention" of democracy in the UK, there are two challenges: to design it, and then to have it adopted by a force capable of forming a government. If Sartori's estimate of public interest in politics is correct, then such a measure will not on its own excite great support. It needs to be part of a wider program. In the UK, at present, the most likely vehicle is the Reform Party. It has been frustrated by "first past the post" in seeking to enter the Commons, but has managed (under its varying identities) to remain a dynamic and radical force in English politics since 2010.

Reinventing Democracy

In their public dimension, American and British democracy both need to be reinvented for the democratic state to recover its vitality. There are significant differences. But the basic problems of the current system in both cases are the unequal distribution of effective voting power and lack of competition for office. Tracing the source of these problems brings us to the strength of the party system—including party-like formations within parties—and party interaction with the state. The forces of democracy are bent by the gravitational pull of the parties and their various fragments. This is not say that parties should not exist. Parties are vehicles to assemble propositions—people and programs—to be offered in elections for government, making use of the resources of the constitution. They are essential. The question is whether the institutional resources of democracy can be strengthened to counter the anti-democratic tendencies of powerful parties.

This is unlikely to be something the existing state apparatus will welcome. It is a task for civil society.

Democracy is modified by culture. Successful states reflect the identity of citizens. Innovations in democracy, such as Swiss referenda and Australian compulsory voting, work because they have become celebrated symbols of "national" culture, and part of the rhythm of public life. They do not translate easily into other situations. Those who craft change must be conscious of the scope for cultural adoption. People need to like what they see in the mirror of politics.

9

Religious Freedom

Christians seek "religious freedom" in order to follow, share, and promote their faith. On the view submitted in this book, this freedom can be protected by the liberal state with equal rights for all. A theonomy, privileging a particular religious perspective, poses a threat to religious freedom, since it must define the version of the truth that it wishes to uphold.

This chapter examines the democracy of the "liberal state" through the lens of recent clashes over sexuality. This includes the experience of a Christian leader of a UK political party. It concludes with a glimpse at new developments in the USA.

The Politics of Sexuality

The Coming of Equality

In the prologue, I explained how I learned that I was the grandson of Jews murdered by the Nazi state. My parents both served in the British forces in the Second World War—a war often seen as one fought to protect democracy. One of the heroes of that war was a pioneering computer scientist called Alan Turing. His genius was applied in reading the enemy's "Enigma" coded signals.

Around the same time that I heard of my grandparents' fate, Turing died, aged just forty-one.

Investigating a burglary, police learned of Turing's private sexual intimacy with a man. Both men were prosecuted for "gross indecency." In those days, British police patrolled meeting places for homosexual men, seeking targets to prosecute. Each year, over a thousand men were imprisoned for this offense.[1] To avoid prison, Turing agreed to take drugs to suppress his sexual appetite. He died soon after. An inquest determined that his death was a suicide.

A few weeks after Turing's death the UK government set up an inquiry, chaired by John Wolfenden. It reported in 1957, recommending that his crime belonged in "a realm of private morality and immorality which is, in brief and crude terms, not the law's business."[2] During my lifetime, this understanding has spread through much of the democratic world.

Same-sex intimacy between adult males was made legal in England and Wales in 1967.[3] The province of South Australia followed in 1975, after outrage over the death by drowning of a gay man, apparently at the hands of "vice" police. Laws against same-sex activity were abolished across Australia by federal legislation in 1994. The US Supreme Court suppressed all such laws in 2003.

Since then, it has widely become unlawful to discriminate against those with diverse sexual inclinations in the provision of services and employment.

The recognition of same-sex couples as legally married has followed. The first state to approve so-called "equal marriage" (EM) nationally was the Netherlands, in 2001. Canada followed in 2005. For England and Wales, the Marriage (Same Sex Couples) Act was passed by Parliament in 2013. Scotland followed in 2014. Massachusetts was the first US state to take this step, through a court ruling in 2004. The federal Supreme Court extended EM throughout the USA in deciding a case in 2015.[4] Australia followed in 2017, with the support of six out of ten taking part in a referendum conducted by post.

"Equal Marriage" and "Free Speech"

Australia

The Australian referendum prompted wide concern among Christians that the coming of EM would threaten religious freedom, so should be opposed by Christians. The Australian right of free speech is generally restricted by laws against "vilification." The state is to restrict free speech to limit damage to collective harmony. Senior Christian politicians feared that any public expression of doubt about EM would be considered vilifying toward individuals in same-sex relationships. Various pieces of legislation were presented with a view to

---

1. Same-sex intimacy being illegal for men but not women under then UK law.
2. UK Parliament, "Wolfenden Report."
3. Extended to Scotland in 1980 and Northern Ireland in 1982.
4. Obergefell v. Hodges, 576 U.S. 644 (2015).

guaranteeing religious freedom, while accommodating Australia's traditional anti-vilification stance. Unsurprisingly, this proved an impossible balance, and no such law was passed. However, research has not found "evidence that those opposed to marriage equality were unable to articulate their views in the public sphere."[5]

USA

The USA has a different perspective on "free speech" from that of Australia. The First Amendment to the Constitution guarantees free expression except where directly inciting crime, or defaming individuals, or in other limited circumstances. The default position in the US is often called "free speech absolutism." This holds that the harms that may arise from free expression are best countered by "more speech" rather than by suppression. Through "more speech," those who disagree with a hostile or hateful comment will use free speech to draw attention to the potential harm and this will shift the balance of opinion.[6]

EM in the USA has given rise to concerns about religious freedom, but with a different focus: on the point at which the right to *express* religion crosses the rights of other groups to equal treatment in the marketplace. The 1993 Religious Freedom Restoration Act (RFRA) said that government should not "substantially burden a person's exercise of religion" unless it was the "least restrictive" way of securing a "compelling government interest."[7] This law applied only at the federal level, so a movement began for corresponding legislation in the states. Under its then governor, the evangelical Christian (and later US vice president) Mike Pence, Indiana was among the states that passed their own RFRA. This made the exercise of religious freedom a "defense in a judicial or administrative proceeding." Many religious and family policy advocates attended a signing ceremony in Governor Pence's office.[8]

However, after protest, and threatened loss of business spending, the Indiana legislators reversed themselves to amend their RFRA so that it would not "authorize a provider to refuse to offer or provide services, facilities, use of public accommodations, goods, employment, or housing to any member or members of the general public on the basis of race, color, religion, ancestry, age, national origin, disability, sex, sexual orientation, gender identity, or

---

5. Gelber, "Free Speech," 84–85.
6. Downing, "Hate," 176.
7. Pub. L. 103–141, 107 Stat 1488 (1993).
8. Fitch, *Church*, 136.

United States military service."[9] This produced an outraged response from church-based "religious freedom" advocates, who said:

> Christian bakers, florists and photographers would now be forced by the government to participate in a homosexual wedding or else they would be punished by the government![10]

Amid the controversy surrounding the act, news broadcasters interviewed the Christian proprietor of a take-out pizzeria. She admitted she would not cater a gay wedding, if asked. Within hours its online review page "lit up" with insults and slurs. Lewd pictures of naked men appeared on its Facebook page, along with threats of murder and arson. The pizzeria announced its imminent closure due to the level of threat. Christian supporters launched fundraising for them. In a few days twenty-nine thousand people gave nearly a million dollars, amounting to a sum greater than all the earnings in the pizzeria's history.

This story come from David Fitch. He reflects:

> That no gay or lesbian couple had actually ordered pizzas for their wedding. In fact it is rare that any couple . . . thinks of take-out pizza as the preferred meal for a wedding reception . . . the pizza parlor had become an absurd and empty symbol toward which could be aimed the hate and vitriol and also the perverse enjoyment of winning a battle for the sake of the Christian nation.[11]

The pizza makers were persecuted for their answer to a hypothetical question, dreamed up by a broadcaster seeking fuel for the fire of culture war. They would have no reason to know if their product would be consumed at an event to which they were not invited. The question was an impertinent piece of entrapment.

However, real legal cases have featured conflict between equality law and free expression for those with religious objections to same-sex marriage. These cases feed the "culture war" and cast doubt on the future of democracy in modern conditions.

Gay Cakes: Masterpiece and Ashers

In 2012 Jack Phillips, owner of Masterpiece Cakeshop in Lakewood, Colorado, was approached with an order for a cake for a celebration of a same-sex marriage. The marriage would happen in Massachusetts. There, unlike in

---

9. Holputch, "Indiana," para. 7.
10. https://www.advanceamerica.com/2015/04/legislature-about-to-destroy-religious-freedom-protection-in-indiana/. Author's record of a since-deleted site.
11. Fitch, *Church*, 136–37.

Colorado, it would be a legally registered union. Mr. Phillips declined, citing his Christian faith. He was taken to court by the state civil rights commission. In 2013, the commission won its claim that the baker had discriminated on grounds of sexuality. The essence of the case against him was that he rejected the order because the customers were gay. He argued that they were welcome to buy anything else he provided. However, requiring him to make his speciality, a custom-created wedding cake, was forcing him to express approval for same-sex marriage.

With the support of the Alliance for Defending Freedom (ADF), the baker pursued an appeal as far as the US Supreme Court, which found in his favor. This did not exactly settle the issue. The court found that the proceedings in Colorado were too prejudiced against his expressed views to consider the case fairly. Had the state authorities "not demonstrated overt hostility" to the baker's convictions, then they might have found differently. The ruling did "relatively little to resolve the conflict between anti-discrimination laws and the right of business owners to decline, out of sincere religious conviction, to provide services in connection with same-sex weddings."[12]

This case is often compared with one in Belfast, Northern Ireland.[13] The Ashers bakery chain was run by a Christian couple. They rejected an order for a cake decorated with the words "support gay marriage" and the logo of a group called Queerspace. The owners, Mr. and Mrs. McArthur, were not expected to create a design: it was provided by the customer. Ashers had the equipment to reproduce it on the cake. The Northern Ireland Equalities Commission (NIEC) supported the customer, Mr. Lee, to claim that the McArthurs were guilty of discriminating on grounds of sexual orientation. This was a claimed breach of the UK Equalities Act of 2010. The claimants won their case in the Northern Irish courts. With the support of the Christian Institute, the McArthurs appealed as far as the UK Supreme Court (UKSC). In 2018, five judges ruled in their favor. They accepted that the bakers did not discriminate against Mr. Lee because he was gay (the McArthurs insisted they did not; in fact he was a regular customer). They were discriminating against the *message* they were asked to reproduce on the cake.

There is an important, but often overlooked, difference between the two cases of Masterpiece and Ashers. Mr. Phillips was asked to produce a cake to celebrate a marriage. The cake ordered from the McArthurs was for an event celebrating the end of a campaign for the legalization of same-sex marriage in Northern Ireland. The Northern Ireland Assembly rejected this legalization in April 2014, in its third vote on the subject. Mr. Lee ordered his cake a few days

12. Movsesian, "Future," 713.
13. For example, Chandrachud, "Bittersweet."

later, for a show of continued defiance of the government of the province. The NIEC shared this defiant stance. The McArthurs did not agree. This was not a wedding cake: it was a political cake. The sexuality of the client was, as the UKSC agreed, irrelevant. UK anti-discrimination law protects people against receiving unfavorable treatment on the grounds of their "religion or belief." It has been left to the courts to sort out what qualifies as a protected "belief." It is now established that, among others, beliefs in left-wing socialism,[14] Darwinism, and the sanctity of the life of a hunted fox[15] are all protected. Could a conservative-minded printer be held to discriminate unlawfully if refusing to design a leaflet for a socialist campaign? Possibly. The Ashers ruling protects against this.

The Ashers ruling falls into a classically liberal defense of rights: it does not privilege religion. It potentially protects a wide range of suppliers who refuse business that promotes a cause with which they disagree.

Mr. Phillips's claim was:

> Requiring him to create a cake for a same-sex wedding would violate his right to free speech by compelling him to exercise his artistic talents to express a message with which he disagreed and would violate his right to the free exercise of religion.[16]

He won his case, but the ruling focussed narrowly on the way his defense had been considered. The ruling did not establish a space of protected religious belief, where people could claim exemption from the demands of equality law.

When Indiana backed away from its apparent plan to create such a privileged space, advocates of "religious freedom" said that "bakers, florists and photographers would now be forced . . . to participate in a homosexual wedding." There is no obligation on anyone to "participate" in a wedding if they choose not to. There are, however, laws that protect groups against discrimination on a variety of grounds, including race, gender, sexual orientation, and religion or belief. People who offer commercial services may not disadvantage customers on account of these (as the UK law calls them) "protected characteristics." Does someone who sells floral arrangements for a wedding "participate" in that event? If so, what about the chauffeur who transports the bride, or the furniture supplier that rents out stacks of chairs, or the energy company whose electricity flows into the building? A modern economy is a network of goods and services provided for ready money. This aspect of equality law says that, in a modern democracy, one person's money is as good as anyone else's.

---

14. McGuirk, "Belief."
15. Landau Law, "Religion or Belief."
16. Masterpiece Cakeshop v. Colorado Civil Rights Commission, 584 U.S. (2018).

However, maybe the creation of a wedding cake, or the photographic assignment, or the floral arrangements, need insight into the personalities involved in the marriage. This might be experienced as "participation."

Suppliers may be selective about the weddings they service. If a baker happens to know that one of the partners is insincere or immoral in entering into a marriage, he or she may wish to reject an order for a cake for its celebration. This would be to discriminate, but not unlawfully. However, if it turns out that this happens with suspicious frequency to (say) Asian customers but not others, then it is possible the baker may be found liable under laws against discrimination on grounds of race or national origin. Jack Phillips wants to refuse cakes for same-sex weddings. This opens him to action for discriminating on grounds of sexual orientation. He protests that he serves gay customers all the time—except when they are marrying each other. A court may find that this amounts to unlawful discrimination—not because he will not "participate" in a same-sex marriage, but because the customers who want this particular product (such as Jack's special "masterpiece") are gay.

In addition to anti-discrimination laws, the United States has the First Amendment right to "free exercise of religion." Part of Jack Phillips's defense was that, in refusing service to a same-sex wedding, he was exercising his religious freedom. How so? Prominent Christian and Jewish organizations submitted an amici brief to explain.[17] Their aim, their brief said, was a "classic American response to deep conflict"—to "protect the liberty of both sides."[18] Jack, they continued, considered all marriages to be "inherently religious" and same-sex unions are "sinful." Therefore, by providing services, he was being required to serve in a sinful act of worship.

> It does not matter that the state or the couple may not understand the wedding as religious. What matters for understanding burdens on religious liberty . . . is the petitioner's understanding.[19]

The state does not, in this case, have a "compelling interest" to override this understanding.

This is a strange argument. Christians understand the lifelong marriage of one man and one woman to be a religious union that depicts and celebrates the union of Christ and his church.[20] We know this is challenging and not always possible—so much so that when they first heard the idea of lifelong

---

17. Berg and Laycock, *Amicus*. In the UK courts this would be called an "intervention."
18. Berg and Laycock, *Amicus*, 2.
19. Berg and Laycock, *Amicus*, 3.
20. Eph 5:32.

union of one man and one woman, Christ's own disciples thought it might be preferable to be single.[21]

We are familiar with proposals that other marriages—those failing to meet the standards of the New Testament ideal—may still be recognized by Christians in one way or another. Currently, there is agonized debate over whether same-sex unions may attract such recognition. Clearly a legal requirement that Christians must recognize same-sex unions in church would breach religious freedom, since it would amount to the state determining theology.

But the Masterpiece amici put the issue the other way round. Even if neither the state nor the participants think they are worshiping God in a union, another person is entitled to say that they are, and then to deny service for that reason. This may take us to strange places. Potentially anything may be deemed "religious." We have seen that "hard" theonomy holds that all law-making is actually religious. Even the "soft" version holds it right to treat law as religious if this serves a moral or evangelistic argument.[22] Any law may potentially be disputed for violating someone's religious freedom. The answer, under the RFRA doctrine, is to claim that nonetheless the state's "compelling interest" is to override that freedom. On this logic, the democratic state will be forced to set itself up in opposition to religion across many parts of society. This is a recipe for culture war.

The scale of current culture war is acknowledged by the amici. Their intervention seeks to defuse a situation where:

> Blue states refuse to protect religious liberty; red states refuse to enact gay-rights laws.[23]

They seek to create religious exemptions from the requirements of "gay-rights laws." However, this solution would displace the conflict across a much broader stretch of territory that anyone may deem "religious."

Mark Movsesian also seeks to understand this cultural divide. Writing in 2018, he observed:

> Over the past two decades, American religion has become polarized between two groups, the Nones, who reject organized religion as authoritarian and hypocritical, especially with respect to sexuality, and the Traditionally Religious, who continue to adhere to organized religion and to traditional religious teachings, especially with respect to sexuality. Each group views the other's values as threatening and incomprehensible. Neither is going away, and neither seems in a

---

21. Matt 19:10.
22. For more on the doctrine of "evangelism through law," see p. 7.
23. Berg and Laycock, *Amicus*, 11–12.

mind to compromise—including in commercial life. This religious polarization has figured very prominently in the public's response to *Masterpiece Cakeshop* and similar controversies.[24]

This religious divide is one feature of wider American polarization. Friendships between Republicans and Democrats are uncommon,[25] and marriages rare.[26] Less than one American in five can understand the case of both sides in the conflict over religious freedom and same-sex marriage.[27] Movsesian suggests that past mutual tolerance was based on an idea of equality that reflected a basic assumption of goodwill across religious difference. Now, for a rising generation of "Nones,"

> [to] refuse to participate in someone else's wedding on religious grounds is to erect a boundary that seems socially incomprehensible. It is to express a judgment that the life events of other citizens are so opprobrious that one cannot take part in them. Such a judgment . . . is likely to be taken as a deep insult to the dignity of other citizens.[28]

The Masterpiece amici recognize this and submit that the "Court must also consider the dignitary harm to the religious objectors."[29]

It seems odd for Christians to feel they are owed "dignity" under the application of religious freedom laws. Christians are called to adopt the attitude of Christ who "being in very nature God . . . made himself nothing."[30] Anyway, "harm" in the context of democratic rights to self-government refers to the equal right of all to exercise those rights.[31] Whether everyone feels "dignified" has nothing to do with it. The notion that free speech is conditional on protecting the dignity of those who are criticized is a radical move away from "free speech absolutism"—a move that goes even further than Australian "anti-vilification" in the direction of restraining free speech.

24. Movsesian, "Future," 713.
25. PRRI Staff, *Bubbles*.
26. Wang, "Marriages."
27. Movsesian, "Future," 730.
28. Movsesian, "Future," 733.
29. Berg and Laycock, *Amicus*, 5.
30. Phil 2:5–6.
31. See p. 7.

Religious Freedom

Equal Marriage and Equal Protection

In 2015, the US Supreme Court directed all states to legalize same-sex marriage, in considering the case of *Obergefell v. Hodges*. Its main basis for this direction was the constitutional principle of "equal protection" of law. Here it had regard to the effect of differing state-level legislation. Mr. Obergefell was the long-term partner of Mr. Arthur. When Mr. Arthur was dying, they were distressed that in his home state of Ohio, Mr. Obergefell could not be named on the death certificate as the next of kin of the deceased. So the couple flew to Maryland, where equal marriage was legal. There, they married, in the plane, as it stood on the tarmac.[32] In another case, a serving soldier, who married in New York before deployment to Afghanistan, found his marriage undone when the couple returned home to Tennessee. A minority of the court dissented from the ruling, on the grounds that this was properly a matter for political legislation, not for their court. However, this would result in continued "unequal protection"—a violation of the constitutional provision put in place after the Civil War to achieve a consistent level of civil rights for all citizens.

This radical difference between legislation in different localities is a feature of the US, but not necessarily of other jurisdictions. However, we may consider the issue of "equal protection" more widely. Could same-sex relationships be granted the same legal protection as marriage, without losing the distinctive recognition of "marriage" as being for opposite-sex relationships? That was the intention of civil partnerships (CPs), introduced into UK legislation in 2004. The then Labour government was clear that "marriage" was to be reserved for opposite-sex relationships. Even so, the Christian Institute (CI) responded to consultation on this proposal with a campaign denouncing CPs as "counterfeit marriage."[33] This left no room to argue for the distinctive status of "marriage" when, a decade later, a Conservative prime minister decided to legislate for same-sex marriage.

The militant stand against CPs is understandable from the thinking of the influential founder-trustee of the CI, David Holloway. The 1957 Wolfenden report, advocating the legalization of male same-sex intimacy, separated law from morality and thus inaugurated a "new morality," which "justified an attack on the right of individuals to have legal support for their moral endeavours . . . Wolfenden was quite wrong."[34] The CI said that in opposing CPs it was seeking to protect the distinctive status of marriage as a union of people of opposite sexes. But it really believed that same-sex union of any kind

---

32. Obergefell v. Hodges, 576 U.S. 644 (2015), at 658.
33. Christian Institute, *Counterfeit*.
34. Holloway, *Church and State*, 47.

should be illegal, as it had been up to 1967. Might heterosexual marriage have been better defended by a campaign that took the government at its word, welcomed the equal protection offered by "civil partnerships," and sought to strengthen firm political commitments to the distinctive status of "marriage"? It is a hypothetical question. But it seems to me that there would have been a more credible defense of the "conservative" position had so much energy not been spent denouncing CPs as "counterfeit."

Forced Speech

Icing the Gay Cake

Ashers bakery was asked to set up its machines to write the words "support gay marriage" on a cake. Was this a case of "forced speech" or "compelled speech"? In other words, were they being compelled to express something they did not believe? If so, this would be a clear breach of the principle of "free speech." It was suggested by some that this was so with Ashers.[35] However, the views on the cake were clearly those of the customer. No one could seriously think that this was the opinion of the bakers.

"Misgendering"

Another area where "forced speech" is alleged is what is called "misgendering." Under UK discrimination law, one "protected characteristic" comes under the heading of "gender reassignment." If someone has begun a process of changing gender, it is unlawful to discriminate against that person on that ground. The courts have agreed that refusing to use their preferred gender in identifying them amounts to such discrimination. This applies in the areas of employment and providing services. There is nothing unlawful in "misgendering" someone in private life. However, if a business calls a customer (say) "Mr." when they say they are to be called "Ms." then that is potentially unlawful "misgendering." Does that make it "compelled speech"?

One case receiving attention in the UK and the USA was that of Dr. David Mackereth. Dr. Mackereth worked shifts as an emergency doctor in the UK National Health Service. He also sought to become an assessor for the Department of Work and Pensions. He would examine people who claimed state benefits due to being too sick or disabled to work. While undergoing training, he learned that it was policy that, in describing a client, he should refer to that

35. M. Jones, "Analysis."

person by their preferred gender. He thought this violated Bible teaching that all people have the gender assigned to them at birth. He left the course and claimed redress for religious discrimination. The US Heritage Foundation, a key part of the "religious right" movement, reported that:

> A 30-year veteran doctor in Britain was fired from the National Health Service for not calling a 6-foot man with a beard a "she."
>
> The employment tribunal that heard his case said his belief that God created human beings male and female was "incompatible with human dignity."[36]

The source for its reporting was Fox News, and Fox's source was Christian Concern. This British organization supported Dr. Mackereth, through its legal arm, the Christian Legal Centre.

Some claims in the report are false. Dr. Mackereth was not "fired from the National Health Service" (or from anywhere else). There was no "six-foot bearded man" involved. But what about the claim in the Heritage Foundation headline: "Compelled Speech Is Hitting Close to Home"? Was Dr. Mackereth right to say that, by remaining on the course, he would be agreeing to speak falsehoods about clients' gender, and this was "forced speech"?

Dr. Mackereth's belief in the immutability of gender was not, at the time, accepted by the courts as qualifying as a protected philosophy. Later, in another case, courts found that a claimant's similar belief did qualify. The appeal court found she was unlawfully dismissed for no other reason than expressing this belief. However, she did not say she would "misgender" clients. The legal position continued to be that such "misgendering" could amount to unlawful discrimination against a transitioning customer.[37] Christians needed to understand this continued legal fact. It was not their own opinion that was involved in the requirement to use the client's gender, but their employer's legal duty to respect the choice of the client.

My published article warned that an employee could still be fired if they refused to follow the law as it applied to their employer.[38] On social media, my article was accused of being a "dog-whistle"—meaning it was rallying people to a political cause. An old friend wrote, accusing me of being like Pontius Pilate (meaning, I guess, that I was washing my hands of the consequences of my analysis). This friend is a director of a life insurance company. I asked him

---

36. A. Jones and Richey, "Compelled Speech," paras. 17–18.
37. *Maya Forstater v. CGD Europe* and others. UKEAT/0105/20/JOJ, June 10, 2021.
38. Lusk, "Christians Can Be Fired."

how the firm protects employees who wish to be exempt from the rule about "misgendering." He did not reply.

I do not think that an employee is submitting to "forced speech" by writing a business letter to a client addressing them by their preferred gender. The employee, like the employer, is following the law that accepts the view of the customer as decisive in this exchange.[39]

Christianity in the Liberal State

"Liberalism" and Religious Freedom

Democracy maximizes personal self-government. This protects religious freedom. This includes the freedom to embrace what is sometimes called "conservative" theology: that is to say, a view of God and man based on the truth revealed in the Bible. This contrasts with "liberal" theology whereby the Bible, though useful, does not have the final word on Christian belief and conduct.

In politics, "liberal" is a shape-shifting word. In the 1870s it meant something different in common American usage from what it does today. Today it tends to be taken in America as meaning "progressive" or "left wing"—including positions that in European terms would be called "socialist." In Europe, generally, the word "liberal" does not imply being on the "left." It is common to find parties of the center or center right calling themselves "liberal."

There is an enduring sense to the word "liberal." A "liberal" political system means one where the state's role is to protect individual liberty and choice as much as possible, subject to the principle that everyone has an equal right to individual liberty. This is sometimes called "classical" liberalism. There are "left" and "right" variants on this position, generally marked by how far state power is used to promote economic equality.

---

39. On Apr. 15, 2025, the UK Supreme Court ruled that a trans person with a Gender Recognition Certificate (GRC) retained their biological sex for the purposes of sex discrimination under the Equality Act of 2010. See For Women Scotland Ltd v Scottish Ministers [2025] UKSC 16. The ruling appears clear that it does not change the protection against discrimination and harassment conferred on people whose "protected characteristic" is gender reassignment. Whether or not they have a GRC, people who have started the process of changing gender remain entitled to this protection. Possibly future cases may change this. My argument is that, in a business context, a requirement to address people by their self-defined gender is not "forced speech," nor a breach of free speech, nor a breach of religious freedom.

Religious Freedom

The British Context

In the USA, there is a tendency to associate "conservative" theology with "conservative" or anti-liberal politics. There is not the same association in the UK. Chris Catherwood is an English evangelical scholar who has lived and worked in the USA. In 2003 he wrote:

> Christians in the USA are always astonished when I tell them that there are active Evangelicals in all of the major political parties in Britain.[40]

British Christians tend toward "social conservatism." But they do not, generally, connect this to voting for a particular party. This nonalignment, Catherwood surprisingly suggested, "gives British evangelicals a far larger influence than those in the USA."[41]

Danny Kruger was reelected in 2024 as a Conservative Member of Parliament.[42] He is also an evangelical Christian. Interviewed by the monthly newspaper *Evangelicals Now*, he explained that faith "makes a good partner for conservatism" but added, "The left have just as good a claim to be in the Christian tradition."[43]

In the United Kingdom, there is a "Liberal Democrat" Party, with "right" and "left" wings. In 2017, this party's leader fell after being targeted for his convictions. This episode has lessons for the protection of religious freedom in liberal democracy.

Leviticus Weaponized: The Fall of Tim Farron

The Liberal Democrat Party is a "third force" in UK politics. It performed strongly in four elections from 1997 to 2010. The party was led by Charles Kennedy from 1999 to 2006, when Kennedy's continuing problems with alcohol abuse led him to resign. The party gained 52 seats in the House of Commons in 2001, and 62 (out of a total of 646 constituencies) in 2005. In 2004 a number of senior Liberal Democrats published the *Orange Book*.[44] This set out a comprehensive manifesto for the "right" of the party, with a strong emphasis on individual choice, free markets, and a smaller state. Kennedy, who was of the "left," did not contribute. The *Orange Book* had two editors. One was Paul

---

40. Catherwood, *Whose Side?*, 96.
41. "Britain" does not include Northern Ireland, which has a different political culture.
42. In 2025 he left the Conservatives and joined Reform.
43. Chapman, "Faith, Politics, Philosophy."
44. Paul Marshall and Laws, *Orange Book*.

Marshall, a wealthy investment banker and committed evangelical Christian. The other was David Laws. After Kennedy resigned, his successor as leader was Nick Clegg, a contributor to the *Orange Book*.

The 2010 general election did not produce a Commons majority for any one party. The fifty-seven Liberal Democrats entered government in coalition with the Conservatives. Kennedy was one of two members of the party's group in the Commons to vote against this coalition. Around a fifth of the group became government ministers. Tim Farron, a member of the group, was not among these. He did not join Kennedy in opposing the coalition. But he voted against a number of government measures.

David Laws joined the 2010 coalition government as chief secretary to the treasury. He was the minister responsible for implementing spending cuts, and thus at the heart of the coalition project to bring the Liberal Democrat "right" into partnership with the Conservatives. Soon he was suspended as a member of the House of Commons, and had to resign as a government minister. His offense was to claim expenses to which he was not entitled. This was for rent paid to his (male) landlord in London. Mr. Laws told the parliamentary inquiry that he lied about the costs because:

> I wanted to keep my sexuality secret, I was having a close relationship with someone who I was denying publicly to be a "*partner*" with ... we presented ourselves as being friends and not partners.[45]

In the general election of 2015, the Conservatives gained a comfortable government majority, and the Liberal Democrats collapsed to hold just eight seats. Nick Clegg lost his Commons seat. The party needed a new leader. In the election for this post, Tim Farron defeated Norman Lamb, who had served as a middle-ranking mister in the Coalition government. Farron was not an "Orange Booker" and led the party from the "left." He is also a well-known evangelical Christian.

On April 18, 2017, the Conservative prime minister, Theresa May, called a general election for June 8. Farron led the party into this election. He tried to focus his appeal to voters on his stance in negotiations with the European Union on the terms for Brexit, and on raising income tax to pay for improved health care. But on April 23 he was waylaid by a radio reporter from a broadcaster called LBC. In four minutes of live interview, the reporter, Vincent McAviney, asked him eleven times if he thought gay sex was a sin. Was he "following Leviticus"? Did he "approve gay people having sex"? Mr. Farron explained, clearly enough, that he, like his party, unequivocally supported

---

45. Standards and Privileges Committee, *Mr David Laws*, s.vv. "Mr David Laws: Introduction," §2; emphasis in original.

equal rights, and that it was inappropriate to expect a politician to rule on theological questions. He tried to explain the meaning of separation of church and state. A few days later, visibly shattered by the experience, Farron sat in front of a camera and announced that he did not think gay sex to be a sin—a position he later retracted. In the election, he improved the party's position only slightly, but well enough to see the return to Parliament of some former ministers. Nine days later he resigned as leader.

> [He] said the struggle to balance his Christian faith with his duties as a political leader was a factor in his decision to step down.[46]

Within hours of the McAviney ambush, a Liberal Democrat candidate, Vince Cable, appeared on television, and said of Mr. Farron's remarks:

> The problem he has as an individual, and it's true of a lot of evangelical Christians and Roman Catholics, is that their religious faith has a certain approach to these problems but they are also public figures who have to represent their constituencies, which are much more diverse.

Dr. Cable was the candidate for Twickenham, the constituency he had previously represented from 1997 until losing it in 2010. He was, at least in principle, commending Mr. Farron to electors as the next prime minister. Yet here he was depicting Mr. Farron as a hypocrite, insincere in his protestations of support for the equal rights of those in same-sex relationships, someone who merely trims to the majority. He was really saying that his leader was not a liberal at all.

Dr. Cable had served as a senior minister in the coalition with the Conservatives. He was a contributor to the *Orange Book*.

After Farron's resignation, David Laws wrote that he was "right to resign" since:

> You cannot be a leader of a liberal party while holding fundamentally illiberal and prejudiced views, which fail to respect our party's great traditions of promoting equality for all our citizens. Many of us have despaired over the last few weeks in seeing all the good work of Liberal Democrats... undermined by Tim's failure to be able to give direct and liberal responses on his own attitudes to homosexuality.[47]

Laws's argument here is that Farron cannot support equality for people in same-sex relationships if he is unclear that such a relationship is not "sinful." The argument is much the same as that of theonomy, which seeks to bring civil

---

46 McDonald, "Farron Resigns."
47. Laws, "Farron," para. 1.

law in line with God's law. Theonomy fears that it is difficult to say that something is wrong if is legal.[48] Laws says that if you think something is properly legal, then you cannot think it is wrong.

As we have seen, David Laws co-edited the *Orange Book*, along with Sir Paul Marshall.[49] Sir Paul was active in the Liberal Democrat Party until parting company over his support for Brexit. He is in the congregation of Holy Trinity Brompton (HTB). HTB is a "conservative" Anglican church that does not endorse same-sex partnerships for Christians. The *Orange Book* was published in 2004, the year the Civil Partnerships Act became law. It seems most unlikely that Laws did not know his co-editor's position on a question of such personal importance. Nonetheless he accepted his co-editor's ability to make an important contribution to shaping "liberal" political thinking. Laws accepted Marshall as a "liberal." Why could he not do the same for Farron? The difference is not in their Christianity, but in their politics. Farron was no "Orange Booker."

Christians—indeed all—who enter politics should prepare for attacks on their identity that are in fact motivated by political competition. Laws knew shame because of his sexuality. Once, it would have been acceptable in politics to try to shame someone on that account. Now it is acceptable to shame someone as a Christian, or, in some contexts, as a Jew. We need to understand such behavior as not, in fact, about these identities. They are about diminishing the influence of political rivals—about winning political argument.

Vincent McAviney, David Laws, and Dr. Cable all violated religious freedom in their assaults on Tim Farron. They refused him the right to follow his faith while fighting for his chosen political cause. The "Liberal Democrat" politicians were unready to defend "liberal democracy" if this did not suit the interests of their faction of the party. Dr. Cable replaced Tim Farron as leader before retiring from Parliament at the 2019 general election.

With a few exceptions,[50] "liberal" voices were not raised in support of Farron's religious freedom. Why so? Here are some reasons. Farron himself was shocked, faltering, and unwilling to expose the hypocrisy of senior colleagues. The church is confused on both the theology and the politics of sexuality. More widely, there is insufficient understanding among so-called liberals of the fundamental principle of liberalism—that we do not legislate on the basis of what we consider to be "wrong." Individuals have the right to take their own view of what is "good." The role of the state is to protect that equal right.

---

48. See p. 68.

49. He was knighted in 2016.

50. One being in the traditionally liberal London *Guardian*. Shariatmadari, "Who Cares?"

Christians understand "sin" as meaning an offense against God. The greatest sin is to reject him. When a nonbeliever asks a believer whether something is a "sin," they are asking: Would this action be an offense against the God in whom you believe, and I do not? The nonbeliever understands "sin" as an offense against "morality" and does not understand that Christians vary in how far they identify "sin" with "crime." Christians who take a theonomic view condemn "sinful" actions by nonbelievers, because they think this is a way to lead them to belief.[51] Christians who favor liberal democracy do not agree with that. To be asked "Is gay sex a sin?" begs the questions: "What do you mean by 'sin,' and what do you think I mean by 'sin'?" To the ear of the modern unbeliever, this sounds like an evasion.

Religious Politics Against Religious Freedom

This book has suggested that, in principle, the liberal state does not align itself with any religious position. If it does so align itself, the state is liable to make a political choice of the religious truth to be applied, and this itself threatens religious freedom. Recent developments in the United States illustrate this tendency.

The state of Louisiana recently passed a law requiring all classrooms in the state's education system to display a specified text in a readable typeface.[52] This text begins with the words "The Ten Commandments." It is the text of Exod 20:1–17, in the English translation known as the King James Version (KJV) or Authorized Version, completed in 1611. The exact KJV text is prescribed, with one omission, using American spelling. To be placed with this text is a "context statement" that describes the Ten Commandments as "part of American public education for almost three centuries." The "context statement" does not say that the words are from the Bible and are a translation from Hebrew. The words omitted are in verse 1, which in the Louisiana law reads "I am the Lord thy God." The omission, which should follow, reads: "which have brought thee out of the land of Egypt, out of the house of bondage"—an important clue as to the real context! The text may, optionally, be accompanied by displays of various American historical documents. The prescribed teaching seems to be that God's law is something passed to America through the court of the English monarchs,

---

51. See p. 7 on "evangelism through law."

52. Louisiana H.R. 71 (2024). On June 20, 2025, the Federal Appeals court found that the Louisiana law violated the US Constitution. ACLU, "Federal Appeals Court." On the same day as this ruling, the Texas state legislature passed a law requiring the Ten Commandments to appear on schoolroom walls, using the same version as Louisiana's, but without the "context statement." LegiScan, "TX SB10."

preserved in an archaic English text. Supporting the law, the founder of the National Association of Christian Lawmakers said:

> This is all born of the leftist culture war tearing down the fabric of the country. . . . We are going to try to rebuild the foundation of this country.[53]

The Bible is thus weaponized in the culture war and its meaning nationalized to meet the political ends prescribed by the state.

In another case, the state of Oklahoma decided to purchase fifty-five thousand "Bibles" for its schools, in the King James Version, with no commentary. The first tender required the "Bible" to contain also the US Pledge of Allegiance, Declaration of Independence, Constitution, and Bill of Rights, all to be bound with the KJV text. This led to protest: it appeared to favor one supplier of such an edition, this publisher being none other than Donald J. Trump. The state then amended its tender to allow these additional documents to be bound separately.[54]

The Bible can be read online. This is how today's students access information. The point of the Oklahoma tender seems to be to confirm a version to be blessed by the state, and to link it with a story of the role of this version in the political life of the "nation."

Defending Freedom

The developments in Louisiana and Oklahoma are minor episodes that can easily be shrugged off. But they are signs of a more militant strategy by theonomic politics to impose a version of the Bible and an understanding of its meaning. This may, in time, threaten religious freedom.

In the UK, the Christian Institute is inspired by a mission "to work for the state to adopt Christian values and to implement godly laws."[55] Its opposition to civil partnerships provided a poor way to achieve its stated objective of defending the distinctive status of marriage. Its support for the Ashers bakery was a hard-won triumph. But this was not a victory for theonomy. It fitted into a classically liberal defense of freedom.

American democracy was founded on the understanding that religious freedom is not well defended by religious establishment. Religious freedom, like all freedom, is best defended by the liberal state with equality for all.

---

53. Rojas et al., "Louisiana."
54. Martinez-Keel, "Oklahoma Changes."
55. Christian Institute, "State," para. 4.

This understanding is tested by the decline of Christian identity and the rise of theonomy. It is important for all who favor liberal democracy to defend and apply religious liberty—even when not in their apparent political interests.

Final Reflections

Modern democracy was founded on religious freedom. It is not for the state to define what beliefs qualify for protection. The only way to ensure religious freedom is to extend liberty of thought and expression to any and every set of values or beliefs. This was the central insight behind the Providence democracy of 1647.

If the state sets out to protect an understanding of Christian truth, the danger is that, sooner or later, some other account of Christianity will find itself on the wrong side of the law. Such risk is already apparent in the USA, in state projects to define an interpretation of the Bible for display in public schools. "Nationalism" and "racism" are weak explanations of the driving force at work here. A more convincing one is "theonomy"—the idea that Christians' political duty is to impose God's law on the wider population.

Theonomy gained strength in reaction to a suspicion that the "liberal" state was bent on suppressing Christianity. This fear was fed by court rulings banning voluntary religious performance in schools—rulings that overinterpreted the lessons of 1647 and "separation of church and state." Self-styled "liberals" have sought to regulate the values that qualify individuals for political leadership, and to exclude Christians who are held to violate these standards. This commits the same error as theonomy. It assumes that the civil law is the application of a moral code.

When citizens mostly identified as "Christian" it was not difficult to base political argument on Christian principles. The fading of Christendom sharpens the need for clarity about the foundations of democratic values. Liberal democracy affirms the "boundless" rights of individuals, provided the rights of others are equally protected. The task of the state in liberal democracy is not to enforce what is "good," but to defend the equal rights of all to pursue "goodness" according to their moral code. This is the best way to protect the freedom of Christians to worship and to spread the gospel. It is not the task of

Final Reflections

Christians to use political power to make fellow citizens obey God's law even though they do not share Christian love for God.

Does this mean there is no Christian "national" culture? We may imagine a society where the gospel is freely taught and accepted, where vibrant Christian organizations serve their communities, and where care for neighbor is widely practiced. In everyday language, in this imagined society, a "Christian" person means someone who professes faith in Christ. This society is, in a sense, a Christian society; we might even be prepared to call it a Christian "nation," as long as it accepts that citizenship alone does not make a person "Christian." But this "Christian nation" does not have a Christian state—it is not seen as the state's job to make people Christian or to assume they should be. Total and equal freedom of belief is nurtured.

If it is true that a "quiet revival" is now reversing the UK's long-term decline in Christian affiliation, then that revival must not expect or pursue a return to Christendom. This is not to call for people of any "theonomic" persuasion to be excluded from public policymaking—their insights and energy are valuable.[1] It is to ask Christians to reject theonomy and to define and defend a liberal alternative—not chiefly for the sake of civil order, but so that the gospel may thrive in freedom.

Four decades ago, Richard John Neuhaus agonized over the "naked public square" and the approaching "crisis of legitimacy unless a transcendent moral purpose is democratically asserted."[2] So a proposed "partnership between responsible religious and secularist leaders"[3] is to result in an "agreed framework . . . for the common good."[4] The danger here is that this "partnership" will allow Christianity to be expressed only insofar as is considered safe for the stability of the state. I prefer Roger Williams's approach: religious freedom is unbounded, and politics must learn to accommodate that.

Christians may largely agree on a vision for the life that should be enjoyed by all human beings, regardless of their faith. This vision may be shared by many "secularists." It may be pursued through multiple avenues—family, friendship, voluntary and community action, employment, commerce, and so on. Some may have the energy and gifting to pursue it through politics.

---

1. I agree with Luke Bretherton (Bretherton, *Politics*, 68) that we should not require those who wish to assert a religious basis for civil law to "translate" their reasoning into liberal language. That said, they should be ready to state their scriptural or other case for imposing a law or custom onto others.
2. Neuhaus, *Naked*, 259.
3. Guinness, *Global*, 193.
4. Guinness, *Global*, 181.

"Politics" means examining the state, its governance, and its relationship with power in society.

At issue in politics is not so much "What is that good vision?" as "What is the proper role of the state in managing its pursuit?" For example: What are the boundaries for state action in dealing with the many obstacles to fulfilling that vision? Can vast state expenditures on private goods (such as health, education and housing), and on income transfer, which are meant to help achieve that vision, be justified and sustained? Christians are likely to be on different sides of debate over these questions. That is at it should be. These issues demand diligent and creative thinking from all perspectives.

Without transcendent moral purpose, what holds a state together? Roger Williams answered that it would be "held by consent." Providence defined its "democracy" that way. People must decide that it is best to associate, and to disagree, together, in the "civil contrivance" of political community.[5] This requires us to consider not just our own conditions for consent, but also those of others, of different moral and political persuasions.

In democracy, the state's role is to maximize the equal self-government of citizens. Some things must be binding on all. These are for the state to deal with. It is the task of politics to establish what these are and how they are to be regulated, financed and run. Rights to associate and to communicate are the foundation of citizen engagement in these questions. These rights are fundamental to democracy. They enable a thriving "civil society" where ideas about common purposes are incubated.

The system for allocating the tasks of public leadership must provide, as far as possible, for the equal voice of all citizens in choosing competent officeholders. Successful political parties will narrow the battlefield in two ways: limiting the range of citizens whose vote is effective, and limiting the talent pool among whom leaders are chosen. These tendencies are apparent in the USA, where two parties maintain their duopoly while seeking to gain advantage over each other. In the UK, party factions limit officeholders to a narrow range of loyal members of the House of Commons.

Political parties are essential to democracy, but they also tend to subvert it. The task of reinventing democracy includes seeking ways to balance the various forces that try to control it.

---

5. P. Miller, *Roger Williams*, 54.

Bibliography

ACLU. "Federal Appeals Court Rules Against Louisiana Law Requiring Public Schools to Display Ten Commandments in Every Classroom." ACLU, June 20, 2025. https://www.aclu.org/press-releases/federal-appeals-court-rules-against-louisiana-law-requiring-public-schools-to-display-ten-commandments-in-every-classroom.
Adams, James Truslow. *The Founding of New England*. Boston: Atlantic Monthly, 1921.
Alexander, Amy C., and Christian Welzel. "Measuring Effective Democracy: The Human Empowerment Approach." *Comparative Politics* 43 (2011) 271–89.
Alinsky, Saul D. *Rules for Radicals: A Pragmatic Primer for Realistic Radicals*. New York: Vintage, 1989.
Anderson, Benedict. *Imagined Communities: Reflections on the Origin and Spread of Nationalism*. London: Verso, 2016.
Australian Election Commission. *Election Funding and Disclosure Report: Federal Election 2022*. Canberra: Australian Election Commission, 2023.
Bailyn, Bernard. *The Ideological Origins of the American Revolution*. 50th anniv. ed. Cambridge, MA: Belknap, 2017.
Balandier, Georges. *Political Anthropology*. Translated by A. M. Sheridan Smith. Harmondsworth, UK: Penguin, 1970.
Balmert, Jessie. "Election 2024: Why Is Ohio Issue 1 Ballot Language Different Than the Proposed Amendment?" *Cincinnati Enquirer*, Oct. 31, 2024. https://eu.cincinnati.com/story/news/politics/elections/2024/10/31/explain-issue-1-in-ohio-ballot-language-was-written-by-opponents/75936806007/.
Bancroft, George. *History of the United States of America from the Discovery of the Continent: Author's Last Revision*. 10 vols. New York: Appleton, 1888.
Barry, John M. *Roger Williams and the Creation of the American Soul: Church, State and the Birth of Liberty*. New York: Penguin, 2012.
BBC. "Brexit: Cameron 'Blocked' Civil Service Talks with Leave Campaigners." BBC, Sept. 14, 2016. https://www.bbc.co.uk/news/uk-politics-37360386.
Bebbington, D. W. *Evangelicalism in Modern Britain: A History from the 1730s to the 1980s*. London: Unwin Hyman, 1989.
Bejan, Teresa. *Mere Civility*. Cambridge, MA: Harvard University Press, 2017.
Bell, Daniel A. *Beyond Liberal Democracy: Political Thinking for an East Asian Context*. Princeton, NJ: Princeton University Press, 2006.
———. "Democratic Deliberation: The Problem of Implementation." In *Deliberative Politics: Essays on Democracy and Disagreement*, edited by Stephen Macedo, 78–87. New York: Oxford University Press, 1999.

Bibliography

Bennett, Anthony. *The Race for the White House from Reagan to Clinton: Reforming Old Systems, Building New Coalitions*. New York: Palgrave Macmillan, 2013.

Berg, Thomas C., and Douglas Laycock. *Masterpiece Cakeshop v. Colorado Civil Rights Commission: Brief of Christian Legal Society, Center for Public Justice, The Church of Jesus Christ of Latter Day Saints, The Lutheran Church–Missouri Synod, National Association of Evangelicals, Queens Federation of Churches, Rabbinical Council of America, and Union of Orthodox Jewish Congregations of America, as Amici Curiae in Support of Petitioners*. Christian Legal Society, Sept. 7, 2017. https://www.christianlegalsociety.org/wp-content/uploads/2022/10/Masterpiece_CLS_Center_for_Law_and_Religious_Freedom.pdf.

Berlin, Isaiah. "Two Concepts of Liberty." In *The Proper Study of Mankind: An Anthology of Essays*, edited by Henry Hardy and Roger Hausheer, 191–242. London: Pimlico, 1998.

Bliss, Nic, ed. *Bringing Democracy Home*. Birmingham: Commission on Co-Operative and Mutual Housing, 2009.

Boda, Mark J., and Mary Conway. *Judges: A Discourse Analysis of the Hebrew Bible*. Zondervan Exegetical Commentary on the Old Testament. Grand Rapids: Zondervan, 2023.

Bodin, Jean. *Six Books of the Commonwealth*. Edited and translated by M. J. Tooley. Oxford: Blackwell, 1955.

Booth, Robert. "Grenfell Residents Were Treated as 'Sub-Citizens', Inquiry Told." *Guardian*, Apr. 19, 2021. https://www.theguardian.com/uk-news/2021/apr/19/grenfell-residents-were-treated-as-sub-citizens-inquiry-told.

Bretherton, Luke. *Christianity and Contemporary Politics*. Oxford: Wiley-Blackwell, 2010.

Brett, Annabel. Introduction to *The Defender of the Peace*, by Marsilius of Padua, edited and translated by Annabel Brett, xi–xxxi. Cambridge Texts in the History of Political Thought. Cambridge: Cambridge University Press, 2005.

Bruce, F. F. "Judges." In *New Bible Commentary*, edited by Donald Guthrie et al., 252–76. 3rd ed. Leicester: IVP, 1970.

Cabellos, Anna. "What Message Is DeSantis Sending with Religious 'Full Armor of God' Rhetoric?" *Tampa Bay Times*, Sept. 14, 2022. https://www.tampabay.com/news/florida-politics/2022/09/12/what-message-is-desantis-sending-with-religious-full-armor-of-god-rhetoric/.

Calamandrei, Mauro. "Neglected Aspects of Roger Williams' Thought." *Church History* 21 (1952) 239–58.

Carey, George, and Andrew Carey. *We Don't Do God: The Marginalization of Public Faith*. London: Monarch, 2012.

Carville, James. "Democrats Need a Plan. Here's One." *New York Times*, July 8, 2024.

Catherwood, Christopher. *Whose Side Is God On? Nationalism and Christianity*. London: SPCK, 2003.

Chandrachud, Chintan. "Bittersweet Judgment: The UK Supreme Court in the Ashers Baking Case." UK Constitutional Law Association, Oct. 15, 2018. https://ukconstitutionallaw.org/2018/10/15/chintan-chandrachud-bittersweet-judgment-the-uk-supreme-court-in-the-ashers-baking-case.

Chaplin, Jonathan. *Faith in Democracy: Framing a Politics of Deep Diversity*. London: SCM, 2021.

———. "An Institutionalist Reframing of the Religion and Public Reason Debate." In "Religious Diversity, Political Theory, and Theology: Public Reason and Christian Theology," special issue, *Social Theory and Practice* 47 (2021) 589–602.

Bibliography

Chapman, Rebecca. "Faith, Politics, Philosophy, Prue Leith and Canada's Conveyor Belt of Death." *Evangelicals Now*, Apr. 1, 2023. https://www.e-n.org.uk/features/2023-04-faith-politics-philosophy-prue-leith-canadas-conveyor-belt-of-death/?access_code

Christian Institute. "Christianity and the State." Christian Institute, 2024. https://www.christian.org.uk/who-we-are/what-we-believe/christianity-and-the-state.

———. *Counterfeit Marriage: How "Civil Partnerships" Devalue the Currency of Marriage.* Newcastle, UK: Christian Institute, 2002.

Chwalisz, Claudia, and Ieva Česnulaitytė. "What Is a 'Successful' Representative Deliberative Process for Public Decision Making? Assessing the Evidence." In *Innovative Citizen Participation and New Democratic Institutions: Catching the Deliberative Wave*, by the Organisation for Economic Co-operation and Development, ch. 4. Paris: OECD, 2020.

Cockburn, Claud. *A Discord of Trumpets: An Autobiography.* New York: Simon & Schuster, 1956.

Common Cause North Carolina. "DRA Analysis: 2024 North Carolina Voting Districts." Common Cause North Carolina, Nov. 11, 2023. https://www.commoncause.org/north-carolina/articles/dra-analysis-2024-north-carolina-voting-districts/.

Co-Operative Development Services. *Building Democracy: Housing Co-Operatives on Merseyside.* Rev. ed. Liverpool: Co-Operative Development Services, 1987.

Corasaniti, Nick, et al. "Voters Are Deeply Skeptical About the Health of American Democracy." *New York Times*, Oct. 27, 2024. https://www.nytimes.com/2024/10/27/us/politics/american-democracy-poll.html.

Coyle, Wallace. *Roger Williams: A Reference Guide.* Boston: Hall, 1977.

Creek, Heather, and Kyle Ueyama. *Why Are Millions of Citizens Not Registered to Vote?* Philadelphia: Pew Charitable Trusts, 2017.

Crick, Bernard. *In Defence of Politics.* 5th ed. London: Continuum, 2000.

Dahl, Robert A. *On Democracy.* New Haven, CT: Yale University Press, 1998.

Danbury Baptist Association. "Danbury Baptist Association to Thomas Jefferson." Founders Online, [after] Oct. 7, 1801. https://founders.archives.gov/documents/Jefferson/01-35-02-0331.

Davis, Michael J. "Religion, Democracy and the Public Schools." *Journal of Law and Religion* 25 (2009–10) 35–56.

Decter, Midge. "Ronald Reagan and the Culture War." *Commentary*, Mar. 1991. https://www.commentary.org/articles/midge-decter-3/ronald-reagan-the-culture-war/.

Democratic Party. "1948 Democratic Party Platform." American Presidency Project, July 12, 1948. https://www.presidency.ucsb.edu/documents/1948-democratic-party-platform.

Diamond, Larry. "Power, Performance, and Legitimacy." *Journal of Democracy* 35 (2024) 5–22.

Domke, David, and Kevin Coe. *The God Strategy: How Religion Became a Political Weapon in America.* Oxford: Oxford University Press, 2007.

Donaldson, Samantha, et al. *The State of Public Trust in Government 2024.* Partnership for Public Service, 2024. https://ourpublicservice.org/publications/state-of-trust-in-government-2024.

Downing, John D. H. "'Hate Speech' and 'First Amendment Absolutism' Discourses in the US." *Discourse and Society* 10 (1999) 175–89.

Dress, Brad. "Boebert Says She Is 'Tired' of Separation Between Church and State: 'The Church Is Supposed to Direct the Government.'" *Hill*, June 28, 2022. https://thehill.

com/homenews/house/3540071-boebert-says-she-is-tired-of-separation-between-church-and-state-the-church-is-supposed-to-direct-the-government/.

Du Mez, Kristin Kobes. *Jesus and John Wayne: How White Evangelicals Corrupted a Faith and Fractured a Nation*. New York: Norton, 2021.

Durham, Christine. *Brief of Amici Curiae Common Cause: In Support of Reversal*. Common Cause, May 19, 2023. https://www.commoncause.org/wp-content/uploads/2023/05/Common-Cause-Amicus-Brief.pdf.

Eatwell, Roger, and Matthew Goodwin. *National Populism: The Revolt Against Liberal Democracy*. London: Pelican, 2018.

Ellis, Richard J. *Democratic Delusions: The Initiative Process in America*. Lawrence: University Press of Kansas, 2002.

Élysée. "The Declaration of the Rights of Man and of the Citizen." Élysée, last updated Dec. 14, 2022. https://www.elysee.fr/en/french-presidency/the-declaration-of-the-rights-of-man-and-of-the-citizen.

Evans, Tim. *Compulsory Voting in Australia*. Canberra: Australian Electoral Commission, 2006.

Explore the Data: Who Is and Isn't Registered to Vote? https://www.electoralcommission.org.uk/who-is-registered.

FairVote. "Proportional RCV Information." FairVote, n.d. https://fairvote.org/our-reforms/proportional-ranked-choice-voting-information/#how-proportional-rcv-works.

Featley, Daniel. *The Dippers Dip't, or, The Anabaptists Duck't and Plung'd over Head and Eares*. London: Bourne and Royston in Ivie-Lane, 1645.

Feldman, Noah. "From Liberty to Equality: The Transformation of the Establishment Clause." *California Law Review* 90 (2002) 673–731.

Field, Jonathan Beecher. "A Key for the Gate: Roger Williams, Parliament, and Providence." *New England Quarterly* 80 (2007) 353–82.

Figgis, John Neville. *Studies of Political Thought from Gerson to Grotius, 1414–1625: The Birkbeck Lectures Delivered in Trinity College Cambridge, 1900*. New York: Cambridge University Press, 2011.

Fisher, Linford D., et al. *Reading Roger Williams: Rogue Puritans, Indigenous Nations, and the Founding of America—a Documentary History*. Eugene, OR: Pickwick, 2024.

Fitch, David E. *The Church of Us and Them*. Grand Rapids: Brazos, 2019.

Fitzgerald, Frances. *The Evangelicals: The Struggle to Shape America*. New York: Simon & Schuster, 2017.

Freedman, Robert. "The Religious Right and the Carter Administration." *Historical Journal* 48 (2005) 231–60.

Freedom House. *Freedom in the World 2024*. Washington, DC: Freedom House, 2024. https://freedomhouse.org/sites/default/files/2024-02/FIW_2024_DigitalBooklet.pdf.

Frum, David. *Trumpocracy: The Corruption of the American Republic*. New York: HarperCollins, 2018.

Gagnon, Jean-Paul. "2,234 Descriptions of Democracy: An Update to Democracy's Ontological Pluralism." *Democratic Theory* 5 (2018) 92–113.

———. "Democracy with Adjectives Database, at 3,539 Entries." University of Canberra, Apr. 15, 2020. https://researchprofiles.canberra.edu.au/en/publications/democracy-with-adjectives-database-at-3539-entries.

Gallup, George. "People Favor Prayers in Public Schools." *Washington Post*, May 16, 1980. https://www.washingtonpost.com/archive/local/1980/05/16/people-favor-prayers-in-public-schools/c700df28-ab4f-41ea-a19e-5e2d2926abdf/.

Bibliography

Gąsiorowska, Adela. "Sortition and Its Principles: Evaluation of the Selection Processes of Citizens' Assemblies." *Journal of Deliberative Democracy* 19 (2023). https://doi.org/10.16997/jdd.1310.

Gelber, Katharine. "Free Speech, Religious Freedom and Vilification in Australia." *Australian Journal of Political Science* 59 (2024) 78–92.

Goss, Dan, et al. *Trustwatch 2024: A Playbook to Rebuild Trust in Politics.* London: Demos, 2024.

Grant, Madeleine. "Labour Has Confirmed That It's Now the Stupid Party." *Daily Telegraph*, Feb. 21, 2024.

Grayling, A. C. *The Good State: On the Principles of Democracy.* London: Oneworld, 2022.

Groves, Stephen. "Trump Suggests He'll Use the Military on 'the Enemy from Within' the U.S. If He's Reelected." PBS News, Oct. 13, 2024. https://www.pbs.org/newshour/politics/trump-suggests-hell-use-the-military-on-the-enemy-from-within-the-u-s-if-hes-reelected.

Grudem, Wayne. *Politics—According to the Bible: A Comprehensive Resource for Understanding Modern Political Issues in Light of Scripture.* Grand Rapids: Zondervan, 2010.

Guinness, Os. *The Global Public Square: Religious Freedom and the Making of a World Safe for Diversity.* Westmont, IL: IVP, 2013.

Gushee, David. *Defending Democracy from Its Christian Enemies.* Grand Rapids: Eerdmans, 2023.

Gutteridge, Neil. "Labour Backtracks over Sue Gray's Announcement on Citizen Assemblies That Will Bypass Whitehall." *Daily Telegraph*, Feb. 19, 2024.

Guttmann, Amy, and Dennis Thompson. *Why Deliberative Democracy?* Princeton, NJ: Princeton University Press, 2004.

Hall, David D. *The Puritans: A Transatlantic History.* Princeton, NJ: Princeton University Press, 2019.

Hansard. "Commons Chamber Volume 444: Debated on Tuesday 11 November 1947." Hansard, Nov. 11, 1947. https://hansard.parliament.uk/Commons/1947-11-11/debates/ac22a8ea-e202-4be6-b2b6-a5a448a12182/CommonsChamber.

Harrison, Rick. "Can Citizens' Assemblies Help Restore Trust in Government?" Yale Institution for Social and Policy Studies, Nov. 20, 2023. https://isps.yale.edu/news/blog/2023/11/can-citizens-assemblies-help-restore-trust-in-government.

Hart, D. G. *From Billy Graham to Sarah Palin: Evangelicals and the Betrayal of American Conservatism.* Grand Rapids: Eerdmans, 2011.

Hauerwas, Stanley. *The Peaceable Kingdom: A Primer in Christian Ethics.* London: University of Notre Dame Press, 1983.

Hazell, Robert, and Peter Riddell. *Trust in Public Life: Restoring the Role of Constitutional Watchdogs.* London: University College of London, Constitutions Unit, 2024.

Hébert, Keith S. "Ku Klux Klan in Alabama from 1915–1930." *Encyclopedia of Alabama*, Feb. 22, 2012; last updated Mar. 15, 2024. https://encyclopediaofalabama.org/article/ku-klux-klan-in-alabama-from-1915-1930/.

Henry, Matthew. *Matthew Henry's Commentary on the Whole Bible in One Volume.* Edited by Leslie Church. London: Marshall, Morgan and Scott, 1960.

Held, David. *Models of Democracy.* 3rd ed. Cambridge: Polity, 2006.

Herman, Alice. "Pete Hegseth, Trump's Pentagon Pick, Sparks Alarm over Far-Right Extremism." *Guardian*, Nov. 15, 2024. https://www.theguardian.com/us-news/2024/nov/15/trump-cabinet-pete-hegseth-defense.

Bibliography

Hilder, Paul. *Seeing the Wood for the Trees: The Evolving Landscape of Neighbourhood Arrangements.* London: Young Foundation, 2005.

Hill, Christopher. "The English Civil War Interpreted by Marx and Engels." *Science and Society* 12 (1948) 130–56.

Himmelstein, Jerome L. *To the Right: The Transformation of American Conservatism.* Berkeley: University of California Press, 1989.

Hobbes, Thomas. *Leviathan or the Matter, Forme and Power of a Common-Wealth Ecclesiastical and Civil.* London: Crooke, 1651. Project Gutenberg Ebook 3207. https://www.gutenberg.org/files/3207/3207-h/3207-h.htm.

Holloway, David. *Church and State in the New Millennium: Issues of Belief and Morality in the 21st Century.* London: HarperCollins, 2000.

Holputch, Amanda. "Indiana Amends Religious Freedom Bill to Put an End to Discrimination." *Guardian,* Apr. 2, 2015. https://www.theguardian.com/us-news/2015/apr/02/indiana-republicans-religious-freedom.

Hudson, Winthrop S. "John Locke—Preparing the Way for Revolution." *Journal of Presbyterian History* 42 (1964) 19–38.

Humphrey, Edward Frank. *Nationalism and Religion in America, 1774–1789.* Boston: Chipham Law, 1924.

Ingersoll, Julie. *Building God's Kingdom: Inside the World of Christian Reconstruction.* New York: Oxford University Press, 2015.

Inoguchi, Takashi, et al. Introduction to *The Changing Nature of Democracy,* edited by Takashi Inoguchi et al., 1–20. New York: United Nations University Press, 1998.

Jefferson, Thomas. "Jefferson's Letter to the Danbury Baptists: The Final Letter, as Sent." Library of Congress, Jan. 1, 1802. https://www.loc.gov/loc/lcib/9806/danpre.html.

Jones, Andrea, and Alex Richey. "Compelled Speech Is Hitting Close to Home." Heritage Foundation, Feb. 4, 2020. https://www.heritage.org/gender/commentary/compelled-speech-hitting-close-home.

Jones, Mark. "Analysis of the Ashers Bakery Ruling." Edward Connor Solicitors, Oct. 15, 2018. www.edwardconnor.com/2018/10/15/analysis-of-the-ashers-bakery-ruling/.

Kaufmann, Bruno. *Modern Direct Democracy.* Geneva: Federal Department of Foreign Affairs, 2018.

Keddie, Tony. *Republican Jesus: How the Right Has Rewritten the Gospels.* Berkeley: University of California Press, 2021.

Kefauver, Estes. "The Electoral College: Old Reforms Take On a New Look." *Law and Contemporary Problems* 27 (1962) 188–212.

Kellstedt, Lyman, et al. "Religious Voting Blocs in the 1992 Election: The Year of the Evangelical?" *Sociology of Religion* 55 (1994) 307–26.

Keswick Ministries. "James Robson: Matthew 8:5–13—Matchless Authority (2/7)—Keswick Convention 2022, Week 1." YouTube, July 17, 2022. https://www.youtube.com/watch?v=g7wZoDNmTKw.

King, Martin Luther, Jr. "The Most Segregated Hour in America." YouTube, Apr. 19, 2014. https://www.youtube.com/watch?v=1q881g1L_d8.

King, Oona. *House Music: The Oona King Diaries.* London: Bloomsbury, 2008.

Kleinfeld, Rachel. "The Rise of Political Violence in the United States." *Journal of Democracy* 32 (2021) 160–76. https://www.journalofdemocracy.org/articles/the-rise-of-political-violence-in-the-united-states/.

Knowles, James Davis. *Memoir of Roger Williams, the Founder of the State of Rhode-Island.* Boston: Edmands and Co., 1834.

Bibliography

Kreitzer, Larry J. *William Kiffen and His World (Part 1)*. Centre for Baptist and Heritage Studies: Re-Sourcing Baptist History: Seventeenth Century Series 1. Oxford: Regents Park College, 2018.

Lafont, Christina. *Democracy Without Shortcuts: A Participatory Conception of Deliberative Democracy*. Oxford: Oxford University Press, 2020.

Lambert, Frank. *The Founding Fathers and the Place of Religion in America*. Princeton, NJ: Princeton University Press, 2003.

Landau Law. "Religion or Belief Discrimination." Landau Law, n.d. https://landaulaw.co.uk/religion-or-belief-discrimination/.

Lane, Melissa. *The Birth of Politics: Eight Greek and Roman Political Ideas and Why They Matter*. Princeton, NJ: Princeton University Press, 2014.

Laws, David. "Tim Farron Held Prejudiced Views—He Was Right to Resign." *iPaper*, June 15, 2017. https://inews.co.uk/opinion/tolerance-not-enough-lib-dems-72778.

Leeman, Jonathan. *Political Church: The Local Assembly as Embassy of Christ's Rule*. Downers Grove, IL: IVP, 2016.

LegiScan. "TX SB10, 2025–2026, 89th Legislature." LegiScan, June 20, 2025. https://legiscan.com/TX/bill/SB10/2025.

Li, Michael, and Gina Feliz. "The Competitive Districts That Will Decide Control of the House." Brennan Center for Justice, Oct. 24, 2024. www.brennancenter.org/our-work/analysis-opinion/competitive-districts-will-decide-control-house.

Liberal Democrats. *Liberal Democrat Manifesto 2010*. London: Liberal Democrats, 2010.

Ligonier Updates. "Bebbington's Four Points of Evangelicalism." Ligonier, Aug. 29, 2020. https://www.ligonier.org/posts/bebbingtons-four-points-evangelicalism.

Lincoln, Abraham. "Gettysburg Address Delivered at Gettysburg Pa. Nov. 19th, 1863." Library of Congress, n.d. Portfolio 244, Folder 45. https://www.loc.gov/resource/rbpe.24404500/?st=text.

Lienesch, Michael. "Right-Wing Religion: Christian Conservatism as a Political Movement." *Political Science Quarterly* 97 (1982) 403–25.

Lijphart, Arend. *Democracy in Plural Societies: A Comparative Exploration*. New Haven, CT: Yale University Press, 1977.

Lipset, Seymour Martin. "Social Conflict, Legitimacy, and Democracy." In *Comparative Government: A Reader*, edited by Jean Blondel, 52–59. London: Macmillan, 1969.

Locke, John. *"A Letter Concerning Toleration" and Other Writings*. Edited by Mark Goldie. Indianapolis: Liberty Fund, 2010.

Lusk, James Paul. "Christians Can Be Fired for Not Using Someone's Preferred Pronouns. Here's What You Need to Know." *Premier Christianity*, July 4, 2022. https://www.premierchristianity.com/opinion/christians-can-be-fired-for-not-using-someones-preferred-pronouns-heres-what-you-need-to-know/13400.article.

———. *The Jesus Candidate: Political Religion in a Secular Age*. London: Ekklesia, 2017.

———. "Leviticus Weaponised: The Assassination of Brother Tim." James Paul Lusk, June 29, 2017. https://jamespaullusk.blogspot.com/2017/06/leviticus-weaponised-assassination-of.html.

———. "Reappraising the English Anabaptists in the Time of the Revolution: Article 50 of the 1646 Confession." *Anabaptism Today* 1 (2019) 15–25.

———. "The State in the Bible." *Anabaptism Today* 2 (2020) 77–84.

Luther, Martin. "To the Christian Nobility of the German Nation." In *Three Treatises: From the American Edition of "Luther's Works,"* translated by Charles M. Jacobs, revised by James Atkinson, 1–112. 2nd ed. Philadelphia: Fortress, 1970.

Bibliography

Lutz, Donald S. *Colonial Origins of the American Constitution: A Documentary History.* Indianapolis: Liberty Fund, 1998.
Manville, Brook, and Josiah Ober. *The Civic Bargain: How Democracy Survives.* Princeton, NJ: Princeton University Press, 2023.
Margolick, David. "Blair's Big Gamble." *Vanity Fair,* June 2003.
Marshall, Paul, and David Laws, eds. *The Orange Book: Reclaiming Liberalism.* London: Profile, 2004.
Marshall, Peter J., and David B. Manuel. *The Light and the Glory: God's Plan for America, 1492–1793.* Rev ed. Grand Rapids: Revell, 2009.
Martinez-Keel, Nuria. "Oklahoma Changes Criteria for Bible Bids." *Oklahoma Voice,* Oct. 8, 2024. https://oklahomavoice.com/briefs/oklahoma-changes-criteria-for-bible-bids/.
Mayflower Society, The. "The Mayflower Compact." Mayflower Society, n.d. https://themayflowersociety.org/history/the-mayflower-compact/.
McAfee, Noelle. Review of *Democracy Without Shortcuts,* by Cristina Lafont. *Contemporary Political Theory* 21 (2021) 55–58.
McAleer, Rhiannon and Rob Barward-Symmons. *The Quiet Revival Swindon: Bible Society,* 2025.
McDonald, Karl. "Tim Farron Resigns as Lib Dem Leader Citing Struggle to Live as 'Faithful Christian.'" *iPaper,* June 14, 2017. https://inews.co.uk/news/politics/tim-farron-resigns-lib-dem-leader-citing-criticism-faith-72702.
McGuirk, Rebecca. "Philosophical Belief Under Equality Act Can Include Left-Wing Beliefs." *Personnel Today,* Apr. 29, 2015. https://www.personneltoday.com/hr/philosophical-belief-equality-act-can-include-left-wing-beliefs/.
McKee, Rebecca, and Jack Pannell. "Citizens' Assemblies: What Are Citizens' Assemblies and How Do They Work?" Institute for Government, Mar. 27, 2024. https://www.instituteforgovernment.org.uk/explainer/citizens-assemblies.
McKellar, Katie. "Utah Supreme Court Hands Big Win to Plaintiffs in Anti-Gerrymandering Lawsuit." *Utah News Dispatch,* July 11, 2024. https://utahnewsdispatch.com/2024/07/11/gerrymandering-case-utah-supreme-court-rules-against-legislatures-ballot-initiative-override/.
McVicar, Michael J. *Christian Reconstruction: R. J. Rushdoony and American Religious Conservatism.* Chapel Hill: University of North Carolina Press, 2015.
Meachan, Jon. "The Editor's Desk." *Newsweek,* Nov. 12, 2006; last updated Mar. 13, 2010. https://www.newsweek.com/editors-desk-106637.
Michael, Chris, and Agencies. "Trump Says He Will Be a Dictator Only on 'Day One' If Elected President." *Guardian,* Dec. 6, 2023. https://www.theguardian.com/us-news/2023/dec/06/donald-trump-sean-hannity-dictator-day-one-response-iowa-town-hall.
Mill, John Stuart. "On Liberty." In *J. S. Mill Utilitarianism, On Liberty and Considerations on Representative Government,* edited by H. B. Acton, 69–162. London: Dent, 1972.
Miller, David. "Deliberative Democracy and Social Choice." *Political Studies* 40 (1992) 54–67.
Miller, Perry. *Roger Williams: His Contribution to the American Tradition.* New York: Atheneum, 1966.
Mohamed, Besheer, et al. *Faith Among Black Americans.* Pew Research Center, 2021. https://www.pewresearch.org/wp-content/uploads/sites/20/2021/02/PF_02.16.21_Black.religion.report.pdf.

Bibliography

Morley, Henry, ed. *The Spectator: A New Edition Reproducing the Original Text Both as First Issued and as Corrected by Its Authors.* 3 vols. London: Routledge, 1891. Project Gutenberg Ebook 12030. https://www.gutenberg.org/files/12030/12030-h/12030-h.htm#toc1.

Movsesian, Mark. "Masterpiece Cakeshop and the Future of Religious Freedom." *Harvard Journal of Law and Public Policy* 42 (2019) 711–50.

Murrin, John M. "'Things Fearful to Name': Bestiality in Colonial America." *Pennsylvania History: A Journal of Mid-Atlantic Studies* 65 (1998) 8–43.

Nagel, Thomas. "Moral Conflict and Political Legitimacy." *Philosophy and Public Affairs* 16 (1987) 215–40.

National Archives. "14th Amendment to the U.S. Constitution: Civil Rights (1868)." National Archives, last reviewed Mar. 6, 2024. https://www.archives.gov/milestone-documents/14th-amendment#transcript.

———. "The Bill of Rights: A Transcript." National Archives, last reviewed Aug. 7, 2025. https://www.archives.gov/founding-docs/bill-of-rights-transcript.

Neuhaus, Richard John. *The Naked Public Square: Religion and Democracy in America.* 2nd ed. Grand Rapids: Eerdmans, 1986.

Noll, Mark A. *The Civil War as a Theological Crisis.* Chapel Hill: University of North Carolina Press, 2006.

———. *God and Race in American Politics.* Princeton, NJ: Princeton University Press, 2008.

Norman, Jesse. *The Big Society: The Anatomy of the New Politics.* Buckingham: Buckingham University Press, 2010.

North, Gary. "God's Covenantal Kingdom." In *Christian Reconstruction: What It Is, What It Isn't,* edited by Gary North and Gary DeMar, 27–79. Tyler, TX: Institute for Christian Economics, 1991.

Norty, Justin. "Most White Americans Who Regularly Attend Worship Services Voted for Trump in 2020." Pew Research Center, Aug. 30, 2021. https://www.pewresearch.org/short-reads/2021/08/30/most-white-americans-who-regularly-attend-worship-services-voted-for-trump-in-2020/.

Obama, Barack. "Super Tuesday." Obama Speeches, Feb. 5, 2008. http://obamaspeeches.com/E02-Barack-Obama-Super-Tuesday-Chicago-IL-February-5-2008.htm.

Open Secrets. "Incumbent Advantage." Open Secrets, based on data released on Sept. 16, 2025. https://www.opensecrets.org/elections-overview/incumbent-advantage.

Parker, Kim Ian, et al. "A King Like Other Nations: Political Theory and the Hebrew Republic in the Early Modern Age." In *The Oxford Handbook of the Bible in Early Modern England, c. 1530–1700,* edited by Kevin Killeen et al., 384–96. Oxford: Oxford University Press, 2015.

Parrington, Vernon Louis. *1620–1800: The Colonial Mind.* Vol. 1 of *Main Currents in American Thought.* New York: Harcourt Brace and Company, 1927.

Partridge, P. H. *Consent and Consensus.* London: Pall Mall, 1971.

Poole, Matthew. *Commentary on the Whole Bible.* 3 vols. McLean, VA: Macdonald, 1985.

Pope, Robert P. *Half-Way Covenant: Church Membership in Puritan New England.* Princeton, NJ: Princeton University Press, 2020.

Posner, Sarah. *Unholy: Why White Evangelicals Worship at the Altar of Donald Trump.* New York: Random House, 2020.

PRRI [Public Religion Research Institute] Staff. *American Bubbles: Politics, Race, and Religion in Americans' Core Friendship Networks.* PRRI, May 24, 2022. https://www.

prri.org/research/american-bubbles-politics-race-and-religion-in-americans-core-friendship-networks/.

———. *Challenges to Democracy: Findings from the 2024 American Values Survey*. PRRI, Oct. 16, 2024. https://www.prri.org/research/challenges-to-democracy-the-2024-election-in-focus-findings-from-the-2024-american-values-survey/.

Przeworski, Adam. "Minimalist Conception of Democracy: A Defense." In *Democracy's Values*, edited by Ian Shapiro and Casiano Hacker-Cordón, 23–55. Cambridge: Cambridge University Press, 1999.

Putnam, Robert. *The Upswing: How We Came Together a Century Ago and How We Can Do It Again*. With Shaylin Romney Garrett. New York: Simon & Schuster, 2020.

Radcliffe-Brown, A. R. Preface to *African Political Systems*, edited by M. Fortes and E. E. Evans-Pritchard, xi–xxiii. Routledge Revivals. Oxford: Oxford University Press, 1970.

Renwick, Alan, et al. *The Future of Democracy in the UK: Public Attitudes and Policy Responses—Final Report of the Democracy in the UK After Brexit Project*. London: University College of London, Constitutions Unit, 2023.

Resh, Richard W. "Alexis de Tocqueville and the Negro: Democracy in America Reconsidered." *Journal of Negro History* [*Journal of African American History*] 48 (1963) 252–59.

Roberts, Mostyn. *Subversive Puritan: Roger Williams and Freedom of Conscience*. Welwyn, UK: Evangelical, 2019.

Robinson, J. H. *Readings in European History*. Boston: Ginn, 1905.

Rojas, Rick, et al. "Louisiana's Ten Commandments Law Signals a Broader Christian Agenda." *New York Times*, June 21, 2024. https://www.nytimes.com/2024/06/21/us/louisiana-ten-commandments-landry.html.

Rushdoony, J. Roussas. *Institutes of Christian Law*. Phillipsburg, NJ: Presbyterian and Reformed, 1973.

Sands, Philippe. *East West Street: On the Origins of "Genocide" and "Crimes Against Humanity."* London: Weidenfeld & Nicolson, 2016.

Santayana, George. *Life of Reason or The Phases of Human Progress*. London: Constable, 1905.

Sargeant, Jess, et al. *Review of the UK Constitution: Final Report*. Institute for Government, Sept. 19, 2023. https://www.instituteforgovernment.org.uk/publication/final-report-review-uk-constitution.

Sartori, Giovanni. *The Theory of Democracy Revisited*. Chatham, NJ: Chatham, 1987.

Schaeffer, Francis A. *A Christian Manifesto*. Wheaton, IL: Crossway, 1981.

Schaeffer, Katherine. "Key Facts About Americans and Guns." Pew Research Center, July 24, 2024. https://www.pewresearch.org/short-reads/2024/07/24/key-facts-about-americans-and-guns/.

Schlozman, Daniel. *When Movements Anchor Parties: Electoral Alignments in American Politics*. Princeton, NJ: Princeton University Press, 2015.

Schoenfeld, William. "Separation of Church and State—a Policy or a Principle?" *North American Review* 189 (1909) 662–74.

Schwoerer, Lois G. "Locke, Lockean Ideas and the Glorious Revolution." *Journal of the History of Ideas* 51 (1990) 531–48.

Seidel, Andrew L. "Christian Nationalism and the January 6th Insurrection: Evidence." GovInfo, Mar. 18, 2022. https://www.govinfo.gov/content/pkg/GPO-J6-DOC-CTRL0000062431/pdf/GPO-J6-DOC-CTRL0000062431.pdf.

BIBLIOGRAPHY

———. "Events, People, and Networks Leading Up to January 6." In *Christian Nationalism and the January 6, 2021 Insurrection*, by Andrew L. Seidel et al., 14–24. Baptist Joint Committee for Religious Liberty and the Freedom from Religion Foundation, 2022. https://bjconline.org/wp-content/uploads/2022/02/Christian_Nationalism_and_the_Jan6_Insurrection-2-9-22.pdf.

———. *The Founding Myth: Why Christian Nationalism Is Un-American*. New York: Sterling, 2021.

Shariatmadari, David. "Does Tim Farron Think Gay Sex Is a Sin? Who Cares?" *Guardian*, Apr. 19, 2017. https://www.theguardian.com/commentisfree/2017/apr/19/does-tim-farron-think-gay-sex-is-a-sin-who-cares.

Shaw, Daron R., et al. *Battleground: Electoral College Strategies, Execution, and Impact in the Modern Era*. New York: Oxford University Press, 2024.

Siedentop, Larry. *Inventing the Individual: The Origins of Western Liberalism*. London: Lane, 2014.

Simpson, Alan. "How Democratic Was Roger Williams?" *William and Mary Quarterly* 13 (1956) 53–67.

Southern, R. W. *Western Society and the Church in the Middle Ages*. Harmondsworth, UK: Penguin, 1970.

Standards and Privileges Committee. *Mr David Laws*. Parliament, May 10, 2011. Report 15. https://publications.parliament.uk/pa/cm201012/cmselect/cmstnprv/1023/102302.htm.

Stanley, Luke, et al. *The Kids Aren't Alright*. Onward, 2022. https://www.ukonward.com/reports/the-kids-arent-alright-democracy/.

Stone, Geoffrey R. "In Opposition to the School Prayer Amendment." *University of Chicago Law Review* 50 (1983) 823–48.

Storm, Lise. "An Elemental Definition of Democracy and Its Advantages for Comparing Political Regime Types." *Democratization* 15 (2008) 215–29.

Sturge, Georgina. "2024 General Election: Turnout." House of Commons Library, Sept. 5, 2024. https://commonslibrary.parliament.uk/general-election-2024-turnout/.

Sullivan, J. W. *Direct Legislation by the Citizenship Through the Initiative and Referendum*. New York: Twentieth Century, 1892.

Syed, Matthew. "The West's Loss of Faith in Liberalism Risks Opening the Door to Great Evils." *Sunday Times*, Oct. 30, 2022.

Taylor, Robert. "Give the Young What They Want: Raise the Voting Age to 55." *Daily Telegraph*, Sept. 7, 2022.

Thompson, Matthew. *Reconstructing Public Housing: Liverpool's Hidden History of Collective Alternatives*. Liverpool: Liverpool University Press, 2020.

Tocqueville, Alexis de. *Democracy in America*. In *"Democracy in America" and Two Essays on America*, by Alexis de Tocqueville, 3–871. Edited by Isaac Kramnick. Translated by Gerald E. Bevan. London: Penguin, 2003.

Tooley, M. J. Introduction to *Six Books of the Commonwealth*, by Jean Bodin, 1–32. Edited and translated by M. J. Tooley. Oxford: Blackwell, 1955.

Towers, Graham. *Building Democracy: Community Architecture in the Inner Cities*. Abingdon: Routledge, 1995.

Trump, Donald. "Trump Speaks at CPAC 2023 Transcript." Rev, 2023. https://www.rev.com/transcripts/trump-speaks-at-cpac-2023-transcript.

Bibliography

Turner, John. "Colonial Religion and the True Revolution in Virginia." In *Faith and Politics in America: From Jamestown to the Civil War*, edited by Joseph Prud'homme, 3–14. New York: Lang, 2011.

Tyler, Amanda. Introduction to *Christian Nationalism and the January 6, 2021 Insurrection*, by Andrew L. Seidel et al., n.p. Baptist Joint Committee for Religious Liberty and the Freedom from Religion Foundation, 2022. https://bjconline.org/wp-content/uploads/2022/02/Christian_Nationalism_and_the_Jan6_Insurrection-2-9-22.pdf.

UK Parliament. "Voting Systems in the UK." UK Parliament, n.d. www.parliament.uk/about/how/elections-and-voting/voting-systems/.

———. "Wolfenden Report." UK Parliament, Oct. 29, 1957. https://www.parliament.uk/about/living-heritage/transformingsociety/private-lives/relationships/collections1/sexual-offences-act-1967/wolfenden-report-/.

University of the State of New York. *The Regents of the University of the State of New York, 1784–1959*. Albany: University of the State of New York Press, 1959.

Vargas, Ramon Antonio. "Trump Tells Supporters They Won't Have to Vote in the Future: 'It'll Be Fixed!'" *Guardian*, July 27, 2024. https://www.theguardian.com/us-news/article/2024/jul/27/trump-speech-no-need-to-vote-future.

Verhaagen, Dave. *How White Evangelicals Think: The Psychology of White Conservative Christians*. Eugene, OR: Cascade, 2022.

Vinayaka, Umang. "Compulsion Emboldens Democracy: A Deep-Dive into Australia's Mandatory Voting." *Harvard International Review*, Oct. 2, 2023. https://hir.harvard.edu/compulsion-emboldens-democracy-a-deep-dive-into-australias-mandatory-voting/.

Wahlquist, Calla. "Teal Independents: Who Are They and How Did They Upend Australia's Election?" *Guardian*, May 23, 2022. https://www.theguardian.com/australia-news/2022/may/23/teal-independents-who-are-they-how-did-they-upend-australia-election.

Waldegrave, William. *A Different Kind of Weather: A Memoir*. London: Constable, 2016.

Walzer, Michael. "The Civil Society Argument." In *Dimensions of Radical Democracy*, edited by Chantal Mouffe, 89–107. London: Verso, 1992.

———. *In God's Shadow: Politics in the Hebrew Bible*. New Haven, CT: Yale University Press, 2012.

Wamba-dia-Wamba, Ernest. "Experiences of Democracy in Africa: Reflections on Practices of Communalist Palaver as a Method of Resolving Contradictions." Libcom, Apr. 14, 2019. https://libcom.org/article/experiences-democracy-africa-reflections-practices-communalist-palaver-method-resolving.

Wang, Wendy. "Marriages Between Democrats and Republicans Are Extremely Rare." Institute for Family Studies, Nov. 3, 2020. https://ifstudies.org/blog/marriages-between-democrats-and-republicans-are-extremely-rare.

Warwick, Robert, et al. "Patent for Providence Plantations." Avalon Project, Mar. 14, 1643. https://avalon.law.yale.edu/17th_century/rio3.asp.

Watson, Ian. "The Dating of the Providence Civil Compact [Part 1]." *American Genealogist* (Jan.–Apr. 2020) 165–89. https://ianwatson.org/the-dating-of-the-providence-civil-compact-by-ian-watson.pdf.

———. "The Dating of the Providence Civil Compact [Part 2]." *American Genealogist* (July–Oct. 2020) 261–83. https://ianwatson.org/the-dating-of-the-providence-civil-compact-by-ian-watson.pdf.

Weale, Albert. *Democracy*. New York: St. Martins, 1999.

Bibliography

Weber, Max. "Politics as a Vocation." In *From Max Weber: Essays in Sociology*, edited and translated by H. H. Gerth and C. Wright Mills, 77–128. New York: Oxford University Press, 1946.

Wegman, Jesse. "Thomas Jefferson Gave the Constitution 19 Years. Look Where We Are Now." *New York Times*, Aug. 4, 2021. https://www.nytimes.com/2021/08/04/opinion/amend-constitution.html.

Welzel, Christian. "Why the Future Is Democratic." *Journal of Democracy* 32 (2021) 132–44.

Welzel, Christian, et al. "Why the Future Is (Still) Democratic." *Journal of Democracy* 33 (2022) 156–62.

Whitehead, Andrew L., and Samuel L. Perry. *Taking America Back for God: Christian Nationalism in the United States*. New York: Oxford University Press, 2022.

Williams, Roger. *The Bloudy Tenent of Persecution for Cause of Conscience Discussed in a Conference Between Truth and Peace*. 1644. In *The Bloudy Tenent of Persecution for Cause of Conscience Discussed: And Mr Cotton's Letter Examined and Answered*, edited by Edward Bean Underhill, 1–364. London: Hanserd Knollys Society, 1848.

———. *A Key into the Language of America: The First Book of Native American Languages, Dating to 1643—with Accounts of the Tribes' Culture, Wars, Folklore, History, Traditions*. Bedford, MA: Applewood, 1997.

Wiredu, Kwasi. "Democracy and Consensus in African Traditional Politics: A Plea for a Non-Party Polity." *Centennial Review* 39 (1995) 53–64.

Wolfe, Stephen. *The Case for Christian Nationalism*. Moscow, ID: Canon, 2022.

Wolin, Sheldon S. "Norm and Form: The Constitutionalizing of Democracy." In *Athenian Political Thought and the Reconstruction of American Democracy*, edited by J. Peter Euben et al., 29–58. Ithaca, NY: Cornell University Press, 1994.

Woodhouse, Arthur Sutherland Piggott, ed. *Puritanism and Liberty, Being the Army Debates (1647–9) from the Clarke Manuscripts with Supplementary Documents*. Chicago: Chicago University Press, 1951. https://oll.libertyfund.org/title/lindsay-puritanism-and-liberty-being-the-army-debates-1647-9.

Woolley, John, and Gerhard Peters. "1948." American Presidency Project, n.d. https://www.presidency.ucsb.edu/statistics/elections/1948.

———. "1968." American Presidency Project, n.d. https://www.presidency.ucsb.edu/statistics/elections/1968.

———. "Voter Turnout in Presidential Elections." American Presidency Project, last updated May 24, 2025. https://www.presidency.ucsb.edu/statistics/data/voter-turnout-in-presidential-elections.

Wright, Lawrence. *The Looming Tower: Al-Qaeda's Road to 9/11*. London: Penguin, 2007.

Wroth, Lawrence C. *Roger Williams: Marshall Woods Lecture, in Sayles Hall, October 26th, 1936*. Providence, RI: Brown University Papers, 1937.

Subject Index

Akehurst, Luke, 101–2
Alabama, 61
Alexander, Amy C., 9, 90
Alinsky, Saul D., 103, 105
Alliance for Defending Freedom, 128
Anabaptists, ix, 11, 13, 14, 16, 17
Anderson, Benedict, 49
Anglican, 29, 35, 62, 71, 140. *See also* Church of England
Ashers bakery case, 128–29, 134, 142
Association, rights of, xiii, 9, 90, 91, 105
Athens (ancient state), 3, 97
Atheists, 31, 32, 44
Attlee, Clement, xiii
Augsburg, Treaty of (1555), 13
Australia, ranked choice and compulsory voting, 113, 117, 123
Australia, equal marriage referendum, 125–26
Australia, election expenses, 116
Australia, vilification and free speech, 125

Balandier, Georges, 75, 82
Baptists, 30, 35, 37, 38, 39, 42, 50, 61
Bailyn, Bernard, 31
Bavaria, 16
Baxter, Richard, 18, 30
Bejan, Teresa, 4, 25, 85
Bell, Daniel A., 2, 100
Berlin, Isaiah, 7, 42, 66
Biden, Joe, 44, 89, 95
Bill of Rights (1791 Amendments to the US constitution), 36, 50, 142
Blair, Tony, 91, 94, 95, 119

Bodin, Jean, 3, 23
Boebert, Lauren, 50
Boston, 20, 23, 29
Bretherton, Luke, 71, 145
Brexit, 98, 121, 138, 140
Bush, George H. W., 43
Bush, George W., 43, 93, 94, 95
Buttigieg, Pete, 104

California, 99
Calvin, John, and Calvinism, 4, 12, 13, 15, 17, 18
Campbell, Alistair, 94–95, 119–20
Canada, 125
Capitol invasion of January 6th, 2021, 45, 51, 89
Carter, Jimmy, 43, 46, 52, 64
Carville, James, 43, 95
Catherwood, Christopher, 137
Catholic 11, 13, 14, 15, 16, 17, 21, 23, 46, 56, 60, 61, 64, 88, 98
Chaplin, Jonathan, 86
Charles I, King, 19, 28
Christendom, 4, 7, 9, 11–19
Christian Concern, 135
Christian education, *see* Education, Christian
Christian Institute. 128, 133, 142
Christian nationalism, 46–51, 66
Church of England, 15, 16, 17, 20, 34. *See also* Anglican
Churchill, Sir Winston, 8
Citizens' assemblies and juries, 100–102
"City on a hill," 17

Subject Index

Civil society, xiii, 9, 89, 91, 104, 106, 111, 113, 123, 146
Civil War (England, also the "war of the three kingdoms"), 10, 11, 18, 30, 31, 32, 152
Civil War (US), 1, 6, 10, 30, 34, 37, 39–40, 42, 56, 66, 133, 155
Clinton, Bill, 43, 44
Cockburn, Claud, 8
Coke, Sir Edward, 20
Common Cause (US), 115
Commons, House of (UK), xiii, 30, 54, 102, 110, 119–23, 137, 138, 146
Commons, House of, as sovereign, 54–55, 117
Compelled speech, see Forced speech
Congregationalism, 16–18, 20, 34, 36
Connecticut, 23, 37
Conscience, 4, 7, 18, 24, 28, 32, 83
Consent, xiii, 3, 4, 6, 9, 10, 22, 26, 28, 33, 42, 44, 50, 53, 55, 59, 66, 75, 86, 87, 88, 90, 10, 106–9, 111, 156.
Consensus, 5, 9, 26, 98, 104, 105, 108
Conservative (political outlook especially in US), 43, 46, 51, 52, 93, 129, 134, 137
Conservative theology, 7, 136, 137, 140
Conservatives (UK political party), xiii, 62, 92, 101, 120, 133, 137, 138
Consociationalism, 88, 98
Constitutions, 1, 36, 39, 50, 53, 55, 59, 60, 61, 73, 91, 99, 114, 115, 121–23, 126, 133, 141, 142
Cotton, John, 24
Cromwell, Oliver, 30
Culture, 4, 11, 21, 24, 38, 41, 48, 49, 52, 59, 60, 61, 63, 64, 66, 68, 88, 107, 113, 123, 144. See also Culture war
Culture war, 5, 6, 10, 34, 41, 42–47, 51, 52, 66, 127, 131, 142

Dahl, Robert A., 2, 88, 90, 111
Danbury letter, 39, 50
Dave's Redistricting App, 115
Davis, Michael J., 53, 54, 58, 60, 62
Decter, Midge, 43, 45

Democracy as successor arrangement "after Christendom," 4, 10, 38
Democracy, Assembly scale, 102–5
Democracy, challenged, xiii, 1–2, 7, 42, 50, 66, 89, 110,
Democracy, definitions, 2, 3, 6, 8, 9, 32, 85, 90–97, 106–9, 111, 136, 146
Democracy, deliberative, 99–100. See also Sortition
Democracy, direct vs. indirect, 90, 91–92, 97
Democracy, elections, voting and voting systems, 40, 44, 90, 96, 98, 111, 112, 116–17, 121
Democracy, fundamental rights, 9. See also Bill of Rights
Democracy, historic origins, 1, 3, 4, 5, 22, 33, 97
Democracy in Bible, 75, 85
Democracy, liberal, 4, 8, 10, 41, 69, 96, 137, 140, 141, 143, 144
Democracy, myth of collective self-government, 106
Democracy, neighborhood level, 103–4, 105
Democracy, procedural, 89, 96, 111
Democracy, role of civil society 91–92, 111, 123
Democracy, state held (legitimized) by consent, 6, 9, 107–8, 111, 146
Democracy, Swiss model, and its use in the US, 98–99, 113
Democracy, UK, problems and solutions, 118–23
Democracy, US, challenges, 113–16
Democrats (US political party), 6, 40, 41, 43, 44, 46, 95, 114, 115, 132
Democrats' split over civil rights, 141
Diamond, Larry, 111
District of Columbia (DC), 37, 39, 89, 114
Divine right of monarchs, 12, 18

Eden, Anthony, xiii
Education, 7, 55–61, 83, 141, 146
Education, Christian, 63–64
Edward VI, King, 15
Engel v. Vitale case, 57, 61

Subject Index

Electoral college (US), 1, 39, 41, 114
Electoral Reform Society (UK), 121
Elizabeth I, Queen, 15, 21
Enlightenment, 3, 32
Equality, 6, 8, 9, 10, 24, 32, 37, 38, 40–41,
    59, 86, 90, 92, 93, 108, 111, 113,
    114, 124, 126, 127, 129, 132, 136,
    139, 142, 144, 145, 146
Establishment of religion, 25, 21, 27, 34,
    35, 36–37, 53, 55. 57, 58, 59, 66,
    142, 150
Evangelical Christianity, 4, 6, 10, 34,
    35, 36, 37, 38, 39, 42, 43, 44, 46,
    47, 62, 64, 66, 71, 77, 126, 137,
    138, 139
Expenses, in elections, 116

FairVote (US), 116, 117
Falwell, Jerry, 42, 64
Farron, Tim, fall from leadership of UK
    Liberal Democrats, 137–40
Featley, Daniel, 29, 30
Fitch, David E., 71, 126–27
Florida, 44
Forced speech, 134–36
France, French, 7, 12, 23, 38, 92, 118
Free speech, 9, 36, 90, 104, 116, 126–27,
    132, 134
Free speech absolutism, 126
Freedom House, 1
Frum, David, 113

Gagnon, Jean-Paul, 2, 3
Gay cakes, *see* Ashers and Masterpiece
Germany, xi, xii, 8, 12, 13, 14, 61
Gerrymandering, 115–16
Gettysburg address, 1, 6
Gideon, 78–80
Goodness and moral consensus, 5, 144
Gray, Sue, 101
Grayling, A. C., 91, 96, 106–7
Grudem, Wayne, 66–67, 151
Guns, 45, 73
Gushee, David, 5

Harris, Kamala, 95
Healthy Democracy (Oregon), 100

Hegseth, Pete, 2
Held, David, 3
Henry VIII, King, 14–15
Heritage Foundation, 135
Hill, Christopher, 32
Hitler, Adolf, xiii; "Little Hitlers," 103
Hobbes, Thomas, 4, 9, 25, 33, 107, 152
Hobson, Paul, 30
Holland, 15, 16
Holloway, David, 133
Holy Roman Empire, 13
Holy Spirit, work of, 37
Hubmaier, Balthasar, 14

Illinois, 36
India, 6
Indiana, 36, 104, 126, 129
Initiative (citizens'), 115
Individualism, 105
Institute of Government (UK), 122
Iraq (2003 invasion), 80, 93–95
Ireland, 18, 28, 48, 88, 125, 128, 137

Japan, 6
Jefferson, Thomas, 35, 36, 37, 49, 106
Jews, xi, 11
Jotham's parable of the trees, 78–79, 83

Kansas, 40, 58
Kiffen, William, 30, 153
King, Martin Luther, 65, 68
King, Oona, 119–20
Knollys, Hansard, 30
Knox, John, 4, 15
Kruger, Danny, 137

Labour (UK political party), xii, 92, 101,
    109, 120–21, 133
Laws, David, 138–40
Lebanon, 88
Legitimacy, 1, 4, 10, 20, 33, 59, 64, 65,
    66, 67, 87–89, 97, 107, 108, 145
Liberal democracy, 4, 7, 8, 10, 124, 141,
    142–43, 144–45
Liberal Democrat Party (UK), 121–23,
    137–40
Liberal theology, 136

Subject Index

Liberalism, 30, 136, 140
Lincoln, Abraham, 1, 2, 6
Lipset, Seymour Martin, 87
Livingstone, Ken, 119–20
Locke, John, 25, 31, 32, 33, 107
Lords, House of (UK), 54, 102, 118, 121, 122
"Lottocracy," see Sortition
Louisiana, 141–42
Luther, Martin, and Lutheranism, 12, 13, 14, 15
Mackereth, David, 134
Madison, James, 2, 27, 35, 36
Maine, 114
MAGA, 91
Marriage, civil partnerships and equal marriage, 125–34
Marshall, Sir Paul, 138, 140
Marsilius of Padua, 26
Marx, Marxism, 7, 32, 88
Mary, Queen, 15
Maryland, 16, 133
Massachusetts, 4, 16, 17, 18, 20, 23, 24, 25, 28, 35, 37, 125, 127
Masterpiece Cakeshop case, 127–31
Mayflower, 16
Methodists, 35, 38, 40
Michigan, 36, 44
Mill, John Stuart, 7
Minimalism, 96–97
Misgendering, 134–36
Misogyny, 5, 51, 52
"Moral Majority," 42
Monarch (UK), 54, 117, 118
Monarchy, 74–76. See also Gideon, Saul
Moravia, 16
Movsesian, Mark, 131–32

Narragansett, 21, 22, 24, 28, 32
Nationalism, 4, 5, 10, 42, 45, 47, 49, 52, 53, 66, 67, 68, 88, 89, 107, 111, 144. See also Christian nationalism
Nazis, xi, xii, 66
Nebraska, 114
Nevada, 63
New Deal, 41, 46, 61

New England, 10, 16
New Jersey, 34
New York, 23, 56–57, 60, 94, 133
Noll, Mark A., 39
Nones vs. Traditionally Religious (US polarization), 131–32
North Carolina, 114–15
North, Gary, 7, 65

Obama, Barack, 93, 103
Obergefell v Hodges case, 133
Ohio, 36, 115–16, 133
Oklahoma, 142
One-party systems, 88, 104
Oregon, 99, 100
Orthodox (church) 11

Paine, Thomas, 36
Palaver, 104–5
Pence, Mike, 126
Pennsylvania, 34, 59
Plymouth, 23
Politics, xiii, 5, 8, 42, 43, 47, 51, 55, 62, 63, 91–93, 113, 123, 136, 137, 140, 141, 145–46
Politics, in Bible, 73–85
Politics, meaning, 10, 70–73
Political parties, role and organization, 91–92, 96, 102, 114–16, 118–21, 146
Prayer, as public ritual, 62
Prayer, in Capitol protest, 45
Prayer, in schools, 6, 53, 56–60
Presbyterians, 35, 63, 64
Priesthood of all believers, 14
Primaries, 96
Protestant 4, 13, 14, 15, 16, 17, 31, 32, 33, 50, 60, 61, 62, 88, 98
Providence, 3, 4, 6, 20, 21, 23, 24, 27, 28, 32, 33, 87, 107, 144, 146
Public and private goods (economic), 86, 89, 109, 146
Puritans, 16, 25, 26, 30, 32

"Quiet revival" (UK), 5, 145

Race, 39, 42, 66, 68, 100, 126, 129, 130

Subject Index

Racism, 5, 10, 42, 45, 51, 52, 53, 61,66, 67, 88,144
Reagan, Ronald, 43, 53, 60, 64
Redistricting (US), 114–16
Referendum vs. plebiscite, 98
Reform Party (UK), 92, 123, 137
Registration to vote, 112–13
Religious freedom, 10, 18, 21, 28, 33, 36, 52, 58, 124–43, 144
Religious Right, 6, 7, 43–47, 51, 52, 53, 63, 64, 65, 66, 67, 68, 84, 91, 135
Republicans (US political party), 6, 40, 43, 44, 45, 46, 50, 51, 52, 91, 114, 115
Revolution (American), 10, 31, 35, 36, 65, 106
Revolution ("Glorious"), 31
Rhode Island, 3, 4, 5, 22, 23, 25, 29, 33, 34, 35, 36
Rice, Condoleezza, 93–94
Richardson, Samuel, 30
Roe v Wade case, 64
Rushdoony, J. Roussas, 7, 63–66

Salem, 21
Santayana, George, xiii
Santis, Ron de, 44
Sartori, Giovanni, 3, 93, 102
Saul, King, 80–82
Schaeffer, Frances A, 7, 64–65
Scotland, 18, 48, 125, 136
Scrutiny, 117
Seidel, Andrew, 45, 47, 49
Separation of church and state, 14, 19, 30, 37, 50, 52, 139, 145
Sexuality, 124–34
Sin, 141
Siedentop, Larry, 105
Singapore, 6
Slavery, 6, 13, 34, 37–41, 46, 66, 74, 97
Socialism, xii, 92, 136
Sortition, 100–102
Soul liberty, 8, 26
Southern, R. W., 12
Starmer, Sir Keir, 101
Spain, 12, 23

State (social institution), xiii, 4, 5, 6, 7, 8, 9,10, 12, 14, 15, 20, 21, 22, 30, 33, 43, 37, 45, 46, 48, 49, 50, 52, 53, 59, 64, 66, 68, 70, 72–80, 83–89, 90, 91, 96, 99, 103, 106–9, 111, 123, 124, 130, 140, 142, 144–46
State and church relations, 15–19, 24, 25, 26, 27, 29–30, 41
State and justice, 64–65, 86
State, definition, 72–73, 76, 89
State, functions, 86, 89
State neutrality in religion, 5, 9, 11, 13, 30, 52, 59, 60, 63, 64, 139, 141, 144
Sullivan, John W., 98–99
Supreme Court (UK), 122, 128, 136
Supreme Court (US), 1, 6, 17, 53–56. 59–62, 64, 115, 116,125, 128, 133
Switzerland, 13, 88, 98–99. *See also* Democracy, Swiss model.

Ten Commandments laws, 141–42
Tennessee, 133
Texas, 63, 65, 101, 141
Theocracy, 15, 33, 78, 80, 89, 107
Theonomy, 7, 8, 10, 64, 65, 66. 67. 68, 89, 107, 111, 124, 131, 139, 140, 142, 143, 144, 145
Tocqueville, Alexis de, 38
Toleration, 25, 30, (Act of) 31, (Essay on) 31
Trump, Donald, 1, 5, 43, 44, 51, 52, 91, 93, 95, 96, 142
Turing, Alan, 124
Two kingdoms (or swords), 12, 15
Tyler, Amanda, 51

Utah, 115

Vietnam, 88
Viguerie, Richard, 46–47
Virginia, 16, 35, 37, 49
Voting systems, 117

Waldegrave, William, 118
Wales, 18, 125
Wallace, George, 41, 46
Walzer, Michael, xiii, 9, 73, 75, 77

Subject Index

Wamba-dia-Wamba, Ernest, 104–5
Wampanoag, 21
Weale, Albert. 92, 107
Welzel, Christian, 3, 9
Westminster model, 117
Westphalia, settlement of (1648), 13
"We don't do God," 94
Weyrich, Paul, 64
Whitfield, George, 35

Williams, Roger, 4, 8, 19, 20–33, 50, 52, 58, 85, 87, 88, 102, 146
Winthrop, John, 17, 22
Wiredu, Kwasi, 104
Wisconsin, 36
Wolfe, Stephen, 48, 49, 68,
Wolfenden Report, 125, 133
Wolin, Sheldon S., 91, 97, 111

Zwingli, Ulrich, 12

Scripture Index

Genesis
11:1–9   68

Exodus
20:1–17   141

Deuteronomy
1:3   74
1:13–16   75
17:14–20   74

Judges
8:2–9   77
8:22–27   77–78
9:1–21   78
9:53–54   80
21   77

1 Samuel
8:19–22   80
9, 10   80–81
10:16   82
11:6–7, 15   81
13:6–13   82
28   82

2 Samuel
12   75

Psalms
32:9   8

Proverbs
15:21–22   84

Matthew
19:10   131

Mark
10:18   5

John
3:3   14
8:3–9   86
13:35   85
18:31   87
18:36   45, 76

Acts
5:29   83
12:2   83

Romans
1:20   84
12:17, 21   9, 84
13:1–7   45, 83

Scripture Index

Ephesians
5:32 — 130
6:11 — 44

Philippians
2:5–7 — 84, 132

1 Peter
2:9 — 14
2:13 — 45

Revelation
5:10 — 14

www.ingramcontent.com/pod-product-compliance
Lightning Source LLC
Chambersburg PA
CBHW030111170426
43198CB00009B/581